AMERICAN LIFE

W9-CZB-686

EACH DOT EQUALS
50 PEOPLE

1790 VILLAGE

NEWTOWN HAD
200 PEOPLE

●●●●●●●●●●●●●●●●●●●●●●
●●●●●●●●●●●●●●●●●●●●●●
●●●●●●●●●●●●●●●●●●●●●●
●●●●●●●●●●●●●●●●●●●●●●

BY 1840
NEWTOWN GREW
TO TOWN OF
4,000 PEOPLE

SOME HAD GONE WEST TO SETTLE

SOME HAD MIGRATED TO OTHER TOWNS AND STATES

SOME WORKED IN NEW MILLS AND FACTORIES

MOST PEOPLE STILL
WORKED ON FARMS
PART OF THE TIME

A FEW TOOK JOBS IN
NEW STORES SELLING
MANUFACTURED GOODS

AGRICULTURE STILL BASIC
MEANS OF LIVELIHOOD
FOR MOST AMERICANS

EMERGENCE OF THE MACHINE

RISE OF FACTORY TOWNS

BEGINNING OF WORKERS'
EFFORTS TO ORGANIZE
NATIONAL LABOR UNIONS

1.⁵⁰ – per copy }
1.⁰⁰ – Paper cover } disc. in
quantity

The
American Story
of
Industrial and
Labor Relations

NEW ENGLAND INSTITUTE
OF TECHNOLOGY
MOUNT ST. JOSEPH
LEARNING RESOURCES CENTER
College Library

New York State Joint Legislative Committee
on Industrial and Labor Conditions

1943

1458839

COPYRIGHT 1943
THE PEOPLE OF THE STATE OF NEW YORK

NO PART OF THIS BOOK MAY BE REPRODUCED IN WHOLE OR IN PART, EXCEPT BRIEF
EXCERPTS FOR REVIEW PURPOSES, WITHOUT PERMISSION FROM THE NEW YORK STATE
JOINT LEGISLATIVE COMMITTEE ON INDUSTRIAL AND LABOR CONDITIONS.

PREFACE

IF SOUND INDUSTRIAL AND LABOR RELATIONS ARE TO BE assured in the America of tomorrow, means for the widest public understanding of the fundamental principles underlying them in practice must be provided. From the very beginning of its activities in 1938, the New York State Joint Legislative Committee on Industrial and Labor Conditions has recognized that legislation alone, no matter how progressive in policy or enlightened in administration, provides no certain guarantee of justice or stability in our economy. In its 1940 Report, it stated its conviction that,

> The most satisfactory and happiest human relationships are the product not of legal compulsion, but rather of voluntary determination among human beings to cooperate with one another. Though we may legislate to the end of time, there will never be industrial peace and harmony without good faith, integrity, a high degree of responsibility and a real desire to cooperate on the part of all parties concerned. Without this spirit of good will, all of the social, economic and labor laws of man will prove eventually to be in vain.*

* Report of the New York State Joint Legislative Committee on Industrial and Labor Relations, 1940, p. 77.

v

This view of its responsibility to the people and the Legislature of New York early led the Committee to consider how public awareness of and interest in the fundamentals of sound industrial and labor relations might be broadened. It has, of course, continuously concerned itself with matters of legislative policy and administrative efficiency in the field assigned to it by the Legislature; its mandate made this its first duty.

The performance of this duty has convinced the Committee that attention exclusively to contemporary legislative or administrative aspects of industrial and labor relations offers no guarantee that they will rest on stable and lasting foundations. If the economic and social conditions of the people of New York are to attain still higher levels in the years ahead, all its citizens—young and old alike, both workers and employers— must share a common understanding of the true character of these relations. This book is a result of this conviction. It is an effort to further popular education in the principles and practices underlying sound industrial and labor relations.

The Committee's educational program, as it has developed so far, is outlined in its 1942 and 1943 Reports. It includes a variety of objectives and activities. One is to provide the state's future citizens—who will become its employers and workers—a more adequate background for appraising state and national policies in the field of industrial and labor relations. This book has been designed for use in the upper high-school years and in introductory college courses.

It may be used as the basis for a specialized course in industrial and labor relations or integrated into existing courses, such as American History or Problems of Democracy. A glance at the table of contents will reveal its scope as well as the possibilities for the use of its different topics in present courses or in a new course in this important aspect of American life.

The Committee here records its conviction that a specific course in industrial and labor relations should be offered in every high school in this state. The current revision of the social studies curriculum, now being developed by the State Department of Education, provides an unusual opportunity for school officials to incorporate this subject in their future programs. An analysis of the Department's own proposals for revision of the social-studies curriculum * reveals that over one-half of the topics suggested are treated in greater or less detail in this book. The treatment of these topics in an integrated course, built around a broad and objective analysis of industrial and labor relations seems to the Committee to offer a significant opportunity to the teachers of the state. Not only would it reflect a further development of the state's present sound educational policies, but it would be an invaluable contribution to improved industrial and labor relations in this state in the future.

These relations will be one of the first concerns of this and future high-school generations when they leave the schools or colleges to make their places in our economy. By providing them—the state's future citizens—with a more informed and comprehensive view of the data and problems in this field, our teachers will be equipping them to meet adult life more effectively. They will also advance the development of sound industrial and labor relations in the postwar world by broadening the perspectives of those who will—as citizens and as employers and workers—determine the character of those relations in our society.

Although this book has been prepared with the primary aim of providing a unit of study in the high schools of New York, the Committee believes that it will be useful to a wider audience.

* University of the State of New York, Bulletin 1189 (1940).

The interested citizen, whether or not he is immediately concerned with the management of a business or with its operation as a worker, will find here a brief but comprehensive review of the way our American economy has developed. He can review the historical evolution of our economic, social, and political ideas within the framework of the changing technological conditions under which Americans have earned their livelihood. He can observe and appraise the course of public policy in the different fields of industrial and labor relations, in the states and in the nation.

The table of contents will indicate at once that the treatment of the materials covered is nation-wide in scope. The account of changes in the American economy over the past 150 years, found in the first four chapters, is "located" in New York. It deals, however, with the processes and results of industrialization on each successive frontier—from Maine to California. Succeeding chapters include data concerning the 48 states, wherever pertinent, as well as the national government.

Special attention has also been given to legislative and administrative developments in New York; separate sections on New York law and administration will be found in various chapters. This arrangement was decided on deliberately, in the hope that the book would prove of equal value to the schools and to general readers in other states. By substituting relevant materials on state law and its administration in particular fields of industrial and labor relations, the book can be fitted to the high-school curricula of any other state. The general reader can do so for himself.

The materials for further study suggested in the appendix are intended to develop a more thorough exploration of problems in the field of industrial and labor relations. They will also serve the general reader as a guide to further lines of inquiry on his own initiative. They will be useful to study groups undertaking a more intensive analysis and discussion of the field as a whole.

The text and materials for further study were produced under the direction of William B. Groat, Jr., Counsel to the Committee. In doing so, he was assisted by Dr. Phillips Bradley, Director of Education and Research, Dwyer W. Shugrue, Chief Assistant Counsel and the other members of the Committee's staff. The design, typography and graphic illustrations were the work of Samuel B. Schaeffer, Graphic Statistician of the Committee's staff. They have also been reviewed by all members of the Committee in 1942 and 1943. Their cooperation in and contributions to the project have throughout its development been indispensable. The text has, in addition, been submitted to representatives of labor and industry in New York, from whom many helpful comments and suggestions have been received. To all those who have cooperated in making this part of the Committee's educational program a more effective instrument for improving industrial and labor relations, I wish to express my own and the Committee's appreciation.

Chairman

*New York State Joint Legislative
Committee on Industrial and Labor Conditions*

CONTENTS

Chapter 5 *(cont.)*

Chapter 7 *(cont.)*

ILLUSTRATIVE MATERIAL

ACKNOWLEDGEMENTS

THE COMMITTEE ACKNOWLEDGES WITH GRATITUDE THE courtesy of the following individuals and publishers for permission to reproduce the illustrations copyrighted or controlled by them. The name of artists and original titles of the sources from which the illustrations have been taken have been included in parenthesis when necessary for identification. Unless otherwise indicated, addresses are New York City. References are to pages in this text.

To the Curtis Publishing Co., Philadelphia, for the illustration at page 8 (W. L. Taylor, "The Travelling Shoemaker", copyright, the Curtis Publishing Co., Courtesy of Ladies' Home Journal). To Paul Dougherty, Carmel, California, for his painting at page 180 ("Deadlocked", exhibited at the Carnegie International Exhibition of Paintings, 1937). To the Farm Security Administration, for the illustrations at page 83 (photos by Lange and Vachon) 105, 285, 287, and 289 (photos by Rothstein). To the Ford News Bureau, Ford Motor Co., Dearborn, Michigan, for the illustration at page 233. To Harper and Brothers, for the illustrations at page 5 (inset, Faneuil Hall, Boston), 8 ("Weaving in Colonial Days"), 14, 17, 28 ("View in a New England Shipyard"), 32 (all from Harper's Encyclopedia of United States History, copyright 1905, 1918, by Harper and Brothers), and 42 (from E. G. Gress, Fashions in American Typography, copyright 1931, by Harper and Brothers). To Peter A. Juley & Son, Inc., and the Old Print Exchange, for the illustration at page 28 (Iron). To the Museum of the City of New York, for the illustration at page 47. To the National Resources Planning Board, for the maps at pages 25 and 74. To the New-York Historical Society, for the illustration at page 43 (*Main Street, 1890,* "A View of Wall Street, New York City, Looking East From Broadway"). To the New York Public Library, for the illustration from the Eno Collection at page 5 (inset, U. S. Subtreasury Building, New York City). To the New York State Labor Relations Board, for the illustrations at pages 143 and 144 (photos by William J. Kridel and Morton Singer). To the Office of War Information and the Office for Emergency Management Defense, for the illustrations at pages 99 and 152 (photos by Palmer). To James A. B. Scherer of Santa Monica, California, and the Schmidt Lithograph Co., San Francisco, for the illustration at page 34. To Everett Warner, Washington, D. C., for his painting at page 217 ("Progress and Poverty", exhibited at the Carnegie International Exhibition of Paintings, 1939). To the Yale University Press, New Haven, Conn., for the illustrations at pages 1, 6, 16, 19 (inset, "Patrick Henry in the First Continental Congress", also in first end paper), 28 (*Textiles*), 32, and 212 (all reproduced from The Pageant of America, copyright Yale University Press). To the U. S. Department of Agriculture, Bureau of Public Roads, for the illustrations at pages 24 and 43, ("The Horseless Carriage", from Highways of History). To Mrs. Florence Kellogg, of Survey Associates, for her aid in gathering photographs.

The data in the text has been obtained from official publications of the United States, the State of New York, and from standard legal-information services. Data has also been supplied to the Committee on request by unofficial agencies, referred to in the texts, either directly or from their recognized publications. Unless otherwise indicated, the data has been brought down to June 30, 1943.

PART I

CHANGING TIMES
CHALLENGING PROBLEMS

A VILLAGE OF 1790   Reproduced from The Pageant of America

1

1790 : Making a New Nation

The Pattern of Living
Farming the Basis of Family Security

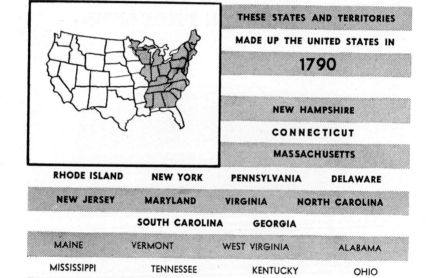

THESE STATES AND TERRITORIES
MADE UP THE UNITED STATES IN
1790

	NEW HAMPSHIRE		
	CONNECTICUT		
	MASSACHUSETTS		
RHODE ISLAND	**NEW YORK**	**PENNSYLVANIA**	**DELAWARE**
NEW JERSEY	**MARYLAND**	**VIRGINIA**	**NORTH CAROLINA**
	SOUTH CAROLINA	**GEORGIA**	
MAINE	VERMONT	WEST VIRGINIA	ALABAMA
MISSISSIPPI	TENNESSEE	KENTUCKY	OHIO
INDIANA	ILLINOIS	MICHIGAN	WISCONSIN

BOLD TYPE REPRESENTS STATES. LIGHT FACE TYPE REPRESENTS TERRITORIES.

IT IS 1790 IN THE FRONTIER VILLAGE OF NEWTOWN. TWENTY-odd log and frame houses, some with detached barns, others with low sheds, border either side of the Mohawk Valley Road.

Fewer than 200 people make up the permanent settlement. The first log cabin in the town still stands—even, in 1790, only a dozen years old. A church, a general store, a cobbler's shop, a blacksmith's forge, a grist mill, and the tavern, which is an overnight stop on the western trail from Albany, face the village green. Most of the families farm their own land; only the minister, the blacksmith, the cobbler, the miller, the storekeeper, and the innkeeper make their living from what today we call the professions and the service trades. When a new house or barn is to be built, all the men turn out to raise the frame and help the new settler or the young farmer, just married, to get started on a farm of his own. There are, perhaps, a doctor and a lawyer in the village; more likely they live miles away and are sent for when they are needed. The village squire, a larger landowner, lives in a brick or stone house and hires some of the farmers to help him harvest his crops in their spare time.

Very few products come into or go out of the village in the course of a year. Most families raise what they need to eat and to wear. Hens, cows, and pigs supply eggs, butter, meat. Sheep provide food and also wool for the family's homespun clothing which is carded, spun, and woven by the women of the family. Of course, some things which do not grow or cannot be produced in the village, like tea or sugar or iron, are needed. These items are brought in by the storekeeper and either sold for cash or traded for the staples raised locally, like wool, wheat, and livestock. As a matter of fact, few actual cash purchases and sales take place in the course of an entire year. The storekeeper does most of the business across his counter on a barter basis and sells the local products which he takes in exchange for his goods in Albany or New York City.

Two or three times a year, perhaps, a peddler comes

through town with new imports from the seaboard towns—silks and brocades for the women, pots and pans for the home, plows and scythes for the farm. If crops have been good, he finds a ready market. The goods which he sells or trades become the models which next year the blacksmith will be turning out himself or the women will be using in designing their homemade furnishings and clothing.

This was the pattern of life for most of the 3,929,214 white Americans in 1790, from the fishing villages clustered along the Maine coast to the farms of the Piedmont country of the Carolinas and Georgia. Most families were self-contained units living on and off the soil, growing what they needed and making what they could for themselves. It took, in fact, the work of 19 farm families on the land to grow enough food to supply one family living in the towns. Farming was still done largely by hand labor with what "power" oxen and a few horses could supply. People raised enough to take care of themselves with only a little surplus, when times were good, to buy the few additional items they needed.

There were few roads of any sort for hauling farm products or town-made goods in or out of the isolated villages and scattered farmhouses or plantations where most people lived. Even the main highways were poor; it took more days (from 5 to 7) to go by stagecoach from New York to Boston than it now takes hours. There were only six "towns" of 8,000 or more population; New York was the only town of over 40,000 in 1790. The people who lived in these towns accounted for only 3.3 per cent of the whole population. Most of them were engaged in local trade, in overseas commerce, or in the wholesale business supplying the back country.

There were, of course, a few small industries. Iron, for instance, was already becoming important in making farm tools, household articles, and stoves. There were iron smelters

4

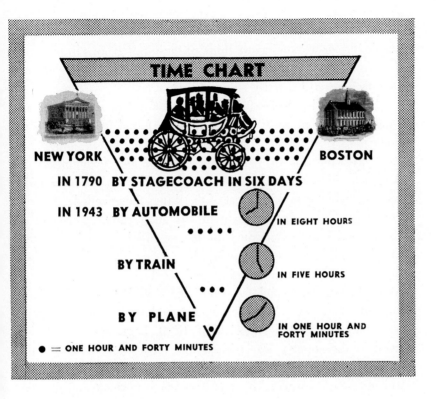

TIME CHART

NEW YORK

BOSTON

IN 1790 BY STAGECOACH IN SIX DAYS

IN 1943 BY AUTOMOBILE — IN EIGHT HOURS

BY TRAIN — IN FIVE HOURS

BY PLANE — IN ONE HOUR AND FORTY MINUTES

● = ONE HOUR AND FORTY MINUTES

and shipyards, ropewalks and barrel factories, where men hired out by the day or week or even by the year. These industries were, however, small and scattered. Often the farmer who lived nearby worked part-time in the small shops or mills without giving up farming as his main job. Few farmers would, indeed, leave their farms to become factory workers.

In the towns there were also a few shops in which shoes and other consumers goods much in demand were made by workmen hired by the season. Master carpenters contracted to build houses for the town dwellers and took on helpers as they were needed. Even in the towns, there were in 1790

5

relatively few people who could be considered as either employers or workers as we think of these two groups in present-day America. Work, whether on the farm, or in the shop or factory, was still usually a family affair.

Most families were fairly large. Four or five children, ranging from one to 20 years old, were found in almost every home. Six or eight (or even more) youngsters under 21 were growing up in perhaps a fifth of the farmhouses of America. These families were really self-contained economic units growing or making most of the things they needed. Every-one helped to keep the farm or the shop running efficiently. Each contributed something to the economic security of the family. Ploughing in the spring, harvesting in the fall, tending the cattle and sheep, clipping and carding and spinning the wool, cutting the wood for fuel—these and many other jobs kept everyone busy from sunup to sundown. Unemployment was unknown in the America of 1790, because no one who lived in the country was without the means for his own sub-sistence. Most families owned their farms outright and so did not have to worry about paying off a mortgage or sharing their crops with the landlord.

It was the same in the villages and towns; the few shops and mills ran on the same day-long timetable. Since, indeed, most of the shops and mills except in the largest towns were part-time occupations for their owners, it was natural that everyone should work long hours.

Reproduced from The Pageant of America

Signs of Economic Change

There were signs on the horizon in 1790, however, that economic life in America was going to be very different in the years ahead. We had gained most of the country (except Florida) westward to the Mississippi by our treaty with Great Britain in 1783. The Confederation Congress had outlined a plan for self-government for new settlers in the northern part of the new territory by the Northwest Ordinance of 1787. Whole families were already on the move into the rich new lands west of the Alleghenies. Dozens of new settlements like Newtown were springing up in the western country. When Jefferson completed the Louisiana Purchase in 1803, the territory under the American flag was nearly doubled and the westward movement of those seeking freedom on the frontier was greatly stimulated.

As we rounded out our frontiers and found ourselves with "a continent to conquer", the new lands opened for settlement beckoned thousands, and then hundreds of thousands, from the towns and farms of the East. This new factor of westward migration was to continue to be important in American life for a century after 1790. Men and women and children could leave their old jobs in the cities or on their worn-out farmlands to seek economic security on the rich prairie soils of the West. Many families began the pioneer life of the early colonists over again in the West, often moving beyond the fringe of new settlements two or three times in a single generation. If conditions were hard where they were, if they could not gain the security they wanted in the East or in the growing frontier towns, they could "go West" to a homestead on the plains between the Appalachians and the Rockies.

This, however, was not the only economic change in the America of 1790. There were rumors coming out of England of new inventions. The stationary steam engine and the

THE CORDWAINER AT WORK

© C. P. Co. courtesy of Ladies Home Journal

EARLY PAPER MAKING IN AMERICA

Courtesy of the Bettman Archive

Courtesy of Harper & Brothers

WEAVING FOR THE FAMILY

new spinning and weaving machines were among the more important, but others had been developed even before 1790. Many others were to follow in the next half-century. England tried to keep these machines at home by forbidding their export or the emigration of anyone who knew about them. They were, nonetheless, soon reproduced over here. Workmen smuggled themselves out of England carrying the plans of the new machines in their minds, and soon set them up in the first water-power textile factories in New England.

Nor were these new machines all imported from England. Americans have always been ingenious at inventing new devices for saving labor or doing jobs more efficiently. This inventiveness was beginning to influence our economy even as early as the 1790's. Eli Whitney's cotton gin of 1793 was the first important American invention which made possible the growth of a new industry, cotton textiles. Many inventions soon followed such as the carding machine and the cast-iron plow in 1797, the high-pressure steam engine in 1799, and the cylindrical paper machine in 1809.* It was, indeed, in the three decades after 1790 that the foundations of our modern machine industry were laid. The ways of earning a living for most people, in factories and shops and service trades instead of on the farm, have, in fact, changed more in the last 150 years than in the previous 1500.

The people of Newtown and other farming villages could not have realized how deeply this shift from agriculture to manufacturing was to influence their own and their children's lives. The shift was already on the horizon in 1790. Decade by decade, it has continued to change the economic and social life of people on the farms no less than in the factories. Many of the children and grandchildren from villages like

* What began then has continued ever since. Up to 1941, over 2,000,000 patents have been issued by the U. S. Patent Office; today they are granted at the rate of about 50,000 a year.

Newtown were going to become workers in these new industrial cities as well as pioneers on the new frontiers of the West.

These economic and social conditions naturally affected the way men and women thought about their stake in the American way of life. How did they view that stake and what were some of the beliefs which they held in 1790 and the early years of the 19th century?

The Pattern of Ideas : Political

Working to make both ends meet was not all that families in the farming villages and the towns of America were thinking about in 1790. The new government under George Washington had just come into being under the Constitution of 1789. Not everyone had been in favor of the new constitution. Most of the back-country farmer representatives in the state ratifying conventions from New Hampshire to Georgia had been against it. Votes had been close in more than one of these conventions. In Massachusetts the new constitution won by only 186 to 168, in New York, by only 26 to 23.

It is hard for us to realize that politics then was very much like politics today and that party differences were as strong and often even more violent. It is difficult because, as we look back, we tend to think of the Constitution of 1789 —the oldest written national constitution still in force today— as the unanimous choice of all the people. That it has weathered many storms is a tribute to the wisdom and the foresight of the Framers who then traced a blueprint of government for us today. That it operates as effectively today for over 130,000,000 people as it did in 1790 when about 3,000,000 white Americans were debating its merits and defects, gives us a deeper sense of its value in these days of challenge.

Despite these differences, however, illustrated by the fact that Rhode Island did not come into the Union until 1790, the people of the 13 states were eager to see the new government succeed. It is true that most of them, even men, could not vote, that only in New York State were the latter free from property or religious restrictions. They had fought a long war and gone through a deep depression. They wanted little more than to settle down to their farming and their crafts, to get on with the main job of making a living. They hoped that the new government would make this possible by keeping peace and good order among the thirteen states.

For these and other reasons, most Americans of 1790 and their children of the next half-century were loyal to the new republican government founded on democratic principles. Some, it is true, wanted to go further than others toward political equality without respect to differences in wealth or religion. The great majority was, however, satisfied to accept the democratic basis on which the constitution rested. The idea that the powers of those holding office should result from the will of the people goes far back in our history—even beyond the founding of Plymouth in 1620. Through a century and a half of our colonial experience, we had become increasingly certain that we did not want a monarchy but a republic, not rule by the will of the few but of the majority.

In the Constitution of 1789, we find these ideas crystallized in a new expression of this faith in government of the people, by the people, for the people. The leaders who framed our Constitution did not depend on force, the totalitarian way of organizing and controlling the people, to govern the new nation. Instead, they based it squarely on the right of the people to govern themselves.

In our Constitution, we find many evidences of this tradition of political democracy. The most important one is the principle of representative government. This principle is that the people shall elect representatives of their own choosing to make the laws under which all shall have equal rights and duties. We did not invent this principle or its practice in the United States. We did, however, give both the principle and the practice their widest use up to 1790, or, indeed, for long thereafter. We have gone on, moreover, during the last century and a half trying to improve the actual practice of political democracy both in the nation and in the states. The people of 1790 believed, as we do today, that political democracy is the soundest basis on which to rest the security of the people. They sought, as we are seeking in the 1940's, to achieve that security through government—for the general welfare.

The Pattern of Ideas : Economic

Other beliefs were strongly held by the families living in the villages of America in 1790 in every state from New Hampshire to Georgia. These beliefs related to their economic activities. Like their political ideas, they resulted from self-reliance, from believing in their own abilities and in their capacity for achieving economic security through their own initiative. These villagers, and the townspeople too, had found that they could generally win security and often prosperity by hard work on the land.

The men of 1790, therefore, based their economic policies on the idea of the individual's right to control and use his own property. Capitalism, as this system of property relations is called, was considered one of the main forces which would help to develop our industrial strength as a nation. It was, indeed, credited by such leaders as Hamilton with being the chief means of increasing our prosperity and security, both individual and national. And why not? We owned a continent to conquer, rich in all kinds of natural resources. These resources only awaited the initiative of the economic pioneer to be turned into the things people wanted.

12

Early in the 1790's, for instance, Moses Brown and Samuel Slater of Rhode Island built a dam for water power and a mill to spin and weave cotton textiles. They and countless others who started new industries in America inevitably made large profits from their enterprises. Our system of private property—capitalism—rests, therefore, on a solid foundation of practical experience which these economic pioneers of the 1790's and their successors gained from their immediate surroundings. They believed that the things people wanted would be made more quickly and cheaply if their enterprises were free from governmental control. Thus, the idea of free enterprise was firmly rooted in the American tradition along with the belief in free government.

During the 19th century, a new industrial order was created by these economic pioneers within this framework of free enterprise. They helped to create, as we shall see, a rising standard of living for many if not for all the people. If the men and women of 1790 could not foresee all the industrial growth of the century ahead, they did establish the pattern of economic ideas which made it possible. They traced a blueprint of a free-enterprise system based on private property. This blueprint remains the basis of our present-day economy.

The Workers' Place in American Life

We may ask one further question before we leave the America of 1790. How far were employers and workers separated into different groups? Were there employers' organizations and labor unions as we think of them today?

In colonial days, as we have seen, most work was performed by individual workmen—shoemakers, millers, tanners, bakers, and others. Sometimes, in the larger towns all the men engaged in a single trade organized a Society or Guild. Practically all industrial work was done by the master craftsmen or skilled artisans, who were the only workers admitted to these societies. Most of these guilds were mutual benefit associations. Their chief purposes were to take care of their members when they were ill or out of work and to provide opportunities for social activities.

During and after the Revolutionary War, more and more people in the towns went to work for the master craftsmen. Two or three workmen, or perhaps a dozen, would hire out to help build a house which had been contracted for by a master carpenter. Again, some apprentice shoemakers might be taken on in rush times in a one-man shop and later become regular wage earners. Since these workers were generally not allowed to join the guilds of the master craftsmen, they formed their own mutual benefit societies or guilds. They were the forerunners of the labor unions of today.

CARPENTER'S HALL   Courtesy of Harper & Brothers   The first group in this country which we should today call a labor union was the Federal Society of Journeyman Cordwainers (or shoemakers) organized in Philadelphia in 1792. In 1799, it carried on an organized strike against reductions in wages which the master craftsmen attempted to impose on the shoe workers. It even paid one of its members to picket outside the master-shoe-makers' shops. After nine weeks, it finally won its demands. The Federal Society was a craft union since it included only the workers in a single craft or kind of skill. This type of union, sometimes called a horizontal union, has been the most usual type of labor organization from 1790 almost to the present. For three-quarters of a century after 1790, it was the only form of labor union which American workers developed.

Until after the War of 1812, these unions were purely local; the workers in a single craft in a single town banded together to try to improve their working conditions. These local groups did not seek to organize either on a state or national basis or in a combination of all the craft unions in a single community until about 1830. They were, in this early period, small, isolated groups, operating locally within a single industry.

One economic factor in this period favored the demands of the workers for higher wages and especially for shorter hours. New industries were springing up almost overnight in New England, New York, and Pennsylvania. It has been estimated, for instance, that, between 1820 and 1825, the amount of capital invested in industry increased from $75,000,000 to $675,000,000. The number of industrial workers rose from about 200,000 to at least three or four times that number. There were, therefore, for most of this period, more jobs than workers available. Although the factories drew people away from the farms to the rising industrial towns and cities the demand for workers was greater than the supply. In fact, the workers often held the balance of power in bargaining with their employers.

Their most insistent demand was for a shorter working day. The twelve-hour day was then common in the new factories.

Because farmers worked from sunup to sundown, no one thought at first of any shorter day for industrial work. But the workers soon tried, through their local unions and even individually, to obtain a ten-hour factory day. A number of strikes were called on this issue during the 1810's and 1820's. By the end of this period, the ten-hour day, if not yet general, had become a major demand of the workers. It was recognized by some employers, and accepted by others in the 1830's. The question of the length of the working day has remained, however, one of the most widely disputed issues even to our own time. It was one of the first aspects of industrial relations which we, the people, sought to regulate through government (see Chapter 10, pp. 210 ff.)

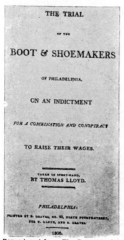

THE TRIAL

OF THE

BOOT & SHOEMAKERS

OF PHILADELPHIA,

ON AN INDICTMENT

FOR A COMBINATION AND CONSPIRACY

TO RAISE THEIR WAGES.

TAKEN IN SHORT-HAND,
BY THOMAS LLOYD.

PHILADELPHIA:

PRINTED BY B. GRAVES, NO. 40, NORTH FOURTH-STREET,
FOR T. LLOYD, AND B. GRAVES.

1806.

Reproduced from The Pageant of America   These early unions were attacked as contrary to law because they were secret. As in England, they were charged with being "conspiracies" * to raise wages or

* We inherited the common law from England. It is the body of principles and rules of conduct which the courts developed from the cases between individuals which were brought to the judges to settle. One of these principles was that no one might "conspire" with others to injure another person or to deprive him of his rights under law. Thus, when workers "combined" to force their employer to give them higher wages or shorter hours, they were held to be conspiring to deprive him of the right to make individual contracts with his workers.

to act in other ways contrary to the public interest. Our state legislatures never passed laws to make labor unions illegal. A few cases, under the common-law doctrine of conspiracy, were, it is true, brought by employers in the courts during the 1810's. Since 1815, the right of workers to join unions of their own choosing has been recognized by our courts. They have, however, held that this right is subject to the terms of the contracts which workers make with their employers. The courts enforced these early labor contracts in the same manner as any other agreement—by requiring that the terms of the contract must be obeyed.* We can say, therefore, that the men and women of 1790 saw this right to join unions established in America although it was over a half-century before unions became an important factor in the workers' efforts to protect and promote their interests.

FRONTIER VILLAGE   Courtesy of Harper & Brothers

* As we shall see, some American courts interpreted labor contracts so strictly that workers were practically deprived of the possibility of joining unions. The workers continued to protest against these decisions of the courts which in effect allowed employers to require their workers to sign a contract by which they agreed not to join a union—or to quit work. In recent years, new laws have guaranteed the right of any man to join a union of his own choosing (see Chapters 5, 6, pp. 100 ff., 124 ff.).

☆ ☆ ☆ ☆ ☆ ☆ ☆ ☆ ☆ ☆ ☆ ☆ ☆

As we look back a century and a half, we can see how different American life was in 1790. Ninety-six out of every 100 people lived on farms in the country or in villages in which farming was still the main occupation of most of the people. Most families grew and made most of what they needed to eat and to wear. The families of 1790 were self-contained economic units largely independent of any outside help to make ends meet. The men and women of 1790 developed their own set of political and economic ideas out of their experience. Political democracy and economic freedom were the watchwords of the people. There were already, however, signs of economic change on the horizon. Machines were soon to create new industries and draw people from the farms into the factories. The workers were becoming concerned about their part in American life, their share and their place in industry. What was America to be like a half-century after 1790? The question was already being asked in the halls of Congress and around the hearths of the townsman and the frontiersman alike. Let us see what changes were to be noted in the America of 1840.

AMERICAN LIFE IN 1790

h figure
resents ten people
of every hundred

96
OUT OF EVERY
100 PEOPLE
LIVED ON FARMS

MOST FAMILIES GREW
AND MADE WHAT THEY
NEEDED TO EAT AND
TO WEAR

Reproduced from The Pageant of America

POLITICAL
DEMOCRACY
AND ECONOMIC FREEDOM WERE THE WATCHWORDS OF THE PEOPLE

2

1840 : Our Economy in Transition

The Pattern of Living
Industry Begins to Draw People From the
Farm to the Factory

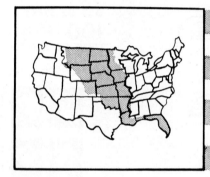

| THESE NEW STATES & TERRITORIES |
| WERE IN THE UNITED STATES BY |
| **1840** |
| LOUISIANA |
| MISSOURI |
| ARKANSAS |

	SOUTH DAKOTA	NEBRASKA	
FLORIDA	OKLAHOMA	IOWA	NORTH DAKOTA
	KANSAS	WYOMING	
	MONTANA	COLORADO	

BOLD TYPE REPRESENTS STATES. LIGHT FACE TYPE REPRESENTS TERRITORIES.

BY 1840, NEWTOWN HAD GROWN TO A TOWN OF ABOUT 4,000 people. The grandchildren of the families of 1790 were now scattered. Some had gone West with the caravans of covered wagons that had begun to stream through the town after the treaty of peace with Great Britain in 1783. Some had gone to the rising industrial towns and cities in New England, Pennsylvania, and in other parts of New York State. A few had remained to work on the Erie Canal, to promote a new railroad, to start a tanning factory or a cotton mill or a nail shop.

Life in Newtown was, however, not very different in 1840 from what it had been a half-century before. The Erie Canal had been opened in 1825 and a new means of transportation provided for the people living in the towns and villages of the Mohawk Valley. Most people still worked on their farms at least part of the time. One or two members of the families living in Newtown perhaps worked in one of the new mills. A few took jobs in the new stores which were opening to take care of the growing demand for manufactured goods. Sometimes they worked for only part of the year; only in a few cases did these new town workers depend for their entire living on their earnings in the stores or factories. Most of them still lived at home and helped out on the family farm, while the rest of the family was still engaged in agriculture. Money, rather than barter, was coming into general use as the basis of exchange both on the farm and in the stores.

This pattern of living was typical of most of the towns as well as of the rising industrial cities of 1840. Agriculture was still the basic means of livelihood for most Americans. Even in 1850, when the census first began to count people in different occupations, fewer than a million out of the more than 23,000,000 people in the United States were factory wage earners.

By 1840, however, the shift from the farm to the factory was well under way. The number of towns of over 8,000 had grown from six to forty-four. In 1790, only a little over three (3.3) of every hundred people in America had lived in these towns; now the number had risen to more than eight (8.5) out of every hundred. Industry was developing throughout the country. It was growing most rapidly in the Northeast—in New England, New York, and Pennsylvania. In these states, and particularly in New England, new towns were springing up around water-power sites. They were the forerunners of the many industrial cities of today. The new textile centers like Lawrence and Lowell in Massachusetts had by 1840 become mill towns in which nearly all the people worked in the factories or in the stores.

A COUNTRY STORE

Signs of Economic Change

What brought about this change in the America of 1840? What forces were at work in the nation which were already transforming, and were to continue to change, the pattern of living for more and more of the people?

One of the forces most responsible for this change in American life was, as we have seen, the War of 1812. During the struggle, a large part of our trade with Europe was cut off and we began to manufacture the goods which had formerly been imported. The conflict also stimulated many new industries. This industrial expansion continued at an even more rapid pace after the war had ended and peace was established.

Thus a new industrial pattern was emerging in the America of 1840. The shift from agriculture to manufacturing, which has continued and accelerated ever since, was already under way.

Except in the largest towns, however, most workers in the new factories could still carry on part-time farming along with their jobs in industry. Land was available near the larger towns and many workers came in from the farms to work in the mills when they were not busy ploughing and harvesting. Most of the new mills, except in the big textile towns, were still small with only a few dozen workers, or a hundred-odd at most, in each mill.

In 1840, most Americans could still count on winning economic security and prosperity for themselves. Whether they lived in the new industrial cities or in the country towns like Newtown, they were able to improve their position in life —their standard of living—largely through their own efforts. There was still land in the West to be had by homesteading, that is, by settlement and use for a few years. A steadily growing population (from 12,866,020, to 31,443,321 between 1830 and 1860) created a rising demand for the products of industry, and made it profitable to establish new factories and trading companies. Before and after 1840, the nation was expanding rapidly both in territory and in population.

Expansion took many forms. One was in territory. We had acquired Florida from Spain in 1819. During the decade of the 1840's, we were to obtain Texas and the Southwest to California by conquest from Mexico and the Northwest by treaty from England. We rounded out our continental frontiers and opened new lands for pioneering settlement and mining discoveries. From 1790 to 1848, we added about 2,104,000 square miles to the 892,135 of the thirteen original states.

NEW HIGHWAYS TO THE WEST

FROM COACH TO BARGE TO RAILROAD

Courtesy
United St
Departmer
Agricultu
Bureau
Public R

TRANSPORTATION AND THE URBAN PATTERN

1840

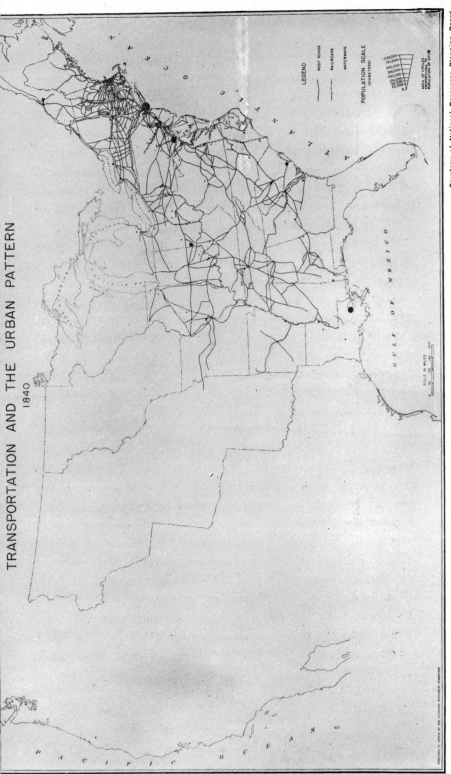

Courtesy of National Resources Planning Board

This westward expansion greatly stimulated one of the rising young industries of 1840—railroads. In 1842 there were 4,026 miles of railroad; by 1850, tney had increased to 9,021, by 1860, to 30,626. We may say, in fact, that westward expansion created the railroads by establishing a demand for two-way transport where canals could not be built or the rivers did not run. Western settlers increasingly wanted the products of eastern factories; eastern city-dwellers depended more and more on western wheat and livestock farms for their food. Thus, railroads were developed out of the need of supplying other industries with quick and efficient transportation, just as busses, trucks, and airplanes have in our time provided similar service to industry and commerce.

Another factor was affecting the pattern of living in the America of 1840. The lure of freedom and free land had already started a new stream of European immigrants to our shores. This stream ran with increasing volume for three-quarters of a century—until, indeed, the War of 1914–1918. Between 1821 and 1830, 143,439 immigrants had come to this country. In the next three decades, the numbers rose to 599,125, 1,713,251, and 2,598,214.

These new Americans often had less security than their neighbors, because they had less to start with. They had come to gain freedom in a democracy. They had also come to win greater economic security for themselves and their families. Some of these immigrants went West to settle on the farms or work on the railroads where they gained a measure of security on the land. Most of them, however, stayed in the cities and took factory or day-labor jobs. They helped to swell the ranks of industrial workers. Decade by decade, they crowded into the slums near the factories and competed with the older immigrants—the earlier Americans—for jobs. Even by 1840, the question of what policy we should follow about immigration was being hotly debated in thousands of homes in hundreds of towns like Newtown from Maine to Missouri.

Thus the pattern of living was changing in America by 1840. New forces—the invention and use of machines and a rising tide of immigration—were already making themselves felt. America was on the move. Our economy was in transition. The prophecies of 1790 that the new machines would change the pattern of life and of work for all the people were coming true. We were on the way toward becoming an industrial nation. How were these changes influencing the way people were viewing the political and economic questions of the day?

The Pattern of Ideas : Political

First, about politics. In 1840, we had just been through what some have called the Jacksonian revolution. Andrew Jackson symbolized the revolt of the frontiersmen, upland farmers, and city workers against the political control of the eastern industrialists and bankers. These groups demanded that the last remaining property and religious restrictions on the right to vote be abolished by the state legislatures. They wanted to establish democracy in the terms of the Declaration of Independence, that "all men are created equal". Free government came to mean the right of every man to vote—for President as well as for constable. Public officers should represent all the people, whatever their economic status or religious beliefs, not just "the rich, the wellborn, and the intelligent", whom John Adams had called the true defenders of sound government.

In this movement of political ideas and party slogans, the people of Newtown shared. They were divided, as were the people in every city and town. Most of the people were still farmers and small tradespeople; only a few of them had part-

27

Courtesy of Peter A. Juley & Son

EXPANDING INDUSTRY

Courtesy of Harper & Brothers

IRON—SHIPS—TEXTILES

Reproduced from The Pageant of America

time jobs in the mills. A majority was in favor of the new ideas about the meaning of democracy in practice. And the same was true of the industrial workers in the cities. For both, property and religious restrictions on voting were no longer tolerable. A new spirit was being forged in the politics of America in 1840. This spirit was to manifest itself in the will of the North to abolish slavery and later of all sections of the nation to guarantee the rights of the workers through government.

The Pattern of Ideas : Economic

In the 1840's, people were also beginning to reshape their ideas about the American economy. Free enterprise as a way of achieving individual security and of developing the resources of the nation was still the basic article of faith in the American economic creed. It was, in fact, considered, as it had been in the earlier agricultural period of 1790, as the chief cause of individual and national prosperity.

There were already, however, voices which questioned the unrestrained exercise of individual initiative as a guarantee of the general welfare. These voices spoke mostly from the ranks of the workers. They had been heard even before 1840. After 1840, they grew in strength and became the basis of a new and increasingly significant factor in American life, the labor-union movement. We may well review, therefore, the origins and growth of this movement.

The Workers' Place in American Life
The Beginnings of a Labor Movement

The new voices beginning to be heard have become, indeed, the chief means through which the workers have sought to gain their ends—to protect and to promote their interests—in an economy in transition. As new industries developed after the War of

1812, as more and more immigrants competed for jobs, some of the new factory workers began to organize on a broader basis than the earlier individual unions, such as the Cordwainers' Society of 1794. In 1827, for instance, 15 local trade "societies" of workers in Philadelphia united to form the Mechanics Union of Trade Associations. This was the first alliance of workers in different occupations into a single city-wide organization. Although its main purpose was to keep wages up and hours low, it soon branched out into politics.

As a result of this movement in Philadelphia, a few state Workingmen's Parties sprang up in 1828 through cooperation between the Philadelphia union and similar unions in New York, Boston, and other rising industrial cities. The movement quickly spread to include workers in all parts of the industrial North. It put a few candidates in the field in the state and local elections of 1830. These workers' political parties were, however, shortlived. With the exception of those in the industrial cities, few succeeded in electing any candidates to public office. Most workers then and since have sought to gain their ends in politics through the national parties, not through separate labor parties.

In March, 1834, the General Trades Union of New York City, another citywide organization, invited all the unions of the country to meet in a national convention. Several such national conventions, attended by delegates from many unions throughout the country, were held during the next two or three years. This was the first effort to create a really national labor-union organization. It collapsed after the Panic of 1837.

A few groups of workers in a single industry or craft also succeeded in this period in organizing along national lines, for instance, the shoemakers, the printers, and the carpenters, all in 1836. None was able to maintain a stable national organization after the Panic of 1837. These early movements were, however, significant for they pointed the way to two types of labor organization which have become increasingly important since. One is the union of all workers in a single craft or industry along national lines. Today these unions are called Nationals or Internationals. The other is the citywide organization of all workers in every type of occupation. These Central Trades or Labor Councils, as they are generally termed, are found in almost every industrial city. Both ways of developing union strength led, as they have more than once since, to the national organization of all workers to protect and promote their interests.

For some time after 1840, the union movement remained weak. It was for the most part organized only locally, and did not concern itself with the broader economic changes confronting the workers. The early drive toward national unions

MAIN STREET — 1840   Courtesy of Harper & Brothers

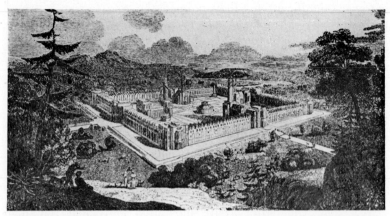

NEW HARMONY, INDIANA   Reproduced from The Pageant of America

could not survive the shock of the Depression of 1837. The first concern of the workers was for jobs and there were not enough jobs to go around in the hard times of the late 1830's and early 1840's.

Several important ideas did, however, emerge in this period to become a permanent part of labor thought in America. Some of these ideas came out of the European movements of the period. For example, Robert Owen, an English manufacturer, came to this country and, in 1825, founded the colony of New Harmony, Indiana. Here he tried to carry out his ideas for a cooperative industrial system. He advocated establishing factories in which the workers would control production and share all the profits of their labor. Although the New Harmony colony survived only a few years, the ideas which started there and in other American groups at about the same time have had a lasting influence within the American labor movement. Among these were free education for all children and shorter hours and higher wages—to insure the worker a just share in the products of his effort.

An American workingman, George Henry Evans, tried to turn these ideas into reality by agitating for definite legislative action. He founded the *Workman's Advocate* in New York City in 1829, a newspaper in which he preached the doctrine of a shorter working day and free land in the West for new settlers. A free-land policy, Evans thought, would give the workers a stronger bargaining position. With free farms available, they would be able to leave their jobs and go on the land if they were dissatisfied with their wages or working conditions.

During this period, too, other ideas, looking toward Socialism were brought to America by German and other workingmen who fled from their homelands before and after the European Revolutions of 1848. These ideas spread in this country and became the basis of new social-reform movements here. These movements have continued to our own time. Many of the ideas originating in the various European Socialist movements have been adopted in one form or another by our American labor movement in the century since 1840. No organized Socialist labor movement, however, has ever attracted more than a small minority of American workers to join its ranks.

America in 1840 was very different from what it had been in 1790—or was soon to be. As we look back a century, we can see how great the changes had been and how great they were to be in the next half-century. The people living in Newtown at that time could look back and see great changes: the western settlements; the new democratic ideas; the emergence of the machine; the rise of factory towns (not yet large cities); the efforts of the workers to organize unions of their own choosing. A new America was in the making.

Few people in 1840 could, however, foresee the changes, political and economic, that were to take place by 1890. The Civil War, the disappearance of the frontier and the closing of western settlement, the growth of immigration, the dominant place of the machine, the emergence of a national labor movement—these were some of the things which the men and women of 1840 could hardly anticipate. These changes were the seeds out of which the America of 1890—and of 1940—was to grow.

WESTWARD EXPANSION REACHES THE PACIFIC

SAN FRANCISCO IN THE 1840's   Courtesy of James A. B. Scherer

AMERICAN LIFE IN 1840

EACH DOT EQUALS
50 PEOPLE

1790 VILLAGE

NEWTOWN HAD
200 PEOPLE

●●●●●●●●●●●●●●●●●●●●
●●●●●●●●●●●●●●●●●●●●
●●●●●●●●●●●●●●●●●●●●
●●●●●●●●●●●●●●●●●●●●

BY 1840
NEWTOWN GREW
TO TOWN OF
4,000 PEOPLE

SOME HAD GONE WEST TO SETTLE

SOME HAD MIGRATED TO OTHER TOWNS AND STATES

SOME WORKED IN NEW MILLS AND FACTORIES

MOST PEOPLE STILL
WORKED ON FARMS
PART OF THE TIME

A FEW TOOK JOBS IN
NEW STORES SELLING
MANUFACTURED GOODS

AGRICULTURE STILL BASIC
MEANS OF LIVELIHOOD
FOR MOST AMERICANS

EMERGENCE OF THE MACHINE

RISE OF FACTORY TOWNS

BEGINNING OF WORKERS'
EFFORTS TO ORGANIZE
NATIONAL LABOR UNIONS

3

1890 : Forging an Industrial Economy

The Pattern of Living
The Factory Displaces the Farm as the
Main Source of Family Security

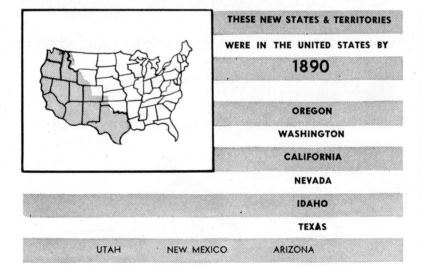

THESE NEW STATES & TERRITORIES

WERE IN THE UNITED STATES BY

1890

OREGON

WASHINGTON

CALIFORNIA

NEVADA

IDAHO

TEXAS

UTAH   NEW MEXICO   ARIZONA

BOLD TYPE REPRESENTS STATES. LIGHT FACE TYPE REPRESENTS TERRITORIES.

THE GREAT-GREAT-GRANDCHILDREN OF THE SETTLERS OF 1790 were growing up in 1890. During the past hundred years, Newtown had grown from a straggling village to a thriving city of about 50,000 people. By 1890, the town of 1840 was almost entirely an industrial and business center. Most of the families who lived in the city were wage earners in the factories and shops. Many of the more fortunate families had moved out to the new suburbs which rimmed the crowded industrial area. Their homes were surrounded by shaded lawns and tree-lined streets.

Beyond the suburbs were the farmlands. The farmers were, however, no longer self-sustaining as their parents and grandparents had been. Instead of growing and making most of what they needed to eat and wear, they now supplied the nearby city markets with many specialized crops, such as fruits, vegetables, butter, eggs, and milk. Like their fellow workers in the factories and shops, they bought most of their clothing, household furnishings, and much of their food in the city's big, new department and grocery stores. Gradually, too, their children were leaving the farms and going to work in Newtown or moving away to other industrial cities. Few now went West to take up farming; the Census of 1890, indeed, noted that "there (was) no longer a frontier in the United States". Opportunity for most boys meant jobs in business or industry, not free land and self-sufficient farms.

What was happening in Newtown was happening all over America. Instead of the 44 cities and towns of over 8,000 in 1840, there were now 445 in which 29 per cent of the whole population lived. The industrial cities were growing rapidly. In 1900, there were three cities of over 1,000,000 and 38 more cities of 100,000, in which 18.6 per cent of the entire population was concentrated. The workers lived in crowded homes, often in slums or tenements. There was little if any room for lawns or gardens. Industry and trade, not farming, now offered the best chance of earning a living for more and more of the people, young and old alike.

There were, however, new frontiers in America—the commercial and manufacturing frontiers, with their factories, shops, and service occupations. These new industries kept pace with the rapidly growing population, beckoning the enterprising youngsters of the cities and towns like Newtown. Both before and after 1890, the pattern of living was becoming geared to the machine and its products. People wanted the thousand-and-one things that machines could make. More and more Americans found security—or insecurity in times of depression —in the factory, not on the farm. By 1890, 4,712,622 people out of a total population of 62,949,714 were wage earners in manufacturing establishments.

But this tells only part of the story. The machine required many people to work for it beside those who worked on it. Many new occupations, especially the professions and the service trades, grew in importance before and especially after 1890. Salesmen, clerks, and office workers were almost as important to industry as the factory workers themselves. Transportation, too, grew rapidly during this period. The network of railroads binding together the different sections of the country had risen from the 30,626 miles of 1860 to 167,191 miles in 1890.

This rapid growth of industry had one very important effect on the position of the workers in America. By 1890, more and more women and children were being drawn into the factories and mills and shops or into domestic service. The number of gainfully employed women over 10 rose between 1880 and 1890 from 2,647,157 to 4,005,532. The number of gainfully employed children between 10 and 15 rose in the same period from 1,118,356 to 1,503,771. Although this trend was to continue for women up to 1940, fewer and fewer children between 10 and 15 have worked since 1900. As we shall see (pp. 210) ff.), we have sought to eliminate child labor altogether in the factories although it still exists on the farm.

Like the girls in the early New England cotton mills, many of the women and children took jobs in order to become independent. Most of the new women and child factory workers, however, entered industry because they had to help balance the family budget. The wages of the man of the family were not enough to support his wife and children. Some of them were forced to accept whatever jobs they could get, often at lower wages than were paid to men for the same work. In good times, there were jobs enough to go around. When depression slowed down industry, on the other hand, many men lost their jobs because women and children were available and willing to work for lower wages. During the decades each side of 1890, the question of wages as well as of hours was, therefore, becoming increasingly important to the workers. It was, in fact, one of the chief causes of the growth of labor unions.

It is clear, then, that the pattern of life in Newtown and towns like it had changed profoundly by 1890. The villages of 1790 had grown into busy industrial cities. No longer was factory and office work or storekeeping a part-time job for people still living on the farms. More and more Americans were crowding into the cities and earning their living by producing or distributing goods made by machines. The farmlands had been pushed out beyond the suburbs and were providing a livelihood for a smaller and smaller part of the population.

As the character of the communities like Newtown changed from farming and trading to industrial and commercial centers, so did the characteristics of the people living in them. The tide of immigration which had begun in the 1820's had by now risen to a flood. In the decade before 1890, 5,246,613 people had come to this country, mostly from Europe. During the next three decades, 18,218,761 more immigrants were to pour into America. It is interesting, too, that the year 1890, which witnessed the end of the American frontier, should also mark the beginning of a new trend in immigration. Fewer and fewer came from northern and western Europe—from England, Ireland, Germany, and the Scandinavian countries. More and more people were coming from southern and eastern Europe— from Italy, Austria, Hungary, Russia and the Balkans. Although most of these newcomers had been peasants in their home countries, when they landed on the shores of America they did not travel West to take up free land or to work as farm laborers. They remained instead in the rising industrial towns and cities to work at the hardest jobs in the mines and iron and steel mills, on road and railroad construction, and in the shipyards. Although they became Americans, most of these European peasants did not bring with them to the cities the self-sufficient, traditions and habits of the American farmers who were also being drawn into industry.

The size as well as the character of our population was changing. As we have seen, during the half-century from 1840 to 1890, we had grown from a nation of 17,069,453 to one of 62,947,714. In every decade since 1790, except the troubled years of the Civil War, the increase of population decade by decade had been over 30 per cent. During the ten years from 1880 to 1890, the increase dropped to 25.5 per cent. It was to continue to drop each decade until it reached a low of 7 per cent in 1930–1940. Only part of the decline after 1920 can be explained by the decline in immigration resulting from the quota of 150,000 a year established by the Immigration Act of 1924. More important was the fact that the country was filling up. It was significant, too, that families were becoming constantly smaller. The families of five or more children were becoming fewer; only two or three children were now found in most homes. As we shifted from agriculture to industry, children were no longer an economic asset—as workers on the farm —as they had been a century earlier.

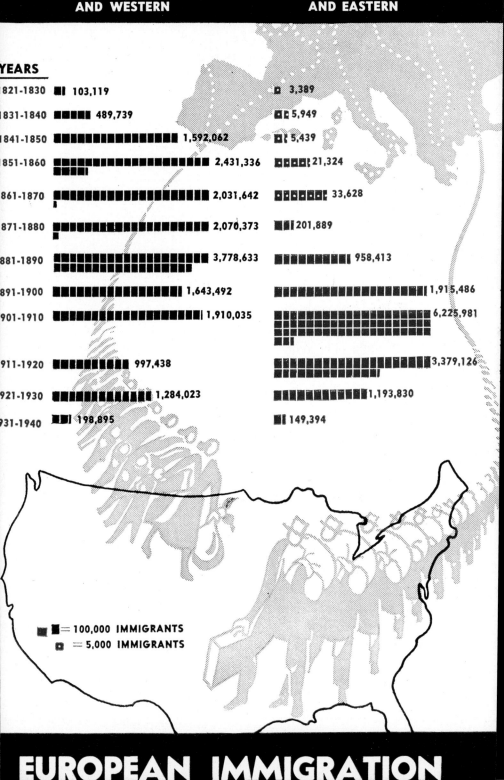

AND WESTERN   **AND EASTERN**

YEARS

	Western	Eastern
1821-1830	103,119	3,389
1831-1840	489,739	5,949
1841-1850	1,592,062	5,439
1851-1860	2,431,336	21,324
1861-1870	2,031,642	33,628
1871-1880	2,070,373	201,889
1881-1890	3,778,633	958,413
1891-1900	1,643,492	1,915,486
1901-1910	1,910,035	6,225,981
1911-1920	997,438	3,379,126
1921-1930	1,284,023	1,193,830
1931-1940	198,895	149,394

■ = 100,000 IMMIGRANTS
□ = 5,000 IMMIGRANTS

EUROPEAN IMMIGRATION

Courtesy of Harper & Brothers

Signs of Economic Change

Other changes were taking place in the 1890's, changes which were to affect the workers even more in the next two generations. Leading all others in importance was the continued growth of industry. The demand for manufactured goods, at home and abroad, was still expanding. New inventions were constantly developing new industries and making older industries more efficient. In the decade of the 1890's, patents reached almost the quarter-million mark (234,956). Electricity was just emerging as a major factor in industry for both power and light. Steam-power from coal had already largely supplanted water-power; oil was soon to become an important source of power for both factories and transportation.

The rapid growth of industry depended not only on the invention of new machines and new sources of power but on the development of great corporations to organize and to manage large-scale industries. The corporation, rather than the single employer or the partnership, became more and more typical of our economic organization in America as well as in other countries. As corporations increased in number they also began to increase in size. Some individuals tried to gain control of an entire industry or, to put it differently, to create a monopoly. Others, deeply concerned over the power of the great

"MAIN STREET — 1890"

Courtesy of The New-York Historical Society

"THE HORSELESS CARRIAGE"

Courtesy of United States Department of Agriculture, Bureau of Public Roads

industrial corporations and trusts, tried to stop this process by which industrial power was concentrated in a few hands.

There were, however, real reasons for the growth of large-scale corporations controlling many factories in the same industry. Management was more efficient because planning and organization could be better done when many units in the same industry could be brought together under a single and uniform production program. Economies in buying raw materials and in selling the output of all the factories could be achieved under a single management. Employment could, in many cases, be more effectively stabilized if many factories were under a unified control.

The development of corporations affected our whole economic structure. In the first place, it became increasingly difficult for an individual to build or buy a factory of his own. The capital necessary to start an industry was much greater than it had been a half-century before. The new machines cost more. The size of a single plant had to be larger in order to be more efficient. Its products were now sold in a national instead of a local market and competition in these markets required large-scale production. All this meant that an investment of thousands, often hundreds of thousands, of dollars was necessary to start an industry. As a result, most new industries were organized on a corporate basis, drawing their capital from many people rather than from one or a few. It was a very different form of industrial enterprise from that which had been typical in 1840.

In the second place, the people who lent money to finance new industries quite naturally demanded a voice, sometimes a controlling voice, in their management. The active organizer of a new plant was becoming less important, the investor more important, in its control.

A third change affected the workers particularly. In the

44

earlier period, the owner had frequently worked side by side with his employees. Even if he did not operate a machine himself, he was close to his workers every day. He knew most of them by their first names and often lived in the same neighborhood and shared in the same amusements as they did. Since both employers and workers generally lived and worked together, their personal relations were close and friendly.

This personal relationship between the employer and his workers had disappeared by 1890 in many industries. Less and less frequently did the owner work in the factory with his employees. The very size of the plant made it necessary for him to devote his entire time to management. Nor did the owner and his workmen any longer share the same community life and recreations. Increasingly, they lived in different parts of the town, the one in the suburbs, the others in the crowded industrial areas of the city. On the whole, the older friendly and personal relations were no longer possible in large-scale industries. This change was one of the most significant in our whole history from the point of view of the place of workers in our society. It is one explanation of the rapid development of the labor-union movement in this period.

Many individuals in America felt that the rise of the great corporations threatened the survival of government by the people. The huge business combinations seemed to be themselves almost independent governments, able to defy the will of the people because of their economic power. If they were to be directed in the public interest, it was felt that somehow they must be subjected to controls determined by the people. The surest way of exercising this control was through the state and national governments. So it was that, in the decades from the 1880's on, the relation of government to our economy became a matter of increasing popular interest and concern, the source of new political movements.

The Pattern of Ideas : Political

It was in this period that new political and economic ideas emerged in America. On the political side, the two decades after 1890 saw the rise of a number of reform movements which sought to insure political control to all the people. Among the more important of these were the initiative and referendum. These two devices were intended to insure to the people the right to control the policies of their state governments. The initiative allows the people to propose and adopt a law by having it placed on the ballot in a state-wide or a local election. The referendum makes possible a popular review of an act passed by a state legislature or a city council, again by a vote of the people.

These new devices were adopted as parts of the new state constitutions and city charters of the period. They provided an opportunity for the people to participate more directly in the framing of policy. At about the same time, a number of states began to use the primary election for choosing party candidates. This was a further step in giving the people power to select the representatives who should run for office—who would manage the people's government through the parties.

These new movements symbolized the desire of many Americans to make political democracy effective. A number of people felt that this was not enough. They believed that the government should regulate economic practices within our free-enterprise system. They insisted that industry must be operated for the general welfare. The next half-century was to see this new attitude toward the relations between government and industry reflected in laws which sought to regulate many business practices. We shall observe in Part II how the changing attitude of the people was reflected in new policies and practices, legislative and administrative.

46

The Pattern of Ideas : Economic

This attitude expressed itself in state and national legislation even before 1890. In the 1870's, the states had attempted to regulate railroad rates and the charges of other industries, such as grain elevators and public utilities. The Interstate Commerce Act of 1887 was the first attempt to bring the railroads under national control in the public interest. The earlier state attempts to control railroad rates had proved ineffective for the reason that most of the railroads were interstate and claimed exemption from state regulations. The state governments were equally ineffective in their attempts to control the practices of the great industrial combinations. Like the railroads, many industries also claimed exemption from state regulation on the ground that they were interstate in character because they had factories in many states and shipped raw materials and goods across state lines. In 1890, Congress enacted the Sherman Anti-Trust Act in an effort to prevent the great monopolies from raising prices by killing competition. In the decades after 1890, this type of law was expanded by both the state and the federal governments into new fields of industrial and business regulation.

All these laws, state and national, reflected a new trend in economic ideas. This new trend was based on the changes in our economy which we have noted: the shift from agriculture to industry; the concentration of economic power in the great

TRADE EXPANDS IN THE 1890's

Courtesy of The Museum of the City of New York

corporations; the separation of the owner-manager and the workers in the large-scale industries.

How did these changes affect the attitudes and the interests of the workers? As in the pattern of our economic life, the period marks a turning point in the growth of the labor-union movement. It may be well to note the events leading up to the new developments after 1890, for these events help to explain how the workers have sought to protect and to promote their interests since that date.

The Workers' Place in American Life
The Knights of Labor

During and after the Civil War, industry, as we have seen, developed rapidly. It was natural that the hundreds of thousands of new workers who were drawn into the factories should again take up the idea of organizing unions to bargain more effectively with their employers. Many local unions and a few national unions in different trades developed during the 1860's and 1870's.

The first effort to revive the national labor movement came just after the war. In 1869, Uriah Smith Stevens, a Philadelphia garment worker, organized the Knights of Labor. On Christmas Day, 1873, a District Assembly of the Knights of Labor was organized with 31 local assemblies in and near Philadelphia. Many local unions joined the new movement which spread rapidly to all the big industrial centers from Massachusetts to Illinois.

After 1875, when it organized its first national convention, the Knights of Labor increased steadily in influence. Like the earlier unions, it maintained itself as a secret organization until about 1878. It used symbols and titles for its members and employed elaborate rituals at its meetings. The reasons for secrecy lay not only in its social and fraternal origins and

48

purposes but in the growing hostility of employers to the new movement. Secrecy, it was thought, would be useful in helping the movement to spread. After 1878, however, when the Knights of Labor was strongly established, it dropped its policy of secrecy.

The principle on which the Knights of Labor appealed to the workers was the one-big-union idea. Stevens and the other leaders of the Knights believed that all the workers in any industry, skilled and unskilled alike, should organize in a single labor union. They felt that, in seeking to get what they wanted through joining one national union, the workers would develop a much stronger bargaining power. Rather than organizing each different craft or group of workers into a separate union they tried to include all the workers throughout all industries. The one-big-union idea made it easier for the skilled and the unskilled to work together for common ends. This idea is the basis for our industrial, sometimes called vertical, unions of today.

The Knights even carried this idea over into agriculture. In its earlier years, the Knights included many farmers' groups which cooperated closely with industrial workers in seeking higher labor standards. The farmers, however, did not play an important part in the industrial struggles of the period and gradually left the Knights of Labor in order to establish their own organizations.

Various other events in this period also showed that a national labor-union movement was beginning to develop. After an unsuccessful effort in 1876 to call a national union convention, the International Labor Union was organized early in 1878 along directly Socialist lines. This was another effort to bring all branches of the labor-union movement together into one big union. The movement was shortlived. The Socialists split into a number of groups, left-wing and right-wing. There

49

were, moreover, deep-rooted differences in outlook between the Socialist groups and the great majority of American workers. These differences have continued ever since to impede these early efforts to organize a single, nationwide labor organization.

In the meantime, the workers in many industries were organizing their craft groups on a city, state, or national basis. Suppose the carpenters, for instance, in a single city had organized themselves in several "locals" and the workers in other trade groups had done the same. All these locals might then organize a "central" for the whole city. Similarly, each of the separate crafts—carpenters, metal workers, plumbers, masons, and the like—might organize a state or national federation of all the workers in that particular craft.

By 1879, 28 cities and a number of counties had organized central trades councils. Eighteen national unions and several railroad unions, many of which were growing rapidly in membership, had also organized. In November, 1881, the Federation of Organized Trades and Labor Unions of the United States and Canada was organized at Pittsburgh. This Federation was the forerunner of the American Federation of Labor of today.

For a time, the Knights of Labor and the new Federation existed side by side. In 1886, the former had over 700,000 members, the latter, over 250,000. During the next few years the Knights of Labor, which up to this time had attracted many local and some nationwide labor unions, began to decline. A Cooperative Board was set up by the Knights and the Federation to work out a basis for joint action, but it did not succeed in bringing about harmony between the two groups.

By 1890, the Knights of Labor had declined to about 100,000 members. This loss of membership occurred mostly in the large industrial centers in which the Federation was making rapid headway. Furthermore, the Knights of Labor refused to cooperate with the Federation in a national campaign for the eight-hour day. Repeated efforts to bring the Knights and the Federation into a single united labor-movement group failed. Too much disagreement had developed over the demands which the two organizations wished to make. By 1893, the Knights of Labor abandoned its labor-union program. It became more a political party than a united workers' front. Its end was only a few years off. It had already lost all real influence both in politics and in the economic struggles of the period.

The new Federation became the real leader of the labor-union movement. In 1886, Samuel Gompers, a cigar maker, who had been one of the chief organizers of the Federation of Trades and Labor Unions, proposed to rechristen the organization as The American Federation of Labor. The basic structure and purposes of the present-day American Federation of Labor took shape, under Samuel Gompers' leadership, in these early years of struggle to forge a really nationwide labor organization.

The American Federation of Labor

From the 1880's to the 1930's, the A. F. of L. has been the dominant force in the American labor movement. Until less than a decade ago it was, indeed, the only important national labor organization. Unlike the Knights of Labor, the A. F. of L. attempted to organize only the skilled workers into craft unions. As we have seen, the craft or horizontal union is the organization of all those workers in a plant, an entire city, or throughout the country who are doing the same job or working with a particular type of tool or machine.

Samuel Gompers was the dominant figure in the A. F. of L. from 1886 to 1924 and served as its president throughout this period, except for one year. He thought that the best strategy for gaining better working conditions and a more adequate social and economic security for the workers was to organize

51

first of all the skilled workers into effective bargaining units.

Until the last few years, Samuel Gompers' philosophy of organizing the skilled workers has been the basis of the A. F. of L.'s philosophy and program of unionism. On the whole, its leaders never considered the unskilled workers' groups as important factors in an organized labor movement. There were a few industrial unions within the A. F. of L., such as the United Mine Workers of America. They were the exceptions, not the rule, however, in the general structure of A. F. of L. craft-unionism.

Why did Samuel Gompers develop this program of unionism principally for the skilled workers? The answer to this question is not unimportant today when we are seeing a revival of industrial unionism. It can be found in the character of our industry in the 1880's and since. When the A. F. of L. was established, his policy was based on sound practical reasons. Relatively few of the automatic machines of today had then been developed. Operating the new power machines was still a highly skilled trade. Unskilled workers could perform only a few of the jobs in most factories. In such an industrial pattern, it was quite logical for Samuel Gompers to promote the labor-union idea primarily among the skilled workers. If they could be effectively organized to protect and promote their interests, the great majority of all industrial workers would, he believed, be included in the new craft-union movement.

Some industrial unions did, in fact, develop at the beginning of the 20th century. In the textile factories, for example automatic machinery, which required little or no skill to operate, had by now come into general use. In this and in other industries, there was a decreasing need for skilled workers. Under such conditions, all the workers, skilled and unskilled alike, sometimes organized into one big union. This is the principle upon which the industrial or vertical union is based.

SOME NOTABLE DATES IN LABOR UNION HISTORY

1794	FEDERAL SOCIETY OF JOURNEYMEN AND CORDWAINERS
1827	MECHANIC'S UNION OF TRADE ASSOCIATIONS
1834	FIRST EFFORT AT A NATIONAL LABOR UNION
1869	KNIGHTS OF LABOR
1881	AMERICAN FEDERATION OF LABOR
1935	CONGRESS OF INDUSTRIAL ORGANIZATIONS

MEMBERSHIP—AMERICAN FEDERATION OF LABOR

1,000,000 2,000,000 3,000,000 4,000,000

Year	Membership
1887	150,000
1897	264,825
1898	278,016
1899	349,422
1900	548,321
1901	787,537
1902	1,024,399
1903	1,465,800
1904	1,676,200
1905	1,494,300
1906	1,454,200
1907	1,538,920
1908	1,586,885
1909	1,482,872
1910	1,502,112
1911	1,761,835
1912	1,770,145
1913	1,996,004
1914	2,020,671
1915	1,946,347
1916	2,072,702
1917	2,371,434
1918	2,726,478
1919	3,260,068
1920	4,078,740
1921	3,906,528
1922	3,195,635
1923	2,926,468
1924	2,865,979
1925	2,638,362
1926	2,714,800
1927	2,759,200
1928	2,808,000
1929	2,769,700
1930	2,745,300
1931	2,743,000
1932	2,497,000
1933	2,317,500
1934	3,030,000
1935	3,317,100
1936	3,542,000
1937	2,994,300
1941	4,569,100

MEMBERSHIP OF SOME REPRESENTATIVE

1941	
F OF L.	
569,100	
. I. O.	
000,000	

OVER A MILLION

UNITED AUTOMOBILE, AIRCRAFT AND AGRICULTURAL IMPLEMENT WORKERS OF AMERICA	1,100,000
UNITED STEELWORKERS OF AMERICA	810,000
UNITED ELECTRICAL AND RADIO MACHINE WORKERS OF AMERICA	600,000
TEXTILE WORKERS UNION OF AMERICA	425,000
INDUSTRIAL UNION OF MARINE AND SHIPBUILDING WORKERS OF AMERICA	385,000
AMALGAMATED CLOTHING WORKERS OF AMERICA	350,000
UNITED RETAIL, WHOLESALE, AND DEPARTMENT STORE WORKERS	140,000
INTERNATIONAL UNION OF MINE, MILL AND SMELTER WORKERS	130,000
TRANSPORT WORKERS UNION OF AMERICA	90,000
NATIONAL MARITIME UNION OF AMERICA	52,000

→ C. I. O. UNIONS

Among the more important of these new industrial unions which became a part of the A. F. of L. were the International Ladies Garment Workers Union, organized in 1900, and the Amalgamated Clothing Workers of America, organized in 1914 under the leadership of Sidney Hillman. The former union soon affiliated itself with the A. F. of L. The latter was long considered by the Federation as a "dual union", because it was formed after a split in the already organized craft union in the men's clothing industry.

Another aspect of A. F. of L. history may be noted briefly. During this period, Socialists of various schools of thought remained active in the labor-union movement. Perhaps the most important Socialist group was the International Workers of the World. Another was the Socialist Trade and Labor Alliance, organized in 1895 after the Socialists had failed to gain control of the A. F. of L. The effort by Socialist groups to gain control of the Federation continued for nearly twenty years after its formation.

In 1901, the various Socialist groups, some of which had already entered politics by nominating their own candidates for office, joined together and organized the Socialist Party of America. For the most part, they ceased their active efforts to organize labor unions, leaving this field largely to the A. F. of L. Only the International Workers of the World continued to have any influence in the industrial field. Its influence declined rapidly after the War of 1914–1918.

These efforts of the Socialists to gain control of the A. F. of L. did much to determine its attitude toward politics. Samuel Gompers and the other leaders of the A. F. of L. avoided direct political action. They emphasized purely economic action (for instance, strikes and boycotts) as the correct basis for the workers' efforts to gain their ends by direct bargaining with their employers. From the beginning, the A. F. of L. pursued a policy of supporting candidates in either major party who promised, if elected, to support labor's demands. Samuel Gompers continued throughout his life to urge the A. F. of L and its affiliated unions not to nominate labor candidates for public office. Rather, he advised labor to exert its influence in politics by supporting candidates of any party who were sympathetic to the labor cause.

The War of 1914–1918 helped greatly to advance the position of labor. As industry expanded rapidly to take care of our war needs, many new workers were drawn into the union movement. The membership of the A. F. of L. rose in this period to 2,726,478.

During the 1920's labor unions were affected by general economic conditions. As prosperity increased, many workers felt that they did not need to join a labor union in order to protect and promote their interests. Wages were relatively high and many workers obtained the advantages of new bargaining agreements won by the unions without the necessity of their joining these unions. When the depression started in 1929, moreover, many workers thought labor unions could do nothing for them. They were, indeed, often unable to pay union dues while they were unemployed. The A. F. of L. lost a large fraction of its membership during this period.

There were other reasons why the A. F. of L. no longer continued to appeal to large numbers of workers. As our industrial system developed toward larger plants and more and more automatic machinery, many workers felt that the craft union could not protect and promote their interests effectively. Many "jurisdictional disputes" between rival craft unions within the A. F. of L., as to which union should do a particular job, weakened the bargaining power of the workers. Many workers who were entirely outside the craft unions involved in such a dispute might be thrown out of work until it was settled.

Furthermore, as factories grew larger and included more and more different operations within a single plant, the craft basis of union organization split the workers into many separate groups. A single employer could often drive a wedge between the workers in his plant by agreeing to bargain with one or more of the craft unions and refusing to bargain with others. Workers, both skilled and unskilled, in the mass-production industries saw increasingly the need for a united front in order to bargain effectively with their employers. Under the A. F. of L., they still lacked a single union in many of our largest industries, such as automobiles, rubber, and steel, through which they could join forces to express their common demands.

Employers Organize Too

Employers also began organizing to protect their interests in this period. Early in the 19th century, as we have seen, the early societies or guilds of master craftsmen often opposed the demands of the new factory workers for shorter hours or higher wages. These guilds, like the early unions, included employers in a single community and were only incidentally interested in their workers' demands. They were primarily mutual benefit societies. It was not until the 1860's that the employers' associations were organized on a statewide basis and sometimes for the definite purpose of limiting the influence of labor unions.

One of the earliest of these associations which took an active stand against the workers was organized during the Civil War. On July 25, 1864, a more or less secret group known as the Employers General Association of Michigan was organized by a group of industrialists in that state. Its governing body included representatives from many different industries. They were subdivided into major groups called "auxiliaries". Each auxiliary was authorized to "fix, grant and regulate" wages and to set minimum prices for its own commodity. The Association was very frank about its attitude toward labor unions. In the preamble to its constitution it stated:

> As a natural result of this system of general and persistent interference . . . our business is thrown into a condition of much uncertainty. . . . If continued for any considerable time (it) must result in widespread beggary with all its attending evils—suffering, bread lines, pillage and taxation.

Similar employer groups, such as the Master Mechanics of Boston and the New York Master Builders Association, established in 1867 and 1869, respectively, held much the same view about the new labor-union movement.

Some of these early employers' associations opposed the growth of labor unions. They used various tactics such as the lockout, the blacklist, and the labor spy to coerce workers into accepting existing or even lower labor standards. During this period, employers' associations were mostly local and often temporary. About 1900, more permanent employers' associations began to develop, at first locally and then on a nationwide basis. 1895, many of these local associations and prominent leaders in the larger industries formed the National Association of Manufacturers. Like the A. F. of L. (and the C. I. O.) for workers, it has become a national representative body for employers. Many employers, too, joined the United States Chamber of Commerce, organized in 1912. The Chamber includes among its members many commercial and business as well as industrial firms.

☆ ☆ ☆ ☆ ☆ ☆ ☆ ☆ ☆ ☆ ☆ ☆ ☆

As the men and women of 1890 looked out on their world, they saw many changes in the half-century after 1840. Large-scale industry, large cities, great corporations organized with large capital investment, new inventions, a rising tide of immigration, a growing labor-union movement, the beginnings of employers' associations—these were some of the changes they and their children observed. These changes had finally shifted the center of the American economy from the farms to the factories. We had become primarily a manufacturing nation; we had forged an industrial economy.

The same forces were to continue dominant in the next half-century. The trends which were already apparent in 1890 were to develop still further. As we look out on the America of 1940, we can see how these forces have helped to shape the nation in which we live today. We can note how these trends are still operating in our present economy.

AMERICAN LIFE IN 1890

GE SCALE INDUSTRY

GREAT CORPORATIONS
AND
LARGE CAPITAL
INVESTMENT

LARGE CITIES

  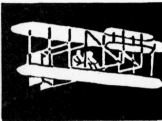

W INVENTIONS

RISING TIDE OF
IMMIGRATION

GROWING LABOR UNION MOVEMENT   BEGINNING OF EMPLOYERS' ASSOCIATIONS

SHIFT FROM FARMS

TO FACTORIES

4

1940 : New Issues, New Directions, in Our Economy

The Pattern of Living
Industry Determines Security for Farmers and City-Dwellers Alike

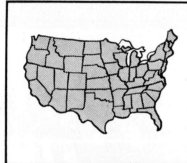

THE UNITED STATES IN		
1940		
ALABAMA	ARIZONA	ARKANSAS
CALIFORNIA		COLORADO
CONNECTICUT	DELAWARE	FLORIDA
GEORGIA	IDAHO	ILLINOIS
INDIANA IOWA	KANSAS	KENTUCKY

LOUISIANA MAINE MARYLAND MASSACHUSETTS MICHIGAN MINNESOTA

MISSISSIPPI MISSOURI MONTANA NEBRASKA NEVADA NEW HAMPSHIRE

NEW JERSEY NEW MEXICO NEW YORK NORTH CAROLINA NORTH DAKOTA

OHIO OKLAHOMA OREGON PENNSYLVANIA RHODE ISLAND

SOUTH CAROLINA SOUTH DAKOTA TENNESSEE TEXAS UTAH

VERMONT VIRGINIA WASHINGTON WEST VIRGINIA WISCONSIN WYOMING

THE NEWTOWN OF 1940 WAS A CITY OF OVER 100,000. THE men and women of 1790—or, for that matter, of 1840—could not have dreamed of what the city of 1890 or 1940 would be like. Even the grandparents of 1890 of the children who were growing up in Newtown in 1940 would have hardly recognized the city of today.

No one could tell where the old city limits were; stores, factories, and apartment houses now spread out across the suburban neighborhoods and farmlands of 1890. Around Newtown, the smaller towns were growing and merging with the city itself. The families which had moved out to them a half-century before to find air and space and light now had to move still farther out to escape the smoke and noise of the new factories in the old suburbs. Around the factories were the cheaper homes and tenements—some of them the old mansions turned into rooming houses—in which most of the workers in the factories and shops lived.

The American city had grown up. It had grown because industry had become the dominant factor in American life. Scattered over the country from Massachusetts to California, there were, in 1940, 92 great metropolitan areas each of which included 100,000 or more people. In these greater cities lived 28.8 per cent of the American people. If we add up all the places of over 10,000 population, we find there were 1077 in 1940, which included 47.6 per cent of the whole population. Less than one-fifth (8,518,124) of the 50,460,700 people gainfully employed or seeking work in March, 1940 were engaged in farming. Most of the other four-fifths earned their living directly or indirectly from industry, commerce, transportation, or the service trades. We had become an urban and an industrial nation; agriculture was still important but secondary to and dependent on industry. A new pattern of life had emerged in the America of 1940.

This new pattern was reflected in the way the city-dweller earned his living. Because of new inventions, machines were being created and improved at a constantly accelerating rate.

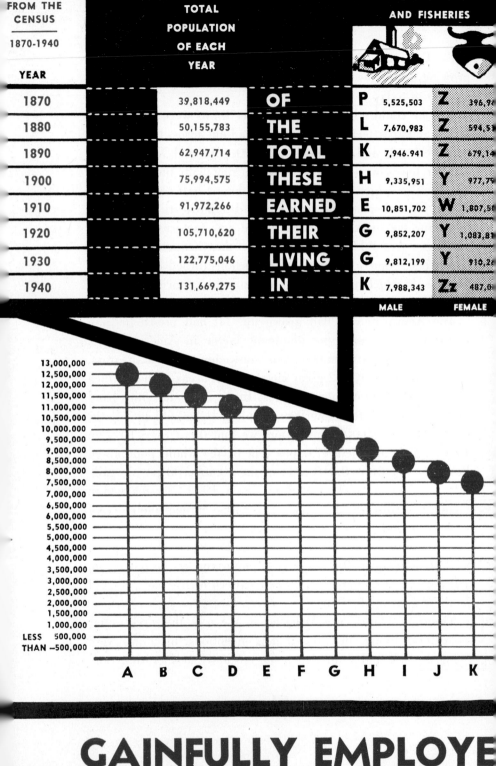

FROM THE CENSUS 1870-1940	TOTAL POPULATION OF EACH YEAR		AGRICULTURE AND FISHERIES			
YEAR				MALE		FEMALE
1870	39,818,449	OF	P	5,525,503	Z	396,9…
1880	50,155,783	THE	L	7,670,983	Z	594,5…
1890	62,947,714	TOTAL	K	7,946,941	Z	679,14…
1900	75,994,575	THESE	H	9,335,951	Y	977,79…
1910	91,972,266	EARNED	E	10,851,702	W	1,807,50…
1920	105,710,620	THEIR	G	9,852,207	Y	1,083,81…
1930	122,775,046	LIVING	G	9,812,199	Y	910,2…
1940	131,669,275	IN	K	7,988,343	Zz	487,8…

13,000,000
12,500,000
12,000,000
11,500,000
11,000,000
10,500,000
10,000,000
9,500,000
9,000,000
8,500,000
8,000,000
7,500,000
7,000,000
6,500,000
6,000,000
5,500,000
5,000,000
4,500,000
4,000,000
3,500,000
3,000,000
2,500,000
2,000,000
1,500,000
1,000,000
LESS THAN — 500,000

A B C D E F G H I J K

GAINFULLY EMPLOYE

ESTIC, PERSONAL AND
OFESSIONAL SERVICES   TRADE
AND TRANSPORTATION   MANUFACTURING
AND MINING

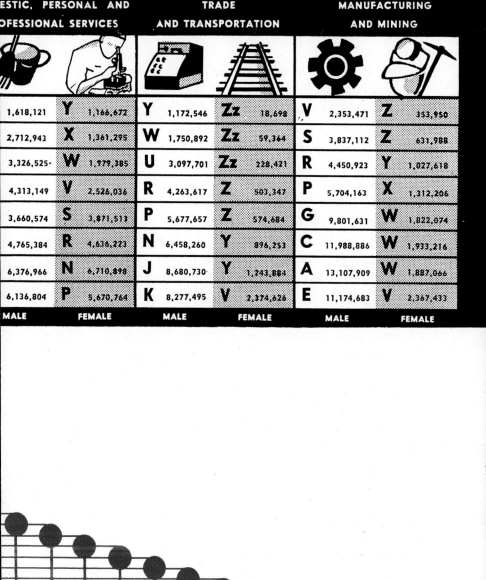

DOMESTIC, PERSONAL AND PROFESSIONAL SERVICES			TRADE AND TRANSPORTATION				MANUFACTURING AND MINING			
MALE		FEMALE	MALE		FEMALE		MALE		FEMALE	
1,618,121	Y	1,166,672	Y	1,172,546	Zz	18,698	V	2,353,471	Z	353,950
2,712,943	X	1,361,295	W	1,750,892	Zz	59,364	S	3,837,112	Z	631,988
3,326,525	W	1,979,385	U	3,097,701	Zz	228,421	R	4,450,923	Y	1,027,618
4,313,149	V	2,526,036	R	4,263,617	Z	503,347	P	5,704,163	X	1,312,206
3,660,574	S	1,871,513	P	5,677,657	Z	574,684	G	9,801,631	W	1,822,074
4,765,384	R	4,636,223	N	6,458,260	Y	896,253	C	11,988,886	W	1,933,216
6,376,966	N	6,710,898	J	8,680,730	Y	1,243,884	A	13,107,909	W	1,887,066
6,136,804	P	5,670,764	K	8,277,495	V	2,374,626	E	11,174,683	V	2,367,433

N O P Q R S T U V W X Y Z Zz

— MALE AND FEMALE

Many of these machines worked almost automatically. One result was a vast increase in the quantity of goods produced by machinery. This meant, of course, a higher standard of living for most Americans. A second result, however, raised certain problems for millions of workers. As machines were improved, fewer and fewer men and women were needed to produce the same amount of goods.

At the same time, more and more people were needed to manage industry, to distribute the goods industry made, and to work in the service trades. As factories became larger and many plants were brought under the control of a single corporation, accounting and sales departments grew in size. As the production of goods which people wanted expanded, more retail outlets were needed. Chain stores and mail-order houses were organized to distribute these goods. As the nation's business increased, the service trades—gasoline stations and garages, beauty parlors, hotels, laundries, radio-repair and other specialty shops—developed even more rapidly than industry itself.

By 1939, there were 6,213,890 people engaged in retail trade and another 1,102,047 in other service trades. In one sense, this whole field was a new frontier of individual initiative. From the 1900's on, many who could not find work in industry, because of the new labor-saving machines, were able to win some economic security for themselves in the new service trades. This is indicated by the fact that of the 6,688,284 people in them, 652,491 were active proprietors of unincorporated businesses.

This new field of gainful employment has meant that new careers have been opened to women. By March, 1940, there were 13,007,480 women, 37.6 per cent of all those over 14, in what is known as "the labor force", i.e. working, or seeking work in factories, shops, and offices. As in the earlier periods, most of these women took jobs because they needed the extra income for themselves or their families. It was still a problem for many mothers to make the family budget balance. The new service trades offered many new kinds of work which they could do as well as or better than men. Most women were, however, engaged in industry and the service trades. Our economy still required women to work and many of these women were competing for industrial jobs which men had formerly done.

The industrial pattern of 1940 also showed that the trend of the 1890's toward large-scale industry had continued. More and more industrial workers were employed in the larger plants. Factories were growing bigger and more plants were being brought under the control and management of the great corporations.*

The changing pattern of American life was reflected in many other aspects of our society. One of the most marked, which we have already noted in the earlier periods, was the dwindling size of the family. By 1940, the average American family had fewer than two children.** Young children were no longer the economic asset to their families which they had been in the agricultural society of 1790 and 1840. The declining rate of population increase—from 25.5 per cent in 1880–1890 to 7.2 per cent in 1930–1940—was presenting serious problems to the nation. On the one hand, there were fewer children

---

* Often, a single corporation controls many "subsidiaries"—other companies (generally smaller) which have been purchased outright or, if corporately organized, a majority of the stock of which has been brought under the "parent company's" control. One typical form of control is the holding company, another, the trust.

** The size of an average American family in 1940 was 3.8. Many people had not married; some families were childless; few American families had 4 or 5 children, as had the typical families of 1790 and 1840.

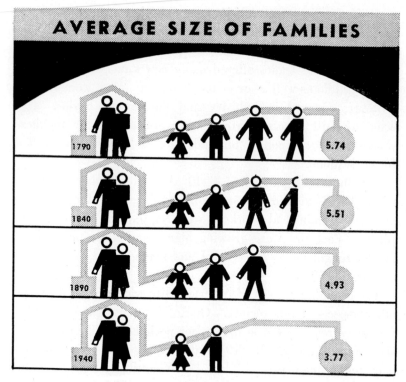

AVERAGE SIZE OF FAMILIES

1790   5.74
1840   5.51
1890   4.93
1940   3.77

of school age and most states were requiring compulsory school attendance until 16 years of age. On the other hand, an even more urgent problem was emerging in the increasing proportion of the people beyond the working age. We were approaching the stage of a stationary population in which there would be fewer children and more old people. Their security was becoming a matter of greater public concern.

These population changes were accelerated by our new immigration policy. By the Act of 1924, which limited future entrants to 150,000 a year, immigration into the United States was almost shut off. In some years since 1924, more people have actually left than have entered the country. This trend not only slowed down the growth of our population; it also indicated the end of an era in which large numbers of unskilled workers were needed to develop and expand our economy. Now we needed skilled workers to run the new machines. We believed that we had enough people in the country to keep our industries efficient, to insure a sound balance between production and consumption. We hoped that we were on the way to creating a stable industrial economy in which all the people would be able to gain security for themselves.

This hope of the 1920's was not fulfilled. We found that a stable economy did not result automatically from a capacity to produce more at less cost. We began to ask why this hope did not work out in practice. What were the economic changes which, during the half-century after 1890, required us to re-appraise the working of our economy?

COUNTRY STORE IN 1890   From Globe

Signs of Economic Change

In a century and a half, America has been made over from a nation mostly of farmers and country-dwellers to a people three-quarters of whom live in cities and work at or for the machine. It is the machine which has made possible the freeing of farmer and factory-worker alike from the drudgery of working from sunup to sundown to make enough to live. The need for day-long toil has been all but ended by the machine.

The machine has also helped us to develop a higher standard of living in America than men and women have known ever before or in any other country. We have created a new world in which steam, electricity, and oil have displaced man and water-power. We have substituted a mechanical hand or an electric eye for many of the human skills which, less than half a cenutry ago, were indispensible to industry and commerce. All these new inventions have helped to increase our material standard of living.

In this process, however, the very machine, which has served us so widely and so efficiently, has created new problems in our economy. Although we have largely conquered man's age-old fears of famine, disease, and lack of adequate shelter through our discoveries and inventions, we have not yet entirely eliminated them from our society. In a nation of 134,000,000 there are still some who do not have enough food, clothing, or shelter to maintain their full health.

How can we explain this dilemma? Why is it that many workers are unemployed part of the time? What causes the recurring periods of prosperity and depression?

These are questions which affect us all, whether or not we are employers or workers. Only as our economy functions smoothly and efficiently, can all the people enjoy the material and mental security which most Americans believe is one of the inalienable rights of free men and women. If all of us are able to work at producing the goods we all want to consume, the relations of workers and employers will be sounder and more stable. We may, then, look at the way our economy has worked in recent years in order to observe the signs of economic change which have occurred.

The Cycle of Prosperity and Depression

As we have seen, the migration from the farms to the factories has meant that for most of the time during the last century there were more workers than jobs available. The new streams of people from the farms (and, until 1924, from abroad) looking for jobs in the cities generally resulted in the supply being larger than the demand for workers. Because, on the whole, wages were set by the demand for and the supply of workers in the industrial cities, many of these workers did not get wages high enough to enable them to save. This was particularly true of the unskilled workers. Their wages were affected by the development of the new automatic machines which required little practice or skill to operate.

Although the new workers might receive more actual cash from working in a factory than on a farm, they had to spend more to live in the city. They were just able to make both ends meet most of the time, and when the factories shut down, even this was impossible. Only when times were good and the demand for workers was greater than the supply, did they enjoy continued economic security.

In good times when wages were high, many of them quite naturally spent their increased earnings on the things they had long wanted to have or to do. When wages went up, moreover, prices also went up so that increased wages often did not mean a real increase of purchasing power among the workers. In bad times, when wages went down and workers lost their jobs, whatever they had saved was soon used up. Thus, there occurred alternating periods of prosperity and depression, sometimes called the business cycle. These cycles, made it more difficult for many industrial workers to gain or to maintain their economic security. The deepest depression in our history began after the stock-market crash of 1929. It

NOTABLE
AMERICAN INVENTIONS

1634 SAWMILL (First American)

1750 FLATBOAT (for Inland River)

1752 LIGHTNING ROD, Benjamin Franklin

1764 SPINNING AND CARDING MACHINE, James Davenport

1775 SUBMARINE, David Bushnell

1785 STEAMBOAT, John Fitch

1793 COTTON GIN, Eli Whitney

1797 PLOW (FIRST U. S. PATENT), Chas. Newbold

1799 SEEDING MACHINE, Spooner

1807 "THE CLERMONT", STEAMBOAT, Fulton

1814 POWER LOOM, Francis Lowell

1816 HAND PRINTING PRESS, Clymer

1826 LOCOMOTIVE WITH MULTITUBULAR BOILER

1829 "TOM THUMB" LOCOMOTIVE

1831 REAPER, Cyrus MacCormick

1835 REVOLVER, Samuel Colt

1837 TELEGRAPH, Samuel F. Morse

1839 VULCANIZATION OF RUBBER

1842 SUBMARINE CABLE, Samuel F. Morse

1843 TYPEWRITER, Chas. Thber

1846 SEWING MACHINE, Ho

1851 HARD RUBBER, Goodr

1858 SLEEPING CAR, Geo. P man

1866 ATLANTIC CABLE, Cy Field

1876 TELEPHONE, Alexander Bell

1877 PHONOGRAPH, Thos. Edison

1878 FIRST LIGHT, Thos. Edison

1882 TROLLEY CAR, F. Sprogue

1884 ELEVATOR PASSENG ELEVATOR, Wm. Baxter

1887 PHOTOGRAPHIC FIL Hannibal Goodwin

1888 KODAK CAMERA, G Eastman

1892 FIRST GAS AUTOMOB

1903 AIRPLANE, W. and Wright

1903 ELECTRIC AUTO STA ER, Coleman

1906 SOUND TRACK F FILMS, Lauste

1906 CRYSTAL DETECT RADIO, Dunwoody

1907 AUDION TUBE, RAD De Forest

1910 GYRO-COMPASS, Spe

1929 POLAROID

NUMBER OF PATENTS
PER DECADE

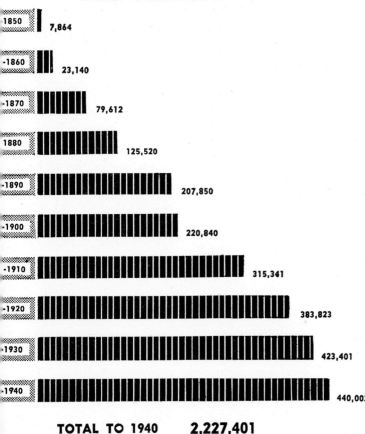

-1850   7,864

-1860   23,140

-1870   79,612

1880   125,520

-1890   207,850

-1900   220,840

-1910   315,341

-1920   383,823

-1930   423,401

-1940   440,002

TOTAL TO 1940   2,227,401

ACH BAR REPRESENTS 10,000 PATENTS

brought the problem of insecurity sharply before the nation.

There have been many attempts to explain these recurring periods of prosperity and depression. One view of the problem of why they occur relates a widespread purchasing power among all the people to the stability of industry. Unless, so it is said, people are able to buy what the new machines can make, the machines themselves will stand idle.

That machines have in fact, often, increased employment and raised our standard of living can be illustrated by many of our most important industries today. For instance, low-cost automobiles, household equipment such as refrigerators or washing machines, and radio are industries which have grown rapidly during the past two or three decades as a result of new inventions and mass-production. The radio industry will illustrate this process.

The first radio broadcast from any station in the United States was from station KDKA in Pittsburgh on November 2, 1920. Twenty-two years later (1942), there were 34 non-commercial and 890 commercial broadcasting stations in the United States. Over 47,000,000 receiving sets were to be found in American homes beside over 9,000,000 automobile radios.

As improvements were made, and costs were lowered by new methods of production, the radio industry employed an ever-larger number of workers. In 1942, more than 245,000 workers were engaged in the industry, manufacturing, distributing, and servicing radios and operating stations. The total payroll in the radio industry was over $350,000,000 a year.

Were this the whole story of radio—and of other industries like automobiles and home equipment—our economy would have remained stable and would, indeed, have advanced still further than it has. As we know, however, the advances made in many of our industries were not maintained. None of our mass-produced goods can continue to be sold in increasing quantities unless people have money with which to buy them. Purchasing power will, in the long run, determine the amount of industrial production. If many people cannot afford to buy radios and other products of the machines, some factories will shut down, the railroads will carry fewer goods, the service trades will lose customers.

The relation of low purchasing power to the stability of our economy can be further illustrated by its effect on the actual consumption of the products of some of our basic industries. If we take the year 1929, in which the largest national income in our history until 1941 was produced, we find that 42 per cent of American families received $1500 a year or less and 59 per cent, $2000 or less. The first group received 17.6 per cent of the national income, the second group, 28.8 per cent. These two groups consumed, on the other hand, respectively, 42 and 68 per cent of all the food, 30 and 53 per cent of all the clothing, and 38 and 64 per cent of all the housing bought in 1929. These three items are produced by some of our largest industries—agriculture and food-processing, textiles and garment-making, construction. Had the income of these groups been larger, these and many other industries would have been able to sell more of their products. More people would have been employed in them, in transportation, and in the service trades.

It is important to note also that a depression affects agriculture today almost as much as it does industry. Although farmers can go on eating the food they raise, they are doubly dependent on the cities in bad times as well as good. First, they have to buy many household items, including many processed-food products, which used to be made in whole or in part on the farm in the America of 1790 and 1840 and even

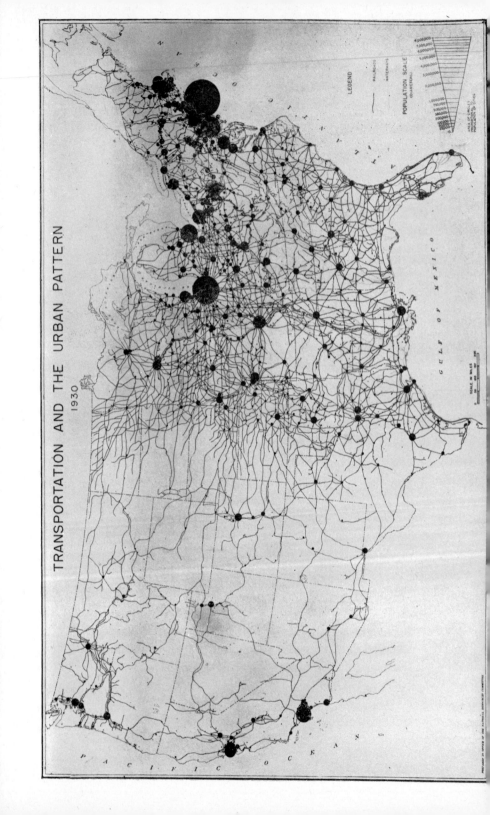

TRANSPORTATION AND THE URBAN PATTERN

1930

GROWTH OF CITIES 1790 1940

POPULATION	8,500 TO 10,000	10,000 TO 25,000	25,000 TO 100,000	100,000 TO 250,000	250,000 TO 500,000	500,000 TO 1,000,000	1,000,000 OR OVER
1790 (94% / 6%)	28	3	2				
1840 (88% / 12%)	123	27	9	2	1		
1880 (71% / 29%)	872	105	57	12	4	3	1
1940 (44% / 56%)	2,387	665	320	55	23	9	5

NUMBER OF CITIES BY SIZE GROUPS

CIRCLES REPRESENT PROPORTION OF RURAL AND URBAN POPULATION

SECTION = RURAL   WHITE SECTION = URBAN

in 1890. Agriculture has, moreover, become more and more mechanized, especially during the last half-century. Farmers have had to use machines instead of human or horse power if they were to compete successfully against the growing number of large-scale farms. The purchase of these machines depends on the farmers' ability to buy. This, in turn, depends on their ability to sell their farm products. Thus, farmers are dependent on industrial prosperity in a second way. A decline in the workers' wages or the growth of unemployment makes it difficult for farmers to sell in the cities. An industrial depression may, indeed, be aggravated by the workers' inability to buy the products of the farms with the consequent decline in purchasing power among farmers.

We can see, then, why the purchasing power of all the people is so important to the stability of our economy. If many wage earners are out of work or receive such low wages that they cannot buy what they need or want, agriculture as well as industry will slow down. If farmers are unable to buy the products of the factories because they cannot sell their own products, industry will suffer and employment decline. The problem of breaking the cycle of depression appears, therefore, to be closely related to the purchasing power of all the people and especially of the low-income groups. As greater purchasing is spread through the whole nation, our industries will operate more continuously and smoothly.

Can Depressions Be Cushioned?

During the depression years after 1929, many plans, public and private, were suggested to meet this problem. Some of these plans attempted to bring the city worker back to the land so that he could raise a part of his food himself. These plans suggest that we are returning to the principle of family security, based on self-sufficiency, of the America of 1790 and 1840.

Some industrial workers have, it is true, gone back to farming when they have lost their jobs in hard times. Often, however, they only helped to spread the depression to the country. Without considerable cash, they were unable to buy the necessary seeds, fertilizer, and machinery to make their farms pay. Moreover, only a small number of the unemployed workers in the cities can move to the farms during bad times. After 1929 more than ever before, the problem of the city worker out of a job has become one of our major national concerns.

Two movements now going on are interesting examples of how we are trying to meet this problem. Both rest on the fact that industrial workers, if they can do so conveniently, are eager to put some of their leisure time into farming for their own needs. They are able not only to keep a job in industry but they are able also to obtain the benefit of growing part of the family's food supply themselves. They may also grow enough to have a little left over to sell in local markets and thus add to their cash income.

One of these movements is individual in the sense that many city workers all over the country have moved to the country and rented or bought farms during the depression of 1929. They have been able to do so because they had enough savings to enable them to invest in a farm. Other workers have been helped by private or government loans. Still others have taken advantage of new private or government projects in cooperative farming. In these projects, a group of workers develop not only their own individual farm plots but a community farm for larger crops or for dairying.

All these experiments seek to find a solution to the problem by giving city workers a stake in the land. These workers continue to work in the cities when there are jobs available. While working they help to build up their own economic security through part-time farming, in good times as well as bad. When bad times come, the workers are better able to meet them because they have recaptured some of the security of the early American farmer—by growing part of their own food needs.

The other movement, which is today of increasing importance, is the transfer of the factories from the city to the country. In some cases, employers are moving their plants to the country because they have discovered that their workers respond to the opportunity to improve their security in this way. The Ford Motor Company, for instance, has moved a number of its units, employing up to several hundred workers each, out of the big central plants to nearby country towns. In moving these units, the company has made it possible for the workers and their families to enjoy homes and gardens of their own instead of living in crowded tenements in the cities. Not only has this resulted in an increased sense of security but it has frequently been shown that this sense of security heightens the workers' efficiency on the job. This is one of the major factors in the stability of an industrial system, a factor which may well become even more important in the post-war period.

This migration of workers and factories to the country is not necessarily a complete cure for unemployment in the cities in hard times. It has not yet gone far enough to give us a complete solution of the insecurity city workers face. It is, however, a significant effort toward restoring an opportunity for greater security to the workers in our factories—in good times as well as bad. It has already demonstrated that this kind of double opportunity will serve as a cushion for the effects of a depression on individual workers and their families.

Factories Can Move—Men Cannot

One other result of recurring booms and depressions is also worth noting. Factories are, on the whole, more mobile than workers. Machines can be moved from one place to another more easily than most workers can move themselves and their families from one industrial center to another. An industry usually has cash reserves or can obtain bank credit to pay for moving its machinery and raw materials to a more favorable location. Most workers are, on the other hand, tied to the places where they live. They are likely, therefore, to lose their jobs if the factory in which they have been working moves to another city.

This element of our economy has been of increasing importance during the recent depression. Many industries have moved from one city to another or from one part of the country to another for what may be called a purely economic reason. For instance, much of the textile industry, formerly concentrated in New England, has moved into the South during the past quarter-century. There, the factories are near the source of the raw-cotton supply and the climate is more favorable for its manufacture. Similarly, a large part of the boot and shoe industry has migrated from New England to the Middle West. There, hides are available without the necessity of carrying them by rail or truck a thousand miles or more before being manufactured. Thus, transportation and other cost factors have played a part in the shifting of American industry.

Additional factors have, however, influenced the movement of industry in recent years. Among them have been the character of state labor and tax laws and the growth of the labor-union movement in the older industrial centers. For example, during the Depression of 1929, some states competed for new industries by adopting or keeping lower labor standards and by exempting industries from various taxes. Employers often avoided locating their plants in areas where labor was strongly organized and built new plants or moved old ones, to states where corporation and other taxes were comparatively light.

These factors are perhaps less important today than they

NEW FRONTIERS FOR AMERICAN INDUSTRY

Year	Key Number to Regions	INVESTED CAPITAL (VALUE OF RAW MATERIALS)	VALUE OF MANUFACTURES
1850	1	$165,695,259.00	$283,372,747.
	2	216,671,473.00	432,493,415.
	3	52,933,513.00	119,414,044.
	4	9,963,482.00	27,934,501.
	5	86,467,781.00	93,892,890.
	6	23,604,617.00	38,876,764.
	7	5,876,729.00	8,485,863.
	8	447,601.00	540,230.
	9	2,010,654.00	15,099,162.
1890	1	792,343,452.00	1,498,797,507.
	2	1,834,364,462.00	3,397,946,143.
	3	1,200,113,693.00	2,314,596,296.
	4	528,147,230.00	855,613,108.
	5	244,988,594.00	496,551,843.
	6	166,377,832.00	307,709,697.
	7	81,788,811.00	151,079,888.
	8	30,683,036.00	64,233,427.
	9	161,954,418.00	296,604,192.
1940	1	2,463,319,806.00	4,891,666,268.
	2	8,684,135,574.00	16,039,272,817.
	3	9,777,614,409.00	17,559,905,003.
	4	2,452,694,136.00	3,815,176,638.
	5	3,156,673,197.00	5,390,420,291.
	6	1,130,137,222.00	1,958,725,580.
	7	1,744,121,604.00	2,567,821,432.
	8	545,186,559.00	819,833,003.
	9	2,206,224,174.00	3,800,203,768.

EACH ■ REPRESENTS $100,000,000 00
EACH ■ REPRESENTS 2,000,000,000.00

X REPRESENTS $100,000,000.00
X REPRESENTS 2,000,000,000.00

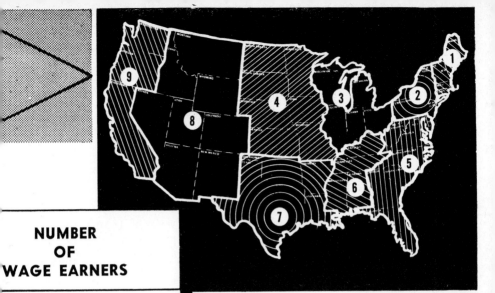

NUMBER
OF
WAGE EARNERS

	304,716
	383,944
▽▽▽▽▽'	92,923
	17,578
▽▽▽▽▽	86,146
	27,705
	8,115
	132
	4,249
	885,132
	1,658,044
	1,064,067
	342,930
	343,141
	279,945
▽▽▽▽▽	87,543
	28,653
	122,806
	1,128,446
▼▽	2,776,954
▼▽	2,711,348
▼	498,548
	1,121,132
	413,138
▽▽▽▽▽'	335,245
	92,273
	545,839

KEY TO REGIONS

1. NEW ENGLAND
MAINE
NEW HAMPSHIRE
VERMONT
MASSACHUSETTS
CONNECTICUT
RHODE ISLAND

2. MID. ATLANTIC
NEW YORK
PENNSYLVANIA
NEW JERSEY

3. E. NO. CENTRAL
WISCONSIN
ILLINOIS
MICHIGAN
INDIANA
OHIO

4. W. NO. CENTRAL
NORTH DAKOTA
SOUTH DAKOTA
NEBRASKA
KANSAS
MINNESOTA
IOWA
MISSOURI

5. SO. ATLANTIC
DELAWARE
MARYLAND
VIRGINIA
NORTH CAROLINA
SOUTH CAROLINA
GEORGIA
FLORIDA
WEST VIRGINIA
WASHINGTON, D. C.

6. E. SO. CENTRAL
KENTUCKY
TENNESSEE
MISSISSIPPI
ALABAMA

7. W. SO. CENTRAL
OKLAHOMA
TEXAS
ARKANSAS
LOUISIANA

8. MOUNTAIN
MONTANA
WYOMING
IDAHO
NEVADA
UTAH
COLORADO
NEW MEXICO
ARIZONA
↓

9. PACIFIC
WASHINGTON
OREGON
CALIFORNIA

ESENTS 100,000   ▽ REPRESENTS 10,000
ESENTS 500,000   WAGE EARNERS

were even a decade ago. New laws, it is true, have been enacted to meet these problems (see Chapter 10, pp. 210 ff.). We must recognize, however, that in the past opportunities for jobs for many thousands of American workers have been affected by such factors. Many industrial centers have prospered or been depressed by shifts resulting from such causes as these. Nor have they even yet been entirely eliminated as factors in the industrial prosperity of our states and cities.

These economic changes had become more than signs by 1940. We had experienced a deep depression; this depression had been more severe for millions of Americans than ever before. We were seeking ways of cushioning depressions and of eliminating unfair competition among states and cities for industrial prosperity. We may ask ourselves how these changes influenced political and economic ideas in America.

The Pattern of Ideas : Political

The War of 1914–1918 and the Depression of 1929 added few new ideas to our political tradition. Each of these periods produced a new slogan—the first, the New Freedom, the second, the New Deal. Each was an effort to express the basic ideas in which most Americans believed; government for the people as well as of and by the people. Each reflected the times in which it was coined. Throughout these years, the feeling was growing among all the people that their government should be concerned with the economic welfare and security of every group in the nation.

As we have seen, efforts were made in the 1890's to regulate the economic activities of the great corporations. This trend continued. The Clayton Act of 1914, for example, was an attempt to strengthen the Sherman Anti-Trust Act of 1890. At the same time, the Clayton Act exempted labor unions from being considered as monopolies in restraint of trade. It was

THE FARMER FEELS THE DEPRESSION   Courtesy of Farm Security Administration

THE CITY DWELLER SEEKS SECURITY   Courtesy of Farm Security Administration

for this reason that Samuel Gompers hailed it as the Magna Charta of labor. As the business boom of the 1920's brought a relatively high level of prosperity to most Americans, however, there was a decline in the trend toward governmental control of industry and finance. When this period of prosperity was rudely interrupted by the Depression of 1929, the American people once again began to demand that industry be regulated in the interest of the public welfare.

As early as 1932, under President Hoover, we began a new experiment in large-scale government lending to industry. In an effort to stimulate industrial production and at the same time to put men and women back to work, the Reconstruction Finance Corporation was created. It was designed primarily to lend money to industries threatened with bankruptcy. As the depression deepened, further laws, both state and federal, were enacted to aid and to regulate industry. Many of these new measures applied directly to industrial relations, for it was clear to many people that peaceful relations between employers and workers would help to stabilize our economy. In later chapters, we shall review some of the policies behind these new laws and try to see how they have operated in practice. Here it is important to recall that these policies formed part of our pattern of political ideas. This pattern was steadily broadening; more and more of the people believed that the general welfare of the nation was directly related to the economic security of all the people.

Another element in the pattern of our political ideas became increasingly important during the 1930's. Ever since the Constitution had been drawn up, we had accepted the idea of representative government, deriving its authority from the will of the people and not from the will of a few self-chosen leaders. Now this principle was challenged by alternative ideas and practices of government. Totalitarian autocracy, not political democracy, was proclaimed as the right principle in more than one country. The decisions of rulers who admitted no responsibility to their subjects, not the choice of representatives responsible to the people, became the political practice of one country after another. The peoples of Russia, Italy, and Germany, to mention only the three major totalitarian nations, were forced to accept various forms of dictatorial government.

As these changes took place in other countries, we observed the physical and political results of the efforts of the leaders to impose totalitarian ideas and practices on their own and other peoples. We became more than ever convinced of the value of our own representative democratic institutions which derived their authority from the consent of the governed. When the European war broke out in 1939, we began to draw closer to the other democratic nations of the world. This understanding had already resulted in close collaboration even before December 7, 1941, when we were attacked by Japan and the other Axis partners immediately declared war upon us. Thus, we were drawn into a worldwide conflict between two irreconcilable political ideas—the democratic and the totalitarian. We shall review the effects of the War of 1941 upon our industrial relations in Chapter 12 (pp. 262 ff.).

The Pattern of Ideas : Economic

Despite the effects of the depression on the stability of our economy, most Americans continued to hold to the principle of free enterprise. We were willing to regulate industry and finance when it seemed necessary to protect the general welfare. We did not, however, abandon our belief in the superiority of an economic system based on private property and individual initiative.

Just as in the political sphere, our economic ideas were challenged by the alternative economic systems of Communism,

Fascism, and Nazism. Both the beliefs and practices of these alternative systems repudiate the basic principles of our economy. Although they have adopted the techniques and achievements of capitalism, such as mass-production and large scale corporate organization and management, they use them within a framework of complete state control of industry.

One reason for the acceptance of Communism, Fascism, and Nazism by the people of Russia, Italy, Germany, (and other countries) is to be found in their loss of faith in the continued efficiency of free enterprise. These alternative systems challenge us in this country to find ways of making our own economic life more effective in terms of the general welfare. We have not lost faith in the values of private initiative and private ownership of property. In a world in which both our political and our economic ideas are being challenged, we are determined that our political and economic practices shall be more efficient and just than those of these competing systems.

The Workers' Place in American Life

We have noted how the growth of industry before and after 1890 resulted in efforts by the workers to organize more effective labor unions. We have already traced the growth of the first permanent nationwide labor organization, the A. F. of L., from its founding in 1886 down to the 1920's. What have been some of the major developments in trade-unionism during the last twenty years?

When the Depression of 1929 occurred, millions of workers, both skilled and unskilled, lost their jobs. Industrial activity declined further than ever before in our history. In the industrial cities like Newtown, whole plants were shut down completely and practically every factory went on short time. Employment fell in 1933 to less than two-thirds of what it had been in 1929; payrolls declined to less than 45 per cent of the peak of four years before. Membership in the A. F. of L. dropped off because many workers could no longer afford to pay their union dues. Many also felt that their unions should be organized differently in order to bargain more effectively with their employers.

The A. F. of L., as we have seen, had followed a policy of not trying to organize the unskilled with the skilled workers in a single union. During the Depression of 1929, there was evidence of a growing conviction among the unskilled workers, then largely unorganized, that the craft form of labor-union organization was not responsive to their demands and expectations. They felt that craft unions were not an effective way of organizing to protect and promote their interests. The semi-killed and unskilled workers began to demand the right to join the A. F. of L. craft unions, most of which until now had admitted only skilled workers. Among the unemployed also, the desire to join unions spread rapidly.

By 1935, there were 18 industrial unions among the 109 A. F. of L. national and international unions. These industrial unions covered only part of the workers in the new mass-production industries.

Now, however, as the depression deepened, these industrial unions began a drive for new members among the unorganized workers. They felt that they had a better chance than ever before to organize strong and effective industrial unions. Congress enacted several laws, especially the National Industrial Recovery Act, which guaranteed the right of workers to join unions of their own choosing. The people acted, through their representatives in Congress, to aid the workers in their century-long struggle to organize themselves without interference from their employers.

The drives in 1933 and 1934 for new members by the A. F. of L. industrial unions were, on the whole, more successful than those by the craft unions. Thousands of workers joined up in the hope of getting jobs or higher pay. This led to an increasing demand by the leaders of the industrial unions that the A. F. of L. itself adopt the industrial-union type of organization for all new unions among unorganized workers. They also urged the older craft unions to admit all the workers in their industries, so as to develop a united front in the unions' efforts to protect and promote the workers interests.

The Congress of Industrial Organizations

At the 1935 convention of the A. F. of L., the issue was brought on the floor for debate. The leaders of the industrial unions strongly urged immediate action by the A. F. of L. to begin a nationwide drive to organize workers in such mass-production industries as steel, rubber, and automobiles. There were already some A. F. of L unions, both craft and industrial, in these and other mass-production industries. They were not, however, very strong; most workers had not joined because they had been afraid of losing their jobs. These unions joined forces in supporting the demand. At the convention, the industrial unions were out-voted by the craft unions. The latter also denied the industrial unions the right to try to organize all the workers in the industries in which they had already been established. The craft unions were unwilling to see industrial unions grow stronger. They still clung to the belief that the surest way to success in organizing unions lay in preserving the old craft basis of the A. F. of L.

The convention gave a general but somewhat vague support to the principle of industrial unionism. Some of the industrial-union leaders, therefore, notably John L. Lewis of the United Mine Workers of America and Sidney Hillman of the Amalgamated Clothing Workers of America, met on November 9, 1935, after the A. F. of L. convention adjourned, to develop the industrial-union program. A Committee for Industrial Organization was formed which was supposed at first to work within the structure of the A. F. of L. President William Green of the A. F. of L. announced, however, that the new Committee had acted illegally. John L. Lewis thereupon resigned his vice-presidency in the A. F. of L. to become chairman of the Committee. The new body now organized as a separate, nation-wide union movement, as the Congress of Industrial Organizations, and elected Lewis as president.

Efforts were subsequently made by various outside groups to bring the two factions together in a friendly and cooperative way to organize all workers in the mass-production industries. President Roosevelt twice sent special messages to both groups urging them to settle their dispute over which type of union to organize. He and many others felt that the dispute was already weakening the whole labor-union movement in America.

In 1936, however, the A. F. of L. outlawed all C. I. O. unions. These unions had grown rapidly in membership and were becoming nearly as strong as the A. F. of L. unions. The A. F. of L. made many demands as to its leadership of organized labor as the condition of a peaceful agreement with the C. I. O. These demands were unacceptable to the C. I. O. Negotiations went on during 1937, 1938, and 1939, but to no avail. Charges and counter-charges, of Communism in the C. I. O. and of obstructionism in the A. F. of L., prevented the two labor movements from reconciling their differences. By this time, the C. I. O. was reported to have about as many members as the A. F. of L., each some 4,000,000.

The C. I. O. first headed by John L. Lewis, and since 1940, by Phillip Murray, continued as the advocate of industrial unionism. In the split with the A. F. of L., two of the largest unions in the A. F. of L. went over to the C. I. O.—the United Mine Workers of America, and the Amalgamated Clothing

Workers of America. In many other fields, the A. F. of L. and the C. I. O. competed for new members. Each actively organized both types of union, craft and industrial.

The C. I. O. is now dominant in many of the mass-production industries, such as steel, automobiles, rubber and textiles. On the other hand, it has adopted the amalgamated or craft-union basis in certain fields, such as those covered by the National Maritime Union and National Association of Die Casting Workers.

Faced by this challenge, the A. F. of L. also developed some industrial unions of its own, in addition to a few which had remained loyal in the C. I. O. split. Among these are the Brewery and Soft Drinks Workers of America and the International Ladies Garment Workers Union. The latter first joined the C. I. O. and later returned to the A. F. of L.

Beside the A. F. of L. and the C. I. O., there are a few independent unions. These are unions which workers in a particular plant, industry, or region organize without affiliating with either of the two national union groups. These unions are generally found in a single plant. Sometimes, workers in various plants in a single industry located in one or several cities have organized in this way. They feel that they can protect and promote their own interests and bargain effectively with their employers without having to join a nationwide union organization. Examples of this type of union are the Independent Union of the Consolidated Edison Company of New York City, the United Telephone Organizations of the New York Telephone Company and similar labor organizations in most other telephone companies in the United States.

Before the various national and state labor relations acts and similar laws (see Chapter 6, pp. 124 ff.), many employers tried to prevent their workers from joining nationwide labor unions by organizing company unions. These company unions,

© International News Photo

organized within a single plant, were frequently dominated by the employers who provided the union with funds or controlled the election of its officers. Company unions were outlawed by the national and state labor relations acts of the mid-1930's. Since then, no employer may in any way interfere with the right of his workers to join a union of their own choosing. The company union has become an historical incident in the long record of the workers' efforts to organize their own unions (see Chapter 6, pp. 124 ff.).

Employers' Organizations Cooperate In Improving Industrial and Labor Relations

As labor unions have grown, so have employers' associations. We have already seen how employers also organized on a nationwide basis in the National Association of Manufacturers and the Chamber of Commerce of the United States during the early 1900's.

In addition to the two major nationwide employers' groups, there are many others which are playing an increasingly useful role in improving the relations of their members with the workers. There were in 1938, about 1,500 national and regional "trade associations", in addition to about 6,500 state and local associations. Of all these groups, about 18 per cent of the state and local, and about 62 per cent of the national and regional associations, represented employers in industry. Of the national and regional groups, more than three-fifths rendered some kind of service to their members in the field of employer-worker relations. In nearly a third of these associations, this service was a major activity.

Among the services which these associations provide are efforts to standardize hours of work, rates of pay for similar work, and vacation plans among their members. They also aid their members to develop more objective and impersonal hiring and firing methods, plans for rating and promoting workers, and orderly practices in handling complaints. Many, too, inform their members about ways of improving working conditions as to health, safety, recreation, and job training.

The main function of employers' associations in these fields is to collect and distribute information to their members. They do not have the power to require their members to adopt any particular plan or to accept the best industrial relations practices already followed by some employers in the association. They do, however, aid in developing better practices throughout an industry by bringing new standards before their members.

This shift away from anti-union activities to cooperative relations with workers on the part of most employers' associations has had important results. These associations can and often have performed a real service in educating their members in ways of cooperating with, rather than combating, their workers. They can become important factors in developing collective bargaining by bringing all the employers in an industry together as a group.

This is, in fact, one of the most important ways in which employers' associations have helped to bring about better industrial relations. The very fact that employers throughout an industry or in a city or state are organized makes it easier for them to sit down with labor-union representatives and work out their common problems. The history of voluntary collective bargaining under which many employers and workers have agreed to settle their disputes without violence is an indication of this new trend in industrial relations. It shows that in America we have already come a long way toward finding a way of adjusting labor disputes through the direct action of the workers and employers themselves. We shall review some of these developments when we note the growth of mediation and arbitration (see Chapter 8, pp. 166 ff.). Here, we may note that the growth of well-organized groups among employers as well as workers has helped to stabilize industrial relations in America.

☆ ☆ ☆ ☆ ☆ ☆ ☆ ☆ ☆ ☆ ☆ ☆ ☆

By 1940, the people of Newtown and of the nation realized several of the major trends already evident in 1840 and 1890. Nearly three-fifths of all the people were listed by the census as urban dwellers. Of the gainfully employed, less than one-fifth earned their living in agriculture. Over four-fifths received wages and salaries from manufacturing and mining, commerce and transportation and the service trades and professions. The latter group had come to play an increasingly important role throughout our economy. The machine had become the dominant factor in our ways of earning a living —on the farm hardly less than in the factory or office. Within industry, the large rather than the small plant, the integrated corporation rather than the single company, became the principal way of organizing production. By the 1930's, however, many large companies were already starting to decentralize their great plants into smaller units.

Employers' and workers' organizations grew in number and size; workers and employers accepted more widely the principles and practices of collective bargaining in their relations with each other. The steady flow of emigrants from Europe decreased during and after the First World War and was sharply limited by the Immigration Act of 1924. Despite the economic and social difficulties created by the War and by the Depression of 1929, the people of Newtown and of the nation continued to maintain their faith in our traditional principles of free enterprise and free government.

Thus far, we have reviewed the pattern of life and the character of the American economy in four periods from 1790 to 1940. In each of these periods we have traced the pattern in a typical industrial city of today from its beginning as a frontier settlement 150 years ago. The story could be told in detail about any industrial city in New York State if we wished only to record these changes of a century and a half. The record would, indeed, not be very different for more than a hundred of our industrial cities from Massachusetts to California. Newtown is a symbol of what has happened everywhere as we have become an industrial nation.

The shift from agriculture to manufacturing, from the country to the city, has had many significant and challenging effects on the pattern of American life. The changes which the shift helped to bring about have not, however, altered our faith in free government and free enterprise.

We have noted in the four periods the various factors that have affected the economic security of different groups within the nation. We have noted particularly the workers' place in American life and their efforts to protect and promote their interests.

All these changes have had much to do with the growing importance, both political and economic, of the relations of employers and workers. We have come to realize that these relations affect the efficiency and stability of our whole economy. We know, too, that they reach further to affect all the people, for, unless these relations are peaceful and orderly, democracy loses some of its value and vitality.

Industrial relations have thus become of first-rate public concern. During the past half-century, we have extended the idea of the general welfare to include these relations as a vital element in the economic security of all the people. We have used our free government to keep our economy free from those individual or group practices which might injure the security of the workers and so defeat the general welfare. Among the efforts we have made to control such practices, to promote the general welfare, the most important have been in the field of industrial relations.

In the following chapters, therefore, we shall review the various fields of industrial relations in which we have acted through government. These fall into three main groups. We shall see, first, how we, the people, have acted, by laying down certain rules to govern employers and workers in their relations with each other. These rules prohibit certain wrongful acts on the part of both employers and workers. Second, we shall note how we have made laws to help workers and employers adjust their differences through the aid of public agencies of mediation and arbitration when their own efforts have failed. Next, we shall analyze how we have acted through our government to regulate the conditions of industrial work in the fields of wages and hours, workmen's compensation, and social insurance. Finally, we shall observe how the War of 1941 has affected these fields of industrial relations, and how the American tradition can be continued in the peace which lies ahead.

AMERICAN LIFE IN 1940

BY 1940 NEARLY THREE FIFTHS OF ALL THE PEOPLE WERE URBAN DWELLERS

ONLY 17 OUT OF EVERY 100 GAINFULLY EMPLOYED EARNED THEIR LIVING IN AGRICULTURE

THE REST WERE EMPLOYED IN MANUFACTURING, TRANSPORTATION AND THE SERVICE TRADES

IMMIGRATION RESTRICTED

THE LABOR UNIONS HAD GROWN STRONG

re and More Employers and Workers Adopted Collective Bargaining

PART II

THE RULES OF THE GAME

Courtesy of Office of War Information

FOR—AND BY—WHOM THE RULES ARE MADE

5

Making Rules for Employers in Labor Relations

THE FIRST WAY IN WHICH WE HAVE ACTED THROUGH GOV-
ernment to regulate the relations of employers and workers
has been to define the rules which they must observe in their
direct dealings with each other. The purpose behind these
rules has been to promote the general welfare by limiting the
actions of private individuals and groups which may have harmful effects on the community, the state, or the nation. The
policies or activities of one side in ,a labor dispute may, for
instance, disturb peaceful industrial relations by using unfair
methods to coerce the other side. When a particular practice
has become sufficiently widespread, we have established new
rules by law—standards of rights and duties—in order to
insure the welfare of all the people.

In the next three chapters, we shall review some of the practices of employers and workers which we have regulated. In
this chapter, we shall note those practices of employers which
have been limited by law because a majority of the people, acting through their legislatures, thought them to be unfair. In
the next chapter, we shall see how the people have also acted

through government to guarantee a special interest of the workers—the right to join unions of their own choosing. In the following chapter, we shall analyze some of the unfair practices of workers and how we have begun to regulate them by law.

Among employers' practices which have caused many industrial conflicts, three have been especially important. First, the kind of contract that some employers have forced their workers to accept in order to get or to keep a job has often led to disputes and sometimes to violence. Under these contracts, some employers attempted to discharge union workers from their plants and to prevent them from finding other jobs. Second, the ways in which some employers have tried to stop their workers from carrying on a strike have more than once disturbed peaceful industrial relations. Third, the practices of certain employers, when a strike has broken out, have frequently affected many people who had no direct interest in the dispute which caused the strike. In each of these areas, we have acted through our state or our national governments to protect the general welfare by setting certain standards of conduct for both. Why have we acted through government and what rules have we made for each coercive practice on the part of employers?

Yellow-Dog Contracts and Blacklisting

When the labor movement was growing rapidly at the end of the 19th century, many employers tried to prevent unions from being organized in their plants. They used two methods. The first method was to require new workers coming to their plants, as well as those already in their plants, to sign contracts agreeing not to join or support a union while they worked for that employer. This type of contract was called a "yellow-dog contract". The second method was to keep a record of workers who were known to be, or suspected of being, union members and to circulate this record among other employers. Some employers thought that by thus "blacklisting" union workers they could prevent the spread of unions.

Labor-union leaders were, of course, opposed to both these practices. Because there were generally more workers than jobs, the first practice was an effective means of preventing the growth of unions. Many workers would abandon their union membership in order to get a job, or to obtain a better one. Similarly, the second practice was a barrier to the growth of unions because workers soon found that, if they were blacklisted, it was almost impossible for them to get any job at all.

The Yellow-Dog Contract in Action

Although yellow-dog contracts were imposed by employers on their workers in many industries, labor-union leaders continued to try to induce workers in these industries to join unions despite these contracts. The first attempt to obtain regulation of yellow-dog conracts was made in the 1890's. Because Congress may regulate railroads under the federal commerce power, it used this power to attempt the first limitation of this practice. The railway unions had become strong enough to press for a law barring this kind of contract from being applied to railroad workers. The Erdman Act of 1898 was enacted largely as a result of the unions' demands. One section of this Act prohibited the railroads from discharging their workers because of membership in a union and prohibited them from making non-membership in a union a requirement for securing employment. In 1908, however, the Supreme Court held that Congress could not impose such a policy on the railroads because it interfered with the "liberty" guaranteed by the Fifth Amendment.*

* Adair v. U. S., 208 U. S. 161 (1908). The 5th and 14th Amendments provide that a person's "life, liberty, or property" may not be taken (that is, regulated or seized) without "due process of law". This restriction has been held by the courts to limit the police power of the states.

By 1910, about 20 states had enacted similar laws. Some of these laws were held unconstitutional in the state courts. In 1915, one of these state laws was brought before the Supreme Court of the United States and was held unconstitutional on the ground that it was beyond the police power of the states under the Fourteenth Amendment.*

Thus, it appeared that, under the Fifth and Fourteenth Amendments, both the state and national governments were prevented from prohibiting yellow-dog contracts. In 1917, the Supreme Court was even more positive in another case. Here it expanded the doctrine of the earlier cases which prohibited any regulation of this type of contract. In this decision, the Court held that union leaders might not encourage workers who had signed such contracts to join a union.**

The Supreme Court did not follow this rather extreme interpretation of the yellow-dog contract in some later decisions. In a case decided in 1921, for instance, Chief Justice Taft, speaking for the Court, stated that it had not meant to prohibit all union efforts to persuade non-union men to go on strike in order to gain the right to join a union. He distinguished the facts in this case concerning a yellow-dog contract from the *Hitchman* case. Here, the union had acted openly in trying to induce the workers to join the union; in the earlier case the union leaders had acted secretly. It was, the Court said, the deceptive means used by the union to induce workers to join it which had been wrong.*** By this decision, the court moved from a strict legalistic doctrine toward a rule of law based on the actual practices in industrial and labor relations in this field.

* Coppage v. Kansas, 236, U. S. 1 (1915).

** Hitchman Coal and Coke Co. v. Marshall, 245 U. S. 229 (1917).

*** American Steel Foundries Co. v. Tri-City Central Trades Council, 257 U. S. 184 (1921).

Some state supreme courts, following this idea to its logical conclusion, began to adopt a new attitude toward yellow-dog contracts. This was particularly true of the New York State courts. In several decisions, they adopted a more liberal point of view on these contracts. In two important cases, the New York courts decided that these contracts were so one-sided that they should not be given the same legal protection as other private contracts. The courts distinguished them from ordinary commercial contracts, in which both sides had a more evenly balanced bargaining power.* Some state courts, notably Ohio, followed the New York lead. Others continued to enforce yellow-dog contracts against the efforts of unions to organize workers who had signed them.

In the meantime, the railway workers continued to press Congress for a law that would protect them from yellow-dog contracts. They were finally successful. In 1926, Congress enacted the Watson-Parker Act. This law, applying to all interstate-railroad workers, guaranteed them the right of collective bargaining. It secured them this right by providing that all labor agreements should be made through union representatives chosen by the workers "without interference, influence, or coercion". In 1930, the Supreme Court held this Act constitutional, this time under the federal commerce power.** The Court found that the Fifth Amendment was not a bar to regulating labor relations. No doubt thirty years' experience with industrial disputes on the railroads, resulting in threats of strikes and other difficulties, had convinced the Court that labor conditions do affect interstate commerce. The Act, beside

---

* Interboro Rapid Transit Co. v. Lavin, 237 N. Y. 65 (1928).
  Interboro Rapid Transit Co. v. Green, 131 Misc. 602 (1928).

** Texas and N. O. R. Co. v. Brotherhood of Railway and S. S. Clerks, 281 U. S. 548 (1930).

Courtesy of Farm Security Administration

guaranteeing the right of collective bargaining, also set up a National Mediation Board, under an amendment in 1934, to adjust disputes which were not settled directly by the railroads and their workers (see Chapter 8, pp. 166 ff.).

In the meantime, a number of states had enacted laws which, although they did not forbid the use of yellow-dog contracts, did prohibit their enforcement in the courts. By declaring such contracts "null and void" or "contrary to public policy", these laws, in effect, made it impossible for an employer to penalize a worker who broke his contract by joining a union. By 1932, 6 states—Arizona, Colorado, New Jersey, Ohio, Oregon and Wisconsin—had enacted such laws. These laws prevented employers from seeking damages from their workers for joining a union or for striking even though they had signed such a contract. These laws also prohibited the courts from issuing injunctions against labor unions merely because they encouraged non-union workers to join. This, in effect, allowed the workers to break their contracts not to join a union without losing their jobs. In 1932, Congress took a further and even more important step by enacting the Norris-LaGuardia Act. This law specifically prohibited any federal court from granting injunctions against those who sought to break yellow-dog contracts. Thus, with respect not only to railroads but to all interstate industries, the use of the injunction to prevent workers from joining unions was limited (see pp. 117 ff.).

The record of how the state and the national governments have regulated yellow-dog contracts indicates that they acted in response to the workers' interest in the right to join unions of their own choosing. In this field, a public policy was established to protect directly this interest of the workers. This policy reflects, too, the interests of the whole community in eliminating one cause of fear, and perhaps of violence, in industrial and labor relations.

The Blacklist in Action

Another industrial practice, the blacklist, is closely related to the yellow-dog contract. As we have seen, some employers have tried to prevent the labor-union movement from spreading in their industry. They did so by circulating to other employers the names of those workers who had joined or were active in a union.

So far as the practice of blacklisting is concerned, much less definite governmental action has been taken. In general, anti-blacklisting laws have provided that the worker must be given a reason for his discharge by his employer. They have also generally provided that a worker may sue anyone for damages who has brought about his discharge from a job by false statements as to his union membership.

More than 30 states have enacted anti-blacklisting laws. These laws have not, however, been very effective in meeting the actual conditions workers face as a result of this practice. Up to 1938, only two criminal prosecutions and fewer than a dozen civil suits against employers were successful. Many of the laws were so vaguely drawn that the courts held them unenforceable. Other courts found ways to avoid applying these laws, holding, for instance, that it was illegal to circulate a blacklist but not illegal to use it once it had been received.

The real difficulty lies in the practical impossibility of proving the use of a blacklist by an employer. It is easy for him to offer a number of reasons for his refusal to hire a certain worker or for the discharge of another. Because a worker rarely has any chance of finding out who supplied the information, he is usually unable to prove his case in the courts.

These anti-blacklisting laws, like the laws prohibiting yellow-dog contracts, were passed in response to the workers' interest in the right to join unions of their own choosing. Taken

together, these laws reflect the people's interest in fair industrial relations and fair employer practices.

Labor Spies and Strikebreakers .

Another practice by which some employers have tried to prevent the growth of unions has been the use of labor spies to
find out what was going on in union meetings. Sometimes, when
an employer thought that a union was being organized in his
plant, he induced one or more workers to join the new union
and report on its activities to him. They would attend union
meetings only for the purpose of obtaining information—undercover—for the employer about the plans and activities of the
union. These "stool pigeons", as they were called, reported
back to the employer and informed him who the union leaders
were and what plans were being made to form or to expand the
union.

The organized use of labor spies in industry dates back more
than half a century. Many examples of this practice have been
revealed at hearings before committees of state legislatures
and of Congress. This is a practice, however, which is very
difficult to eliminate by law. One reason is that under the common law an employer may hire whom he chooses. Therefore,
the hiring of labor spies was, until recently, entirely lawful.*

Before 1933, five states and a number of cities tried to abolish this practice. Private detective agencies were required to
obtain licenses from the state or the city in order to operate.
Under these laws and ordinances, good character was made the
test for obtaining a license. The state or city could then revoke
the license of any agency which did not live up to this test.

---

* Although the National Labor Relations Act does not specifically declare the
hiring of labor spies to be an "unfair labor practice", it has been held to come
within the prohibitions of the Act by the National Labor Relations Board. Section
704, subdiv. 1, of the New York State Labor Relations Act, on the other hand,
specifically prohibits the hiring of labor spies.

These laws have been held constitutional by both state and federal courts. They have not been very effective, however, in preventing this practice, largely because it is so difficult to prove the existence of what is really an undercover activity.

Another employer practice of which workers disapprove is the use of strikebreakers during a strike. Here, as in the case of the labor spies, some employers faced with a strike have used private agencies for supplying them with workers. Often, however, this practice has gone beyond the entirely proper one of obtaining the workers they needed to keep their plants running.

Some of these agencies have supplied "workers" who were often used to threaten the striking workers by strong-arm methods. This practice became widespread during the 1920's and 1930's. Sometimes, these organized strikebreaking groups were equipped with armored cars and weapons. They did little more "work" than to break picket lines, with or without police protection, and to visit the homes of striking workers, often late at night, in an effort to intimidate them.

The transportation of professional strikebreakers across state lines was prohibited by Congress, under the federal commerce power, by the Byrnes Anti-Strikebreaking Act of 1936. The Act prohibits anyone "knowingly" transporting or aiding in transporting persons across a state line with the intent to employ such persons for strikebreaking purposes. As the Act puts it, such transportation must be to obstruct or interfere with the right of peaceful picketing during a labor dispute. There have been very few cases brought to the courts under this Act. Its effect has been whittled away in these cases by interpreting the word "knowingly" very broadly. Strikebreaking agencies have generally asserted that they were merely filling the request of an employer for ordinary workers and did not know that they were to be used to break a strike.

Here, then, is a second field in which we have acted through our state and national governments to make rules about the labor practices of employers. No law can, perhaps, eliminate all unfair practices in these or other fields of industrial relations. The laws noted here will do something to correct the evils they were designed to meet. The solution, however, lies deeper—in the will of all the people to end such practices.

The Labor Injunction

Strikes, Picketing and the Secondary Boycott

The most effective weapon which workers possess in seeking to protect and promote their interests is the strike. The strike is really a war measure in the industrial struggle. It should be a last resort, employed when all other means of settling a a dispute have failed. Before the passage of the national and state labor relations acts (see Chapter 7), the strike was often used to force employers to recognize this right. It is, of course, a weapon which can be used also for protecting or promoting many other interests, for instance, those regarding hours, wages, and working conditions.

If workers merely stopped work and left the factory, the strike might not prove a very effective weapon in trying to enforce their demands on their employer. The employer could hire new workers. True, looking for new workers might cause him some inconvenience. But because, as we have seen, more workers than jobs have usually been available, the employer could generally find workers to take the place of those on strike.

Workers have, therefore, gone further than merely leaving their jobs. They have engaged in active measures to bring further pressure on their employer. They have, for example, "picketed" the plant where they worked. Picketing means that the striking workers and often sympathetic workers from other factories or unions march up and down outside the plant. Often,

110

they carry placards stating their demands and criticizing the employer for his unfair labor practices. Sometimes, the pickets try to keep other workers from entering the plant, either by calling them unpleasant names like "scab", or even by threats of force and sometimes by actual force. When pickets form not a single line or two but a solid group all around the plant, their activities are called mass-picketing. This type of picketing is intended to attract the attention of other workers and the whole community to the dispute.

The pressure of the strike on the employer is thereby made more severe because other workers and perhaps the whole community take sides in the dispute. The employer is directly affected, because his own workers persuade other workers not to take their places. He is also indirectly affected, because the dispute is brought out into the open so that other people in the community are more or less influenced in their attitude toward the employer or his workers. In this way, striking workers try to, and often do, bring the pressure of public opinion to bear on the employer, forcing him to give way to their demands. For

PEACEFUL PICKETING © Keystone View Company of N.Y.

these reasons, picketing has become an important and powerful weapon in the hands of the workers.

As labor unions have grown, other ways of bringing pressure on the employer have been used in order to make a strike more effective. Among these methods is the "secondary boycott". Workers in the same craft or industry may refuse, for instance, to work on products made by an employer who refuses to recognize a union in his plant. That is, if the local union which is striking is a member of a national union, whether craft or industrial, members of the same national union in other cities will help the local union. It will require all the other local unions to stop work on any jobs in which the employer, against whom the strike has been called, is interested. Thus, if a strike in a single plant occurs, workers in other plants, often in other communities, will refuse to handle or to work on the products of the plant where the strike is going on. This may result in further strikes and picketing, often reaching a whole industry and even related industries in many parts of the country.

A special form of secondary boycott has also been developed by labor unions—the "sympathetic strike". Here, workers in other crafts or industries, generally located in the same community, will go out on strike at the same time. They do so in order to aid their fellow workers who are striking in a plant with which the sympathetic strikers have no direct relations. Here again, picketing may spread and cause wide public concern about the original dispute. Both these ways of making the strike and picketing more effective add to the power of the workers to enforce their demands against their employer.

What the Injunction Is

To counterbalance these powerful weapons in the hands of the workers, employers have sought to forge weapons of their own. They have found that their strongest weapon was the injunction. This is an order of a court which requires the person or persons to whom it is directed to do or to refrain from doing certain acts. To understand how powerful a weapon the injunction is, we must trace its origin and its nature.

Ordinarily, before a court acts to protect a person's property or other rights, those rights must have already been impaired by some other person. If, for example, someone is injured in an automobile accident or is not paid what is owed to him under a contract, he may go into court to seek the court's aid in recovering for the damage he has suffered.

This is not, however, the only kind of injury which one may suffer. The harm may not have yet occurred or it may not be measurable in money damages. For instance, spreading false rumors about a person may affect his chance of getting a job, perhaps for the rest of his life. Or again, if striking workers, by using violence or threats of violence, make it impossible for an employer to run his plant, he may lose the goodwill of the community and perhaps be put out of business.

It is to prevent just this sort of probable or future injury that the courts possess the power to issue injunctions. Whether or not the injunction will be granted usually rests in the court's sense of justice and fair play. The granting of an injunction is always in its discretion. If a court issues an injunction, it defines what the party against whom it has been issued may or may not do in the given situation.

How do the courts compel obedience to this type of order? If anyone against whom an injunction has been issued wilfully refuses to obey the court's orders defined in the injunction, he may be brought before the court in what is called a "contempt proceeding".

In a contempt proceeding, any interested person who believes that the terms of an injunction have been disobeyed by the party against whom it was issued may bring that party before the court. Evidence is submitted by both parties. If the court is convinced that the injunction has been disobeyed, it may impose penalties for "contempt" of its previous order, the injunction. The court has complete discretion in imposing these penalties. It may punish the party who has disobeyed the injunction by a fine, imprisonment, or both. The court acts alone; it is the judge of both the law and the facts—without a jury. Thus, the injunction is a powerful weapon in the hands of the courts for controlling the future actions of individuals.

Injunctions were often sought from the courts by employers in order to prevent a strike by their workers or to limit their activities while they were on strike. Both state and federal courts adopted the practice of issuing what are called temporary injunctions. A temporary injunction may be issued on the basis of no proof other than affidavits—written statements under oath. Because no proof need be submitted to support the statements, there is no way of telling whether they are true or not. Later, perhaps after several weeks or months, the question of making the injunction permanent may come up for trial. Only then must further proof of damage, likely to result from the strike or the activities of the workers while on strike, be submitted to the court.

The right to obtain a temporary injunction has been much abused by employers in seeking to prevent their workers from striking or picketing. The found that it was very easy to obtain a temporary injunction in most courts. Because workers' weapon of the strike generally depends for its effectiveness on being used quickly, a temporary injunction against striking was generally enough to dull the edge of its threat to the employer. Once employers had secured a temporary injunction, they often did not seek to make it permanent, for they had gained their end by breaking the strike.

The labor injunction has been for more than half a century the chief weapon used by employers to combat strikes by their workers. In using injunctions, employers have attempted to reach both the strike itself and the picketing activities of their workers. They have sought, first, to obtain injunctions against the workers' striking for any purpose. Second, they have sought to limit the kinds of picketing which workers might use.

Labor unions, too, have used injunctions to enforce their demands against employers. Workers have sometimes applied to the courts for injunctions requiring employers to live up to the terms of their collective-bargaining agreements. They have obtained injunctions, for instance, to prevent an employer from disregarding the terms of the agreement as to such provisions as seniority rights, working conditions, or the discharge of workers for reasons not provided for in the agreement. In general, however, the injunction has been a weapon more often used by employers than by workers.

The practice by employers of seeking injunctions to limit the activities of their workers began in the 1880's. Its use developed most rapidly after 1920; nearly half of all the injunctions issued before 1930 occurred in that decade.

Workers—and many other people—opposed, for several reasons, the granting of injunctions in labor disputes. First, the action of the court was often based merely on affidavits. It was argued that these affidavits supporting a request for an injunction did not give the court sufficient information. Further, it frequently turned out that the person who had obtained a temporary injunction based merely on affidavits could not prove the statements made in them when a hearing for a permanent injunction was later held before the court.

Second, judges often issued "blanket" or "omnibus" injunctions which prohibited the striking workers or their sympathizers from doing many things which most people

PEACEFUL PICKETING

© International News Phot

thought entirely proper. In the famous *Debs* case*, in 1895, for instance, the court's order restrained not only the actual strikers, but also "all persons combining or conspiring with them, and all other persons whomsoever, absolutely to desist and refrain from in any way or manner interfering with, hindering, obstructing, or stopping any of the business of any of the following named railroads". Some of the more detailed injunctions which have been issued in both state and federal courts have made almost everything but eating, sleeping, and getting dressed, on the part of the strikers and "whomsoever", illegal.

In the *Bedford Stone Company* case,** for instance, many actions lawful and harmless in themselves were forbidden.

* In re Debs, 158 U. S. 564 (1895).

** Bedford Stone Co. v. Journeymen Stone Cutters' Ass'n., 274 U. S. 37 (1927).

Such acts as striking in concert, calling or advising a strike, paying strike benefits, offering to pay transportation costs back home to strikebreakers, peacefully persuading others not to work for or patronize employers, mentioning the existence of the dispute in periodicals or in meetings, or "in any way interfering with the operation of the complainant's business" were prohibited.

We Act Through Government to Limit the Injunction

Workers and others who believed that the use of the injunction in industrial disputes had become unfair sought to have laws passed which would limit this broad power of the courts. The history of these efforts is an interesting example of how we, the people, develop new rules through our state and national governments in the field of industrial relations.

The Sherman Anti-Trust Act of 1890 made illegal "combinations in restraint of trade". Congressional leaders who drew up this Act had in mind the great industrial corporations which were, as we have seen, at this time creating popular distrust and suspicion. Unfortunately for the labor unions, the courts held that they could also become "combinations in restraint of trade". This meant, of course, that many of their strike activities could be prohibited by injunctions issued by the courts at the employers' request.

In order to free unions from this interpretation of the Sherman Act, the Clayton Act, passed in 1914, specifically declared that unions should not be considered as "illegal combinations in restraint of trade under the anti-trust laws". The results for labor, however, were disappointing. This purpose of the Act was whittled away by interpretations of the Supreme Court which still held many sweeping injunctions in labor disputes proper. Workers and others still felt that the use of injunctions in labor disputes should be further limited.

THE STATES A

*IN SOME STATES A SINGLE LAW

MAY COVER MORE THAN ONE OF THESE PROVISIONS

● SYMBOL REPRESENTS	◑ SYMBOL REPRESENTS	✿ SYMBOL REPRESENTS
LABOR RELATIONS ACTS	**MEDIATION AND ARBITRATION ACTS**	**ANTI-INJUNCTION ACTS**

REGULATE LABOR RELATIONS*

☙ SYMBOL REPRESENTS	§ SYMBOL REPRESENTS	☯ SYMBOL REPRESENTS
WORKMEN'S COMPENSATION ACTS	**PROHIBITION OF YELLOW-DOG CONTRACTS**	**UNION REGULATORY ACTS**

In response to this widespread feeling, Congress in 1932 enacted the Norris-LaGuardia Act which covered all aspects of the issuance of injunctions by federal courts. The Act lists the situations in which a federal court may not issue injunctions. If, however, workers use fraud or violence in their strike activities, a court may still issue an injunction restraining these activities despite the Act.

The Act applies, of course, only to the federal courts. It has served, however, as a model for many new state laws. A number of the states which had already enacted laws in this field soon strenghtened them by including rules similar to those in the Norris-LaGuardia Act. Still other states enacted new anti-injunction laws between 1932 and 1943, so that in that year there were 26 in all.*

The most important provisions in these laws relate to what activities on the part of workers may not be prevented by injunction. Section 4 of the Norris-LaGuardia Act, for instance, prohibits any federal court from enjoining workers, singly or in combination, from

(a) ceasing or refusing to work;

(b) becoming or remaining a member of a union, regardless of any promise not to do so;

(c) paying or withholding strike or unemployment benefits;

(d) aiding by lawful means any person participating in a labor dispute who is involved in court action;

(e) giving publicity to the facts of any labor dispute by advertising, speaking, or patrolling, or any other method not involving fraud or violence;

* Arizona, Colorado, Connecticut, Idaho, Illinois, Indiana, Kansas, Louisiana, Maine, Maryland, Massachusetts, Minnesota, Montana, New Hampshire, New Jersey, New Mexico, New York, North Dakota, Oklahoma, Oregon, Pennsylvania, Rhode Island, Utah, Washington, Wisconsin, Wyoming.

(f) assembling peaceably or organizing to act in promotion of labor interests in a labor dispute;

(g) advising or notifying any person of intention to do any of the acts just mentioned;

(h) agreeing with other persons to do or not to do any of the above acts;

(i) advising, urging, or otherwise inducing without fraud or violence other persons to join in doing or not doing the above acts, regardless of any previous promise made by the other persons to employers or to others.

The Norris-LaGuardia Act, as did the Clayton Act, also specifically exempts persons taking part in a labor dispute from being considered engaged in a conspiracy under the Sherman Act or under the common law. The Act went even further in broadening the definition of a "labor dispute", by defining it as:

any controversy concerning terms or conditions of employment, or concerning the association or representation of persons in negotiating, fixing, maintaining, changing, or seeking to arrange terms or conditions of employment, regardless of whether or not the disputants stand in the proximate relation of employer and employee.

Further, the Act attempts to prevent the issuance of injunctions in some cases of secondary boycott. It defines the relation of the striking workers to a labor dispute, however, in such a way as to leave open the use of injunctions in other cases of secondary boycott. Injunctions may not be granted by a court against workers who are "participating or interested" in a labor dispute. To be interested one must be "engaged in the same industry, trade, craft, or occupation", or be an officer or agent of a labor union similarly engaged. Machinists in New York City, for example, may now strike in aid of machinists on strike, say, in Illinois, because they are "engaged in the same industry". New York City painters or carpenters, not being engaged in the same industry, may not, however, join in this strike. A sympathetic strike of these workers may still be enjoined under the Act.

The second important provision of the Norris-LaGuardia Act and similar state acts relates to the procedure which must be followed in granting injunctions. The courts may no longer issue either a temporary or a permanent injunction merely on the basis of affidavits. They must hear the testimony of witnesses in open court with opportunity for both sides to cross-examine the witnesses. Thus, evidence of the reality of future damage must be given by those seeking an injunction. The opportunity to refute this evidence can, therefore, be submitted in open court at the time the first injunction proceedings are held.

The third important provision in these laws relates to the power of the courts to punish for contempt. Formerly, as we have seen, the courts alone decided whether a person was guilty of contempt. Under the Norris-LaGuardia Act and most state laws, there must now be a jury trial in all cases in which a person is charged with contempt for disobeying an injunction. Thus, a contempt must be actually shown to the satisfaction of a man's peers, the jury. Together, these three aspects of the anti-injunction laws give the workers protection against the unfair use of injunctions by employers in labor disputes.

☆ ☆ ☆ ☆ ☆ ☆ ☆ ☆ ☆ ☆ ☆ ☆ ☆

The new rules we have established through government to regulate those practices of employers which we, the people, believe interfere with the general welfare cover a wide field of industrial relations. In these rules we have sought to guarantee a more fairly balanced bargaining power in labor disputes. The use of yellow-dog contracts and blacklisting and of labor spies and strikebreakers has been prohibited. The labor injunction, as a weapon of coercion, has been limited by narrowing its character and the scope of its use. In regulating these practices of employers in their relations with their workers, we have modified some of the rules of law which we inherited from a pre-industrial past. These rules were developed to control the relations of people who were, so the courts thought in making the rules, in a more or less equal bargaining position in their dealings with each other. As industrial progress during the past century and a half has changed the actual bargaining position of employers and workers, the older rules of law no longer preserved a real equality between them. In modifying these older rules of law by legislation, we, the people, have sought to make their operation more equal in practice. In the next chapter, we shall see how the workers' general interest in the right to join unions of their own choosing has been guaranteed by law.

6

Unions of Their Own Choosing

IN MAKING RULES REGULATING EMPLOYERS IN THE PAST, WE have acted through government only when some special type of activity or some particular practice seemed to the majority of the people to be harmful to the general welfare. The activities we noted in the last chapter have been regulated by law, because they interfered with peaceful industrial relations. Sometimes they have hindered the workers from gaining one of the aims they most desired—the right to join unions of their own choosing. In addition to regulating one by one the practices of employers, which prevented workers from joining labor unions, we have also sought to protect this right by a general guarantee.

As we have seen (see Chapter 5, pp. 100 ff.), our state and national governments first attempted to meet this problem by what may be called negative action. Many separate laws were enacted, prohibiting employers from discriminating against workers because they formed unions. During the past decade, this negative policy has been translated into a positive policy of protecting directly the interest of the workers in organizing unions of their own choosing. The history of this new trend of policy will indicate how far we have acted through government to secure the general welfare of the whole community in this respect.

We Act Through the National Government

The first step which we took toward a positive policy of protecting the worker's interest in joining a union of his own choosing was through the national government. We had already enacted, as we have seen, under the federal commerce power, various special laws to protect this interest (see Chapter 5, pp. 100 ff.; see also Chapter 8, pp. 166 ff.). Now we acted, again under this power, to insure this interest by general—and positive—laws.

National Industrial Recovery Act

The first attempt to give nationwide protection to this interest of the workers was in the National Industrial Recovery Act of 1933. Section 7(a) of the Act became, in fact, the basis of most later laws in this field, state as well as national. It declared:

> (1) That employees shall have the right to organize and bargain collectively through representatives of their own choosing, and shall be free from the interference, restraint, or coercion of employers of labor, or their agents, in the designation of such representatives or in self-organization or in other concerted activities for the purpose of collective bargaining or other mutual aid or protection;
> (2) That no employee and no one seeking employment shall be required as a condition of employment to join any company union or to refrain from joining, organizing, or assisting a labor organization of his own choosing.

This was the broadest statement of policy which had so far been made in any American law. It seemed to guarantee completely the right of the worker to join a union of his own choosing. Under the Act, all employers in a single industry elected a committee to draft a code of fair competition for the whole industry. To secure governmental approval, every code had to include the guarantees of section 7(a) of the Act. Only those companies which complied with the code for their industry received the right to display the Blue Eagle of the National Recovery Administration.

It soon became evident, however, that this guarantee would not be worth much unless some agency were created to deal with labor disputes which might arise under the Act. Many industries, although they wrote into their codes of fair competition the terms of section 7(a), were not willing to apply these general principles when it came to bargaining with their workers.

In order to make the guarantees of section 7(a) effective, the President appointed on August 5, 1933, a National Labor Board. This Board, with an impartial chairman representing the public, was composed of an equal number of employer and worker representatives. Its duty was to "consider, adjust and settle differences in controversies that may arise through different interpretations" of the codes. The Board by its own action limited this broad power by considering only those labor disputes in which the workers charged that there had been violations of section 7(a).

The Board was soon faced by many disputes under the codes, especially regarding the right of workers to join unions. In order to settle these cases more promptly, the Board set up 20 regional boards, composed of representatives of employers and workers, each with an impartial chairman representing the public. These boards held hearings and tried to adjust disputes on the spot, rather than to refer them all to the Board itself at Washington.

The Board continued to function for a little less than a

year—to July 9, 1934. It made a fine record, however, in settling many of the disputes which arose under section 7(a). During these eleven months, the Board and its staff succeeded in settling 1,019 strikes involving 644,209 workers and aided in preventing 498 strikes involving 481,617 workers. Besides those disputes which were, or almost became, outright strikes, the Board helped to settle about 1,800 labor disputes in cases in which there were no strikes. In a great many other cases, the Board held hearings and made recommendations, most of which were accepted by the parties, in disputes in which no formal settlement was sought.

If its decisions were not accepted by an employer, the Board recommended to the Compliance Division of the National Recovery Administration that the right to display his Blue Eagle be taken away. This Blue Eagle was the symbol of an employer's compliance with the Act. By taking an employer's Blue Eagle away, it was hoped that the pressure of public opinion would force him to accept the Board's decision.

On June 29, 1934, the President set up a National Labor Relations Board and transferred the powers and duties of the National Labor Board to it. This new Board was really the same board under a new name and with the same purposes. This step was taken not because the National Labor Board had failed, but because Congress had enacted a new law providing specially for dealing with disputes arising out of section 7(a) of the National Industrial Recovery Act. This law established clear-cut rules for making the guarantee of the section operate effectively. The new National Labor Relations Board was to hold hearings and make findings of fact regarding violations of this section, to act as a voluntary arbitration board, and to make specific recommendations for the settlement of all labor disputes. Congress limited the life of the Board to one year (June 16, 1935); it was not yet ready to establish a

127

permanent agency for settling this kind of labor dispute.

The new board expanded the previous system of regional boards and provided them with more adequate staffs to handle the rapidly increasing number of cases before it. It also laid down a more definite procedure for handling labor disputes in each region by creating a panel of three members (one representing the employers, one the workers, and one the public) to deal with each labor dispute. When, on May 27, 1935, the Supreme Court held the National Industrial Recovery Act unconstitutional, the new National Labor Relations Board had, of course, no further power to act.*

Like the earlier board, however, it had made a very creditable record. It had settled 703 strikes involving 229,640 workers and had helped to avoid threatened strikes in 605 cases involving 536,398 workers. In addition, it settled about 1,400 disputes in cases in which no strikes or threats of strikes had occurred.

This Board also developed a policy which was later to become important in guaranteeing the right of workers to join unions of their own choosing. It established the practice of conducting secret elections for determining the workers' choice of a "collective-bargaining representative".** These elections afforded all the workers in a plant in which a dispute was going on the right to determine what union, if any, a majority of the workers wished to join. The Board held elections in 579 different plants involving 56,814 workers to determine which was the true collective-bargaining representative of all the

* Schechter Poultry Co. v. U. S., 295 U. S. 495 (1935).

** The "collective-bargaining representative" is that union or person which is finally chosen by a majority of the workers to represent them in bargaining with their employer.

workers in a plant. As a result of these elections, the employers promptly recognized the workers' elected representatives in 306 cases; in 278 cases completely harmonious relations were immediately brought about. Compliance with the decisions of the Board were secured in 46 other cases; in still others, the employers did not accept the Board's action. The Board's life ended before some pending cases could be finally settled.

Here we see the beginnings of a system under which organized workers themselves elect representatives to bargain for them and their fellow workers, without interference on the part of their employer. This practice of holding elections was a real step toward further guaranteeing the workers' interest in the right to join unions of their own choosing. The Board thus developed a new and democratic procedure for giving workers a right to make their own decisions.

During this period, several other labor relations boards were established by the national government to deal with labor disputes in particular industries. Among the more important were the National Bituminous Coal Labor Board, the Newspaper Industrial Board, the Automobile Labor Board, the National Steel Labor Relations Board, and the Textile Labor Relations Board. A National Longshoremen's Board (dealing only with labor disputes on the Pacific Coast) and a Petroleum Policy Board were also created by special orders of the President. Several other boards were organized independently under the National Industrial Recovery Act codes by the employers and workers themselves.

By section 7(a) of the National Industrial Recovery Act, Congress had shown that it really intended to provide a uniform, nationwide guarantee of the workers' right to join unions of their own choosing. Experience had shown that this purpose could be best achieved by a single agency, specifically charged with this function.

The demand for a uniform policy protecting this interest of the workers led to the passage of the National Labor Relations Act (approved by President Roosevelt on July 5, 1935). This new law was the most significant step toward a general guarantee of the workers' right to join unions of their own choosing. It also became the model for state laws in the same field.

We may ask at the outset what power the national government has to regulate this aspect of industrial relations. The Supreme Court had just held the National Industrial Recovery Act unconstitutional. It had done so principally on the ground that Congress could not extend the interstate commerce power to include the regulation of labor relations in the field of manufacturing. This power, said the Supreme Court, applied only to the stage of actual interstate commerce, not to acts which happened before or after goods had actually moved from one

© International News Photo

COLLECTING THE BALLOTS IN A N.L.R.B. ELECTION

state to another. This view had long been the basis of the Supreme Court's interpretation of the scope of national power in this field. In fact, the Court had held that regulation of manufacturing, even as to products which later crossed state lines, was beyond Congress' power because interstate commerce had not yet begun.*

Congress tried to meet this view of the interstate commerce power by relating labor conditions in industry directly to the flow of commerce. It introduced the National Labor Relations Act by a "statement of policy", setting forth its view of the relationship:

> Experience has proved that protection by law of the right of employees to organize and bargain collectively safeguards commerce from injury, impairment, or interruption, and promotes the flow of commerce by removing certain recognized sources of industrial strife and unrest, by encouraging practices fundamental to the friendly adjustment of industrial disputes arising out of differences as to wages, hours, or other working conditions, and by restoring equality of bargaining power between employers and employees.

> It is hereby declared to be the policy of the United States to eliminate the causes of certain substantial obstructions to the free flow of commerce and to mitigate and eliminate these obstructions when they have occurred by encouraging the practice and procedure of collective bargaining and by protecting the exercise by workers of full freedom of association, self-organization, and designation of representatives of their own choosing, for the purpose of negotiating the terms and conditions of their employment or other mutual aid or protection.

* U. S. v. E. C. Knight Co., 156 U. S. 1 (1895).

In stating the purposes of the Act in this way, Congress undoubtedly hoped to persuade the Supreme Court to accept its view of this question. By asserting that all stages in the industrial process were so closely related that they could not be separated by state boundaries, Congress returned to its own earlier constitutional doctrine about interstate commerce. When it had sought to regulate child labor in 1918, it had acted on the same principles which it stated again in 1935.* These principles were made more precise and applied to the broader field of industrial relations as a whole in the National Labor Relations Act.

Many employers refused, however, to accept this view. Indeed, before the National Labor Relations Act had been brought before the Supreme Court for review, an important group of private lawyers had announced their opinion that it was unconstitutional. The main basis of their opinion was that Congress was trying to exercise what amounted to a police power over industry, rather than its proper authority over interstate commerce.

For over thirty years, the Court had held that Congress might not regulate industry in any way, prior to the actual starting of the movement of manufactured goods in interstate commerce. It had maintained this view in declaring the National Industrial Recovery Act unconstitutional just a month before the National Labor Relations Act was introduced in Congress.

Two years later, on April 12, 1937, the Supreme Court handed down a series of five decisions affecting a newspaper press association, bus drivers, steel workers in an Ohio mill, clothing workers in New Jersey, and workers in a bus-trailer

* Hammer v. Dagenhart, 247 U. S. 251 (1918).

factory.* In all these fields of industry, the Court, by a five-to-four majority, upheld the right of the national government, under the National Labor Relations Act, to regulate labor relations in so far as they affected "the free flow of commerce."

Since then, many similar cases have come before the Court. In all of these cases, many industries located and operating for the most part within a single state have been found to come within the Act by the National Labor Relations Board. The Supreme Court has not reversed the Board in a single case on the ground that these industries should be considered local and, therefore, not within the interstate commerce power of the national government.

We may never know what led the Supreme Court originally to adopt this liberal view of the national power under interstate commerce, or to expand it, as it has since. In these decisions, the Court did, in fact, extend national power to cover more and more industries which it had hitherto held were local in character. These industries had until now been subject to regulation only by the states under their police power. In some of its later decisions the Supreme Court has extended the Act to cover "labor disputes" of a very broad—even vague—nature. It has, for instance, approved national control of labor disputes in which the workers are themselves not hired by the employer with whom they claim at the time to have a dispute.** Thus, labor disputes which had before been considered a matter purely of state under the police power, were during the

---

* Associated Press v. N.L.R.B., 301 U. S. 103; Washington, Virginia and Maryland Coach Co. v. N.L.R.B., 301 U. S. 142; N.L.R.B. v. Jones and Laughlin Steel Corp., 301 U. S. 1; N.L.R.B. v. Freedman-Harry Marks Clothing Co., Inc., 301 U. S. 58; N.L.R.B. v. Fruehauf Trailer Co., 301 U. S. 49 (all 1937).

** New Negro Alliance, et al v. Sanitary Grocery Co., Inc., 303 U. S. 552 (1938).

first few years of interpreting the new Act, brought under national control—through the federal commerce power.

The National Labor Relations Board

The Act is administered by a National Labor Relations Board of three members appointed for five-year overlapping terms by the President, with the advice and consent of the Senate. The Board has a large staff of experts, lawyers, and field representatives. Its central office is in Washington; it functions also through 22 regional offices, each covering one section of the country. The Board's function is, broadly, to apply the guarantees of the Act to any labor disputes which are referred to it. Under the Act, the Board may make its own rules and regulations. This power is granted to the Board so that it can develop a procedure which will make it possible for it to carry out the purposes of the Act.

Guaranteeing the Right to Join a Union

The Board is charged, first of all, with the duty to see that the workers' right to join unions of their own choosing is not interfered with by their employers. This right of the workers is stated in the Act itself:

> They shall have the right to self-organization to form, join or assist labor organizations, to bargain collectively by representatives of their own choosing, and to engage in concerted activities for the purpose of collective bargaining or other mutual aid or protection.

To guarantee this right under the Act, the Board may hold an election to determine the workers' collective bargaining representative. Before conducting an election, which is by secret ballot, it must first determine what the proper bargaining unit for the election is—one group of workers within the plant, the whole plant, or a group of plants. The Board will hold an election if it finds that an employer and his workers cannot agree on whether a union which claims to represent the workers really does so.

The workers, in the bargaining unit determined by the Board, decide, in this election, among several alternative choices—the A.F. of L., the C.I.O., an independent union, or no union. To obtain a place on the ballot, a union must show that it actually represents at least some workers in the unit. No outsider may simply walk in and demand a place on the ballot.

Suppose, for instance, an election is held in a unit with 90 workers. Suppose, further, that 16 vote for an A.F. of L. union, 16 for a C.I.O. union, 12 for an independent, and 46 for no union. In this case, the Board would find that a majority of the workers desired no union representative for bargaining with their employer. If, on the other hand, a majority of the workers, in this case, 46 or more, voted for some union representation, the Board has made it a practice to hold a run-off election. In this election, all the workers may vote. The ballot will afford the workers a choice among the three unions. A majority of all the workers' votes is necessary for selecting a union bargaining representative. If necessary, a second run-off election between the two highest unions has sometimes been held to decide which union is desired by a majority of the workers.

Preventing Unfair Labor Practices

To make certain that the right of a worker to join a union is not interfered with by the employer, the Act defines certain employer practices which we, the people, have come to believe unfair. This is the second major function of the Board. The Board is required by the Act to prevent an employer from continuing any of these practices. If his workers complain that he is engaging in them and if these practices are proved against the employer, the Board may then order him to stop these practices. If he does not end these practices, the Board may then take him into the proper federal court and enforce its order through the court.

The unfair labor practices which are prohibited by the Act include: (a) interfering with, restraining, or coercing workers in exercising their right to join a union; (b) interfering with or dominating any labor organization within a plant or industry, or contributing financial or other support to it; (c) discriminating in hiring or firing workers, or encouraging or discouraging their membership in any particular union; (d) discharging or discriminating in any other way against a worker because he had made a complaint or given testimony to the Board; and (e) refusing to bargain collectively with the elected representatives of his workers. The Board may find other employer practices to be unfair because they interfere with the rights guaranteed to the workers by the Act. If it does so, it may also prohibit these activities. The Act allows an employer to enter into a closed-shop agreement if the majority of his employees indicate their desire for this type of contract.

In dealing with the complaints which come before it, the Board has a wide discretion in what it may order an offending employer to do. An employer may, for instance, try to prevent his workers from joining a union of their own choosing by starting or fostering a company union. The Board can require him to disband it or to cease giving it any support or recognition. Thus, one of the chief interests of workers—to be free from having to join a union dominated by their employer— has been protected by the Act and guaranteed by the policy of the Board. Since 1937, when the Act was held constitutional, there have been fewer company unions formed or continued than before the Act became effective.

Similarly, many of the special practices in which employers have engaged (see Chapter 5, pp. 100 ff.) have been regulated by the Board. If a worker, for instance, is fired by his employer for union activity, the Board may order the employer to rehire him, with or without back pay. Thus, employers can no longer interfere with the workers' efforts to form unions by the simple process of firing union leaders or representatives.

The Record

How well has the National Labor Relations Act worked? The record shows that from October, 1935 to July, 1942, 45,993 cases brought to the National Labor Relations Board were closed in one way or another. Of this number, 39,577 (86.1%) were closed without formal action. As compared with the above, there were only 6,416 cases (13.9%) disposed of by formal action, that is, after hearings or court action. Of these, 345 cases were taken to the courts and 289 either enforced the orders of the Board in full or with modifications; the remaining 56 cases were decided against the Board. The record shows that less than 1% of all the cases closed reached the courts, and 86.1% were closed without formal action.

This brief account of the National Labor Relations Act shows how we have acted through the national government to provide a general guarantee of the workers' interest in joining unions of their own choosing. The general guarantee of the Act has not replaced the older special guarantees we noted in Chapter 5. Rather, they make these special guarantees more effective by giving general authority to a single agency, the National Labor Relations Board. This authority covers not only the general guarantee of the right to organize unions but the regulation of a wide range of unfair practices. We may now ask what has been done by the states in the same direction. As we have seen, the national government regulates industrial and labor relations only under the commerce power. The states regulate these relations under their police power.

The States Follow Suit – New York Takes the Lead

When the National Labor Relations Act was held constitutional by the United States Supreme Court, several states enacted similar laws applying to statewide—intrastate—industries. These acts were intended to bring about more friendly labor relations within the states. By making similar rules and by providing the machinery for settling disputes concerning the workers' rights to join unions of their own choosing, every industry throughout the country would be covered. Although only nine states have enacted their own labor relations laws, they are among the more important industrial states.*

Unless a state does enact such a specific law, any general guarantee of the right to join a union will be of little use to those workers who are engaged solely in an intrastate industry. Some of the state acts are not as inclusive or as definite as the National Labor Relations Act. New York State, however, has led the way with one of the broadest and most effective state acts.

The New York State Labor Relations Act

The New York State Labor Relations Act, enacted on May 20, 1937, follows rather closely the pattern of the National Act. Its primary principle, like that of the National Act, is the guarantee of the right to organize. By Section 703:

> Employees shall have the right of self-organization, to form, join, or assist labor organizations, to bargain collectively through representatives of their own choosing, and to engage in concerted activities, for the purpose of collective bargaining or other mutual aid or protection, free from interference, restraint, or coercion of employers, but nothing contained in this article shall be interpreted to prohibit

---

* Colorado, Massachusetts, Michigan, Minnesota, New York, Pennsylvania, Rhode Island, Wisconsin, Utah.

HOW THE STATE LABOR RELATIONS ACT WORKS

WORKERS CLAIM AN UNFAIR LABOR PRACTICE

WORKERS DEMAND RIGHT TO BARGAIN COLLECTIVELY

WORKERS PRESENT THEIR CLAIMS TO THE BOARD

BOARD'S REPRESENTATIVE DISCUSSES CLAIMS WITH BOTH EMPLOYERS AND WORKERS

BOARD'S REPRESENTATIVE HOLDS FORMAL HEARING IF THE CLAIMS ARE NOT ADJUSTED

BOARD DECIDES WHETHER THERE IS AN UNFAIR LABOR PRACTICE

BOARD DECIDES WHETHER TO HOLD AN ELECTION

COURT MAY ENFORCE OR OVER-RULE BOARD'S DECISION

BOARD CONDUCTS AN ELECTION

employees from exercising the right to confer with their employer at any time, provided that during such conference there is no attempt by the employer, directly or indirectly, to interfere with, restrain or coerce employees in the exercise of the rights guaranteed by this section.

The last part of this section is especially interesting. When the Act was first passed in 1937, it did not include the right of workers "to confer with their employer at any time" so long as no coercion was exercised by the employer. The National Act does not include this provision. It was added to the New York State Act in 1940 because the people thought that employers and workers should be free to talk over their mutual problems. Under the national and the original state laws, an employer might be found guilty of an unfair labor practice if he consulted his workers in any direct way about a grievance or dispute. This principle had been placed in these laws in order to prevent any effort by an employer to coerce or intimidate his workers. The people of New York State have recognized by this change that employers can act fairly toward their workers when dealing directly with them. The workers' right not to be coerced is, however, still one of the central principles of the Act. It is enforced by the State Labor Relations Board in any case in which unfair coercion is shown in a complaint made by the workers or their representatives.

The State Labor Relations Board

The Act created a Labor Relations Board of three members, appointed by the Governor, with the advice and consent of the Senate, for six-year, over-lapping terms. The Board is an agency of the State Department of Labor, although it acts as an independent commission. Its principal office is in New York City because this is the largest industrial center in the state. It also has regional offices in Albany and Buffalo. Like the national board, its staff includes labor relations examiners, chosen under the civil service system as experts on labor problems, and lawyers to try cases submitted to the Board.

Guaranteeing the Right to Join a Union

The first principle of the New York State Act—the workers' right to join unions of their own choosing—is guaranteed through the Board's authority to hold elections to determine the workers' bargaining representatives. The State Board follows, in general, the same procedure as the National Board. This

-2. 2-26-42-25,000 (6-C511)

EMPLOYEES' PETITION FOR AN ELECTION

STATE OF NEW YORK

Before the NEW YORK STATE LABOR RELATIONS BOARD

Matter of—

Employer

and

Petitioner

CASE NO................E................

PETITION BY EMPLOYEES FOR INVESTIGATION AND CERTIFICATION OF REPRESENTATIVES PURSUANT TO SECTION 705 OF THE NEW YORK STATE LABOR RELATIONS ACT

and address of employer...

al nature of business..

oximate percentage of sales, if any, made to points outside New York State.........................

facts concerning interstate business, if any...

oximate total number of employees...

types, classifications or groups of employees which the petitioner claims constitute the appro-

ing unit or u....

procedure insures, as we have seen, that the workers will be free to make their own choice as to what unions, if any, they will join.

There is one interesting difference between the national and the New York State Acts. Under the national law, only the workers may demand an investigation by the national board to determine whether there is a dispute between an employer and his workers as to their proper bargaining representative. When the state law was enacted in 1937, it provided that the *Board* might investigate this question if requested by an employer. This was changed in 1940 to *require* the Board to investigate the existence of a dispute over this question.

Preventing Unfair Labor Practices

The New York State Labor Relations Act defines a number of unfair labor practices—a list even more inclusive than that of the national act. Besides those unfair labor practices stated in the national act in which the employer may not engage, the New York State Act includes (but is not limited to): (a) spying; (b) blacklisting; (c) refusing to discuss grievances with representatives of his workers; (d) doing any acts (beyond those already defined in the law) which "interfere with, restrain or coerce employees in the exercise of the rights guaranteed" to the workers.

As in the case of the national act, the parties may appeal to the courts to modify or set aside a decision of the State Labor Relations Board. Also, as in the case of the National Board, the State Board must go to the courts to secure enforcement of its decision. The courts review the entire record of a case. If the Board's findings of fact are supported by the evidence, the courts accept them. The courts may modify or set aside the decisions of the Board only when they do not conform to the State Constitution or the Act.

142

THE NEW YORK STATE LABOR RELATIONS BOARD
CONDUCTS AN ELECTION

THE BOARD IDENTIFIES AND REGISTERS THE VOTERS

THE WORKER MARKS HIS BALLOT IN SECRET

THE WORKER CASTS HIS BALLOT

THE BOARD SORTS THE BALLOTS

THE BOARD COUNTS THE BALLOTS

Courtesy of the New York State Labor Relations Board
THE BOARD TALLIES THE VOTE AND THEN ANNOUNCES THE RESULT

Let us see how well the New York State Labor Relations Act has worked. From July, 1937, to July, 1943, 10,258 cases which were brought to the State Labor Relations Board have been settled in one way or another. Of these cases, 9,132 (89%) were settled without formal hearing, and 5,710 (55.6%) of this number were adjusted directly between the employers and the workers with the Board's consent to the agreement. Of the remaining 3,422 cases, 1,856 were withdrawn by the workers or their representatives who brought them before the Board; 509 were dismissed by the Board because they were found not to have merit; 547 were dismissed because the complainants or petitioners did not appear to follow up their charges; 510 were dismissed because they were referred to another agency (for instance, the National Labor Relations Board or the State Mediation Board) or for other reasons. Only 1126 cases went to a formal hearing. Of these 1126 cases, 298 more were adjusted during or after a hearing by the Board with the employers and the workers concerned—without the necessity of a formal decision. Of the remaining 828 cases, 245 cases concerned unfair labor practices. Of this total, compliance was secured in 166 cases; 64 cases were dismissed on the merits; 11 cases were closed in one form or another and in only 4 cases did the courts refuse to enforce the Board's order. The remaining 584 cases concerning representation petitions were disposed of as follows: 148 were dismissed because they were found not to have merit; 82 were dismissed for lack of a union majority after an ordered election; 109 resulted in certification of a union without an election and 244 resulted in a certification after an election was held.

In the six years of the Board's existence, it is significant to note that out of the total of 10,258 cases that have been closed by the Board, only 195 resulted in court action of one form or another. Of these court cases, the Board was successful in having its order upheld in 139 matters; the court refused to enforce the Board's order in 16; and 40 were withdrawn or settled before final court decision.

☆ ☆ ☆ ☆ ☆ ☆ ☆ ☆ ☆ ☆ ☆ ☆ ☆

We, the people, have acted through government to guarantee the workers' interest in the right to join unions of their own choosing. We have acted through both our state and our national governments. The policies we have established show that we have been continually concerned to promote the general welfare by insuring peaceful industrial relations. We have progressed in New York and other states, as well as in the nation, from special laws prohibiting particular unfair labor practices to general laws guaranteeing the workers' right to join unions.

This is, however, only part of the story. Beside the unfair practices of employers toward workers, we have come to feel that some practices of the workers have been unfair to employers. In the next chapter, we shall note some of their practices and how we have regulated them through government.

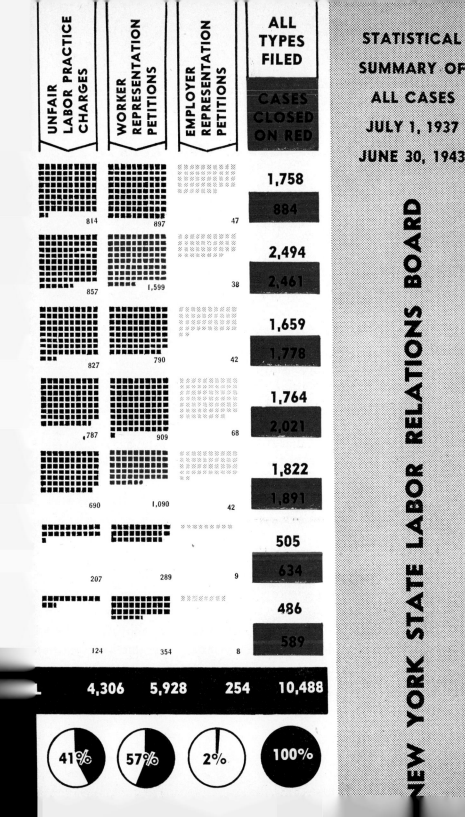

7

Making Rules for Workers in Labor Relations

IN THE LAST TWO CHAPTERS, WE HAVE SEEN HOW WE HAVE acted through government to protect the workers' interest in the right to join unions of their own choosing. We have protected this interest in two ways. First, we have enacted specific laws about particular labor practices of employers which a majority of the people had come to believe were unfair—such as yellow-dog contracts, labor spies, and the labor injunction. Second, we have made general laws guaranteeing workers the right to join unions and defining unfair labor practices on the part of employers—the national and state labor relations acts. We have acted through government in both these ways because we wished to promote the general welfare by insuring, as far as possible, peaceful industrial relations.

In limiting the activities of employers in these ways we have found by experience that the workers' bargaining power has been strengthened. Sometimes, however, the workers' power has proved so strong that they could coerce their employers into accepting demands which a majority of the people came to believe were unreasonable.

We must remember, moreover, that as labor unions have grown in number and membership, their officers have become more and more independent of the rank and file. This seems to happen in all large organizations; it is true of large corporations and of government itself. In government, however, we have developed a system of checks and balances designed to make it possible for the people to control and direct their representatives. These checks and balances are intended also to prevent any one branch of government from becoming too powerful. In our labor unions, a system of checks and balances has not been worked out so completely. The rank-and-file have not always been able to control their elected officers.

The record of some labor unions is not unlike that of some of our cities. Both political bosses and labor-union leaders can grow irresponsible in the use of the power granted them by the people in government and in labor unions. The members of some labor unions have been criticized, just as have the members of political parties in some cities for the acts of leaders who fail to represent the interests and the will of the majority.

We have had many examples in local government where the people have used the ballot to throw the bosses out of office. As yet there have been few examples of the rank-and-file union members acting in the same way to rid themselves of leaders who do not represent their real interests. This explains in part why the labor-union movement as a whole has been condemned for the acts of some irresponsible leaders.

There have been, however, enough examples of unfair practices by labor unions or their leaders to arouse the concern of many people. It is not merely that the balance of bargaining power between employers and workers may swing too far in favor of the workers. The concern goes deeper than that. It goes to the very root of our will to promote the general welfare —by limiting those actions or practices of any private individuals or groups which may be harmful to the whole community.

In this chapter, we shall review some of the practices of workers which we, the people, have come to think are unfair.

Abuses by Labor-Union Leaders
Dictatorship Within the Union

Attempts have been made by labor-union leaders to control their unions so as to prevent the members from criticising or removing them. An example, which was recently brought to the New York State courts, was that of a union in which there had been no election for 30 years. When some of the members had tried to have the officers call an election, the officers refused. The members used every means which was open to them under the Union's charter. Finally, they asked the court to order an election and to investigate how the funds of the union had been used. As a result of the court action, an election was held.

The election was controlled by the old officers, however, who saw to it that they were re-elected to office. In this way they defeated the attempt of the individual members to obtain an honest election. As re-elected officers, they went further and voted down a proposal to hold an election every five years. The old leadership went so far as to place another rule in the charter allowing them to charge the costs of a suit of this kind against the members who had brought it. The workers actually had to pay for finding out what their rights really were!

Also, union leaders are known to have prevented the rank-and-file members from discussing their policies or actions in open meeting. They refuse to recognize members who might raise embarrassing questions. If these members persist, the officers may try to expel them for "insubordination" or on some other pretext of having acted illegally. This type of leader can usually build up a loyal following by granting small favors to some members or by appointing them to offices in the union.

They can, therefore, often maintain their control of the union against the attempts of a majority to challenge their actions.

Misuse of Union Funds

As the example noted above shows, some labor-union leaders have been dictatorial in their actions even toward the members of their own union. In this case, in fact, it was brought out in court that over $160,000 of union funds—dues and other assessments collected from the members—had been spent by the officers in two years. No accounting was made to the members. This is one of a number of cases in which it has been proved that large amounts of money, paid into a union treasury by its members, have been used by the officers for their own purposes. Expense accounts of the officers and their friends may be padded. High salaries may be paid to officers who perform few real services for the rank-and-file. Special assessments may be charged for particular activities which are never actually carried out, the leaders frequently pocketing the money themselves.

To meet this problem, it has been suggested that unions should be required to incorporate under state law. Incorporation, it is said, would impose a sense of responsibility on the leaders for their actions because the officers and members would be legally liable for any damages resulting from union activities.

A more direct and effective way of achieving the same end would be to require unions to keep and publish regular accounts for all their funds. Many unions now do so as a matter of course. If the members of a union are sufficiently alert and interested, they can force their leaders to have open and public accounting simply by writing such a requirement into the union charter. Legislative action, to require public accounting, was taken in 1943 by several states (see p. 163) and has been suggested in others.

AMERICA IN THE 1940's

Courtesy of OEM D

Racketeering

Too many union leaders have found an easy way to make money for themselves by engaging in various kinds of racketeering against both their own members and employers. They have organized "protective associations" and threatened workers in their own union and other workers with loss of their jobs if they did not contribute. Similarly, they have threatened employers in an industry, in which such a protective association was organized, with loss of business and property or personal violence for failure to join the association.

A recent New York County grand jury described this type of racketeering activity as follows:

> We find that most of the rackets in this city are based on the systematic extortion of money from business by the criminal underworld, through pretended trade and protective associations, labor union racketeers, or plain intimidation. The various legal immunities given to labor unions have unfortunately made them, in a number of instances, a particularly attractive instrument for extortion and coercion by criminals. We have found that many labor unions and their helpless members are being mercilessly exploited by corrupt leaders and gangsters who run the unions for their own profits, preying upon both business and union workers.

Some of these practices have become so outrageous that the people have acted directly through the courts to break them up. Many rackets carried on by labor unions have been attacked as contrary to existing law. Prosecutions in New York City and elsewhere have shown that the people can act, under existing laws, to limit some of these unfair practices.

The national Anti-Racketeering Act of 1936 is further evidence that we desire to limit this type of activity on the part of labor unions, or their leaders. The Act was passed under the federal commerce power of the federal government and applies, therefore, only to rackets in industries located in or covering more than one state. Many rackets cover several states in the same way as do large industries. This Act, in substance, prohibits anyone from obtaining, or attempting to obtain, money for protective services by the use of or threats to use force, violence, or coercion.

A recent case was brought in the courts which suggests that this Act is an effective means of breaking up interstate rackets. Union leaders, some living in the eastern states, forced the movie companies to pay them huge sums of money for protection in order to stay in business. When the facts were proved, the union leaders found guilty under the Act were sentenced to long prison terms and ordered to pay heavy fines.*

On March 2, 1942, the Supreme Court held that the Act did not apply to the acts of a teamsters' union in New York City which had been using violence against employers and other workers to gain its ends. The union had forced the truck owners to pay them a service charge for every truck brought into the city. The union members did not load or unload these interstate trucks. In numerous cases, they lay in wait for the trucks, jumped on board and beat up the out-of-state drivers. Chief Justice Stone, who dissented, found that the payments were made to the union "to purchase immunity from the violence . . . and for no other reason." The majority did not agree with his finding; they held that the payments were a part of an ordinary business deal between employers and workers.** As a result of this decision, a number of bills were immediately introduced in Congress to tighten up the Anti-Racketeering Act.

As yet, there are no similar state laws designed to reach this

* U. S. v. Bioff, 40 Fed. Supp. 497 (1941).

** U. S. v. Local 807 of the International Brotherhood of Teamsters, etc., 315 U. S. 521 (1942).

special type of labor-union abuse—racketeering. The criminal laws have also been used in some states to curb this abuse.

Labor-Union Coercion of Employers

As labor unions have strengthened their bargaining position, they have sometimes used unjustified pressure on employers. Some of these practices have been thought so unfair that the people have acted to regulate them by special laws. Other practices have been resisted by employers under existing laws.

Extortion

Just as some labor-union leaders have coerced the members of their unions through various kinds of undemocratic and racketeering practices, others have also adopted the same practices toward employers. As we have seen, some of these practices have been regulated specifically by such laws as the national Anti-Racketeering Act. Sometimes the practices can be controlled through existing state criminal laws, such as those prohibiting extortion.

On occasions, too, labor-union leaders have cooperated with some employers in an industry to hold up outside employers and non-members of the union. Employers and a union may, for instance, join forces to control the market for their goods and services. The union may refuse to handle or work on the products of any but the favored employers. This would automatically prevent any other employer from bidding on a contract because the contractor knows that he cannot do a job without bowing to the union's demands.

Again, a union may force employers to do unnecessary work in order that it may supply additional workers to complete a job. Most electrical equipment, for instance, is now completely assembled in the plant where it is manufactured. An electrical union may force the employer to take the equipment apart so that its members can have extra work in installing it. Another of these instances occurred in St. Louis where an A.F. of L. union boycotted a small-arms manufacturer who needed sand and gravel. It forced him to buy his materials at a higher cost from a quarry employing A.F. of L., not C.I.O., workers. The same situation has occurred with the roles of the A.F. of L. and the C.I.O. reversed.

These instances are, however, only part of the story. Stand-by workers, who do no work, are sometimes forced on employers as the price of obtaining the workers they need. Some brick-layers' unions require mortar to be carried in a hod rather than a wheelbarrow as a condition of working on a job. In Chicago, stone cutters require that all stone used in construction work be locally cut, although it is cheaper and more efficient to cut it at the quarry.

Many unions, too, by threatening to strike, resist the use of new and improved machinery in order to make more jobs. Another device sometimes used in order to obtain more jobs, and also to resist the use of new and improved machinery, is the "slow-down." Even without an actual strike, workers can simply slow down their work to the point where a plant may be practically shut down. This kind of stoppage has been frequent in recent years. It is often difficult to determine whether a slow-down is going on from the way a plant in operation is actually running. It will show up in the balance-sheet of production, however, very quickly.

These and many other practices are important weapons in the hands of the workers in enforcing their demands against their employers. They are, in one sense, monopoly powers which workers can use just as unfairly as employers to interfere with peaceful industrial and labor relations. They may produce the same reaction on the part of the people as monopoly practices of employers—because they are just as harmful to the general welfare. If the principle of an equal bargaining position between employers is a part of that welfare, then monopoly power for either group is unfair.

Unauthorized or Unjustified Strikes

Another practice in which some labor unions have engaged is the calling of unauthorized or unjustified strikes. An unauthorized strike is one which is called contrary to a collective-bargaining agreement. An unjustified strike is one which is not based on a real dispute over working conditions between an employer and his workers.

There are many examples of these tactics being used by labor unions. Some, for instance, in aircraft plants, have agreed not to call any strikes contrary to an agreement in force throughout the industry. Others have, however, been unwilling to follow such a rule in dealing with their employers. Sometimes, too, a local union has disobeyed its national officers and called a strike contrary to their advice, or even against their orders.

It is no doubt easier to say when a strike is unauthorized than when it is unjustified. Certainly when a union has entered into a collective-bargaining agreement, it seems unfair to permit it to call a strike contrary to its terms. True, an employer may seek to obtain an injunction which will prohibit his workers from striking. The anti-injunction laws have, however, as we have seen (see Chapter 5, pp. 100 ff.) been interpreted by the courts in such a way as to make it difficult for him to obtain an injunction against any kind of strike by his workers.

Some states have attempted to meet this problem by establishing a "waiting period" before a strike (or lock-out) may be called. Several states (not including New York) have enacted laws imposing on workers and employers a requirement of notice to an official state agency before calling a strike or a lockout. Some of these laws also require a certain period, up to 30 days, before action on the notice is taken. These laws are intended to promote the peaceful settlement of labor disputes, but they also serve to prevent unauthorized strikes.*

Unjustified Picketing Methods

A third practice, as we have seen, which labor unions have used in seeking to enforce their demands has been picketing. In picketing a plant, the striking workers will march or walk around the nearby streets, often carrying placards with slogans sympathetic to their cause. If picketing is orderly, that is, does not obstruct the streets or injure people in other ways, the courts generally do not interfere. What the courts have defined as "peaceful picketing" varies from state to state. The definitions have differed with the circumstances. No general rule has been laid down in court decisions. On the whole, our state courts have tended to restrict picketing activities to the point at which the judges believe that other people's rights will not be interfered with.

Sometimes, however, picketing becomes so violent that it threatens the public peace. Mass-picketing, that is, a solid cordon of strikers which blocks traffic or access to a plant, has often resulted in mob violence. Again, carrying false or abusive placards in front of an employer's plant or office may lead those who do not know about the dispute to take sides against him without knowing the true facts.

A number of states have enacted laws limiting picketing in one way or another. Some have defined how many pickets may

* A similar waiting period is found in the National Railway Labor Act of 1926 and its amendments. A waiting period, up to 30 days, was provided for disputes subject to review and decision by either the National Board of Adjustment or the Mediation Board. A National Railway Labor Panel of nine members was established by executive order on May 22, 1942, under section 10 of the Act. No action may be taken by the parties to a dispute for 30 days after it has been submitted to the Panel. The Panel has "exclusive and final jurisdiction of the dispute and shall make every reasonable effort to settle it". See also the War Labor Disputes Act, pp. 280 ff.

PERCENTAGE OF TOTAL WORKERS INVOLVED	STRIKES	INVOLVED WORKERS	MAN-DAYS IDLE
4.2	1,897	373,499	x
4.9	1,839	567,719	x
2.1	2,186	302,434	x
x	x	x	x
x	1,593	x	x
8.4	3,789	1,599,917	x
6.3	4,450	1,227,254	x
6.2	3,353	1,239,989	x
20.8	3,630	4,160,348	x
7.2	3,411	1,463,054	x
2.0	1,301	428,416	x
1.8	637	182,975	3,316,808
1.6	810	341,817	6,893,244
1.8	841	324,210	10,502,033
6.3	1,695	1,168,272	16,872,128
7.2	1,856	1,466,695	19,591,949
5.2	2,014	1,117,213	15,456,337
3.1	2,172	788,648	13,901,956
7.2	4,740	1,860,621	28,424,857
2.8	2,772	688,376	9,148,273
4.7	2,613	1,170,962	17,812,219
2.3	2,508	576,988	6,700,872
8.4	4,288	2,362,620	23,047,556
3.09a	3,120	787,000	4,565,000
.31	195	90,000	
.14	210	42,000	170,000
.25	260	72,000	230,000
.74	395	200,000	675,000
	395	620,000	1,275,000

● = 25%   ▲ = 500 STRIKES   ▨ = 300,000 INVOLVED WORKERS   ■ = 5,000,000 MAN-DAYS IDLE

is figure is only for eleven months as the October figure is not available)

ans—Statistics not available

join a picket line. Others have limited the activities of picketers by providing, for instance, that no violence, threat, or intimidation may be used against other workers who stay at work. Further, the carrying of false or abusive statements on placards by pickets has been prohibited by law. Thus, we have acted through government in various ways to regulate unjustified picketing methods.

Rival Unionism
Raiding

As we have seen, rival union activity has increased since the 1930's. It has occurred, first, because of the liberal laws which we have enacted protecting the rights of all workers to join unions of their own choosing. These laws have been interpreted to prohibit interfering with the workers' efforts to form unions, even when a union was already in existence in their plant or industry. Second, it has resulted from the rapid increase in the number of workers who have joined unions. Almost inevitably, new unions began to compete for members and even to try to win members away from other unions. The split within the ranks of labor—between the A.F. of L. and C.I.O.—has caused each group to try to persuade members of the other group to leave the one and join the other.

Thus, under the protection of these liberal laws, an employer was often exposed to rival union activities. He might have already reached an agreement with one union representing a majority of his workers. Another union might succeed in inducing a majority of them to leave the union with which he was already bargaining.

Many employers have resented this sort of interference with their business. They had indicated their willingness to bargain with one union representing a majority of their workers. Why should they now be harassed by another union's interference with an agreement with their workers already accepted?

This type of union activity is called "raiding." We have not enacted laws to control raiding directly. We have, however, become concerned that our present laws be so interpreted by the courts as to prevent the practice of raiding. Without limiting the true purposes of unions, it is possible for union members themselves to regulate this type of activity through their own action. Unless they do so, the people will, sooner or later, act through government in this situation, as in others, to promote peaceful industrial and labor relations—whenever the need becomes recognized.

Cross-Picketing

Another type of activity which has grown out of rival union activity is "cross-picketing". A typical example is the case of two unions which claim to represent a majority of the workers in a certain plant. The employer is willing to bargain with the majority of his workers. It makes no difference to him which union represents them. The parties decide to bring the matter before a labor relations board, state or national, to see which union does, in fact, represent the majority. The board holds an election and declares one union to be the proper bargaining agency. The employer, acting in good faith, signs an agreement with that union. The defeated union, however, refuses to abide by the board's declaration and pickets the employer's place of business in order to coerce him into breaking his agreement with the majority union.

The employer, faced by this situation, finds himself in a dilemma. Even though he has already signed a collective-bargaining agreement with a majority of his workers, he is now picketed by the defeated union. If he deals with this minority union, he may be guilty of an unfair labor practice under the state or national labor relations laws. In any case, he may be prevented by the majority union through court action from breaking his contract with it. If he tries to stop the defeated union from picketing him, by seeking an injunction against it, he is faced with the anti-injunction laws. Most courts have interpreted these laws as prohibiting the issuance of an injunction in this sort of situation (see Chapter 5, pp. 100 ff.).

From the early 1930's to the present, employers have faced increasing difficulties from these tactics of rival unions. An entire plant—often, indeed, many plants—have been threatened with complete stoppages because of these practices. In Oregon, for example, the entire lumbering industry was seriously affected by the bitter rivalry of competing A.F. of L. and C.I.O. unions in that state. A large body of public opinion was aroused at this unfair—because unnecessary—action of two rival unions.

The people, acting through their representatives have, in some states, enacted laws limiting these activities of unions. Since 1937, three states—Oregon,* Pennsylvania, and Wiscon-

* The Oregon law was held unconstitutional by the Oregon Supreme Court on the ground that it interfered with the right of free speech—A.F. of L. v. Bain, Oregon Supreme Court, October 22, 1940.

MASS PICKETING IS NOT PEACEFUL

sin—limited their anti-injunction laws by redefining a "labor dispute" more strictly. In effect, these laws provide that the anti-injunction laws shall not apply to any labor dispute which does not directly involve a majority of the workers of a given employer. Thus, in these states, an employer may now obtain an injunction restraining the defeated union from picketing his place of business.

So far, we have not acted through government in New York State to regulate this practice. A bill was introduced in the Legislature in 1941 but was later withdrawn. Many public hearings have been held which have helped to bring this problem of cross-picketing into the forum of public discussion. The pressure of public opinion—especially during the war—has been brought to bear on a practice about which a growing majority of the people is clearly concerned.

In this chapter, we have seen how we have acted through government to limit unfair practices of labor. In some cases, we have regulated particular practices by specific laws; other practices have not as yet been directly regulated.* In seeking to promote the general welfare by insuring peaceful industrial relations, we have, indeed, regulated employers' practices more strictly than the workers'.

---

* In 1943, several states (Arkansas, Colorado, Idaho, Kansas, Minnesota, South Dakota, and Texas) enacted laws which restricted the activities of labor unions and labor-union leaders. Among the new rules limiting labor-union practices are: workers may not strike unless a majority of those affected have voted for the strike; unions must incorporate under the same laws as other business units; unions must file financial reports and their officers must register with the proper state agency. The constitution and by-laws of the union must also be filed with the state. Certain labor-union practices are also defined as unfair by these laws, such as: closed-shop agreements unless a majority of the workers have voted for them; collecting excessive dues or assessments; secondary boycotts; interference with the rights of union members to vote in union elections. These laws have been attacked in the courts of these states by the labor unions and others; there has been no final decision in any of these cases.

This is not, however, the only way in which we have acted through government. Another means for bringing about peaceful industrial and labor relations has been to offer to both workers and employers the services of impartial governmental representatives to help them settle their disputes. In the next chapter, we shall note how we have sought to promote the general welfare in this way.

AMERICA IN THE 1940's   © Underwood-Stratton

8

Helping Workers and Employers Settle Their Disputes – Mediation and Arbitration

SO FAR WE HAVE BEEN CONSIDERING THE FIRST WAY IN WHICH we, the people, have acted through government to regulate industrial relations. Wherever the unfair tactics of employers and workers have affected not only their own relations, but the welfare of the whole community, we have enacted laws governing them. Most of these unfair practices, on the employers' side, have related to their efforts to prevent workers from joining unions of their own choosing. On the workers' side, they have grown out of unjustified attempts to coerce employers into granting workers' demands.

Now we turn to another way in which we, the people, have acted through government to regulate industrial and labor relations. Here a different principle applies from that underlying the laws we have so far analyzed. Instead of establishing by law specific standards of conduct for employers and workers, we have developed machinery for aiding them to settle their differences or disputes among themselves.

On the one hand, we have given the force of law to voluntary agreements between workers and employers—generally called

collective-bargaining agreements.   Under existing or special
laws regulating contracts, we have made it possible for one
group to require the other to live up to its obligation, freely
accepted, to confer about such questions as working conditions,
wages, or seniority rights on the job.   Thus, we have placed
government behind the principle that peaceful industrial and
labor relations will be promoted by voluntary agreements
between workers and employers to adjust their differences or
disputes among—and by—themselves.

On the other hand, we have also created public agencies to
help them adjust disputes which they are unable to settle by
themselves.   These agencies have been established in order to
provide an additional safeguard for peaceful industrial and
labor relations.   Through these agencies, a friendly and impartial government representative is placed at their disposal to talk
over the dispute with them.   He may first try to induce them to
agree on a friendly settlement satisfactory to both sides.   Second,
if they cannot agree and if both parties consent, he may be
authorized by them to settle the dispute in a manner which he
thinks fair and just.   The first procedure is called mediation, the
second, arbitration.

This way of acting through government to reconcile the disputes of employers and workers is based on the two American
principles of free government and free enterprise.   In keeping
with these principles, it leaves as much freedom as possible to
every employer and every worker group within the nation to
work out its own problems.

Collective Bargaining

We may first observe how this principle of self-government
in industry has worked out in practice with respect to voluntary
collective bargaining.   There is a growing number of employers
and workers who are trying to settle their disputes among them-

167

selves through such agreements. They have developed a wide range of successful experiments in cooperative rather than competitive industrial and labor relations.

Cooperation between workers and employers has followed two main directions. On the one hand, workers have adopted agreements to aid their employers to increase the efficiency of their individual plants, or a whole industry. On the other hand, employers and workers have adopted regular procedures for settling immediate disputes over working conditions—again all the way from a single plant to an entire industry. Both ways of cooperating have shown that workers and employers can, in the long run, work out their problems peacefully—and so more profitable for both.

Working Together to Improve Industrial Efficiency

In the first type of cooperation just noted, workers in several industries have aided their employers to develop more efficient production and selling methods. They have realized that they would be more likely to find and keep jobs if the industry in which they worked were efficiently run and so better able to compete for business. If their employer were unable to sell his product he would sooner or later go out of business, and they would lose their jobs. How have these agreements worked?

We may note, in general, that the unions which have cooperated with employers in this way have tried to stabilize employment for their members. Instead of trying to restrict the use of labor-saving machinery or improved operating standards, they have helped their employers to install them. They have, for instance, made time-studies of the different operations in a plant and then adopted standards of efficient work, on which to base the wages of the workers. These standards were worked out cooperatively by joint committees representing the employ-

OW COLLECTIVE BARGAINING WORKS

EMPLOYER AND UNION SIGN
COLLECTIVE BARGAINING
AGREEMENT

EMPLOYER APPOINTS LABOR RELATIONS
COMMITTEE . . . UNION APPOINTS
PLANT GRIEVANCE COMMITTEE

WORKER AND SHOP STEWARD
PRESENT GRIEVANCE TO
SHOP FOREMAN

IF UNSETTLED, GRIEVANCE IS TAKEN
UP WITH PLANT SUPERINTENDENT BY
PLANT GRIEVANCE COMMITTEE

F UNSETTLED, PLANT GRIEVANCE
OMMITTEE CONFERS WITH LABOR
RELATIONS COMMITTEE

PLANT GRIEVANCE AND LABOR
RELATIONS COMMITTEE HOLD JOINT
HEARING; 3 MEMBERS OF EACH COM-
MITTEE MUST AGREE ON DECISION

IF COMMITTEES FAIL TO AGREE,
RIEVANCE IS REFERRED TO UNION
REPRESENTATIVE AND GENERAL
MANAGER

IF THEY FAIL TO AGREE, "FINAL
AND BINDING" DECISION IS MADE
BY AN ARBITRATION COMMITTEE

ers and workers. Detailed plans for changing the standards, as new machines were installed or as new methods were developed, were agreed to by both sides. Further, both agreed to settle disputes as to how the standards should operate under different conditions, on the basis of conference or of arbitration.

Workers in some industries have gone even further in helping employers to improve their efficiency. They have suggested new operating methods, even if these methods meant short-cuts on jobs. They have aided in improving handling, accounting, and selling methods to cut down overhead costs and to make it easier for their employer to find a market. There are enough examples of this kind of successful cooperation between workers and employers to indicate that, if both sides act honestly and fairly, each will gain in the long run. Among the unions which have found cooperation helpful to themselves as well as to their employers are those in the men's and women's clothing industry and the railroads.

It is true, of course, that if one side takes advantage of the other, cooperation will break down and disputes over rights will occur. Workers, who have made increased profits possible, through aiding in improving an employer's plant efficiency will be justifiably dissatisfied if they do not share in the resulting earnings. To be successful, cooperation must rest on mutual confidence and good faith. Sometimes, too, the problems of keeping a job or maintaining wages cannot be solved merely by increasing the efficiency of a plant. General economic conditions, the cycles of booms and depressions, affect the workers' chances for jobs and for stable wages. Within these broad limits, however, cooperation between workers and employers to improve industrial efficiency will help to promote sound industrial and labor relations. Whenever a formal agreement including any cooperative plan is made between employers and workers, it can be enforced as any other contract—through the courts.

170

Settling Disputes Peacefully

The second way in which employers and workers have cooperated to work out their mutual problems is by developing their own peaceful procedures for settling their disputes. These agreements are made voluntarily by workers and employers in order to adjust their differences entirely "within the family". The number and scope of these agreements have increased in recent years, especially since the passage of the national and state labor relations acts (see Chapter 6, pp. 124 ff.).

Working Conditions are Defined by Agreement

In general, these agreements include two types of provision regarding the settlement of disputes. The first type defines the kinds of dispute covered by the agreement. The second creates machinery for handling these disputes.

These agreements are usually part of a contract between a union and one or more employers covering such questions as conditions of work, wage scales, efficiency rating plans, and hiring and firing. Most questions which may give rise to disputes are, therefore, specifically covered by a collective-bargaining agreement. Many such agreements include, however, a general provision covering any kind of a dispute which may occur between workers and their employers. These collective-bargaining agreements are increasing both in number and in scope.

One example, typical of many of these collective-bargaining agreements, is that between Vultee Aircraft, Inc., and the C.I.O. unions in the airplane industry (signed on November 25, 1940). This agreement goes into great detail on all the important questions concerning working conditions. Among the provisions are, first, those granting the unions the right to appoint shop stewards, in the ratio of one to every 40 workers. These stewards act as the workers' representatives in seeking to adjust all their grievances. Second, the company agrees to maintain safe and healthful conditions in the plant. A safety committee of three workers is allowed to recommend improvements and to review each month, with the company's safety engineers, any complaints about accidents or safety conditions in the plant. Third, there are specific regulations covering such questions as seniority of workers, discrimination against workers for union activities, leaves of absence, transfers within the plant, hiring and firing procedures, vacations, illness, and military service. Fourth, there are rules about apprenticeship, training schools for workers, and minimum and overtime wage rates. Fifth, the employer agrees not to "cause or sanction a lockout", and the workers agree not to engage in or permit any "sit-down, stay-in, slow-down or sympathy strike". Finally, a definite procedure for settling grievances and other disputes is established.

Because agreements of this type are really contracts between employers and workers, they can be enforced by either party against the other. In the past, some courts have held that such agreements were not so much a contract as an "understanding". In recent years, however, the courts have come to recognize that both the employers and the workers are bound to observe their written agreements. If one of the parties refuses to arbitrate under an agreement including an arbitration clause, the other party may, at least in New York State, request a court to require compliance with the arbitration clause. This in itself means that such agreements help to make the relations of workers and employers more stable, and so, more cooperative.

The parties may, and must, if the agreement includes an arbitration clause, try to settle their grievances and disputes by themselves. Some procedure for arbitration is usually defined in these agreements. This is the second type of provision which has been included in recent labor contracts. The parties may use a public agency or establish one of their own.

In the Vultee Aircraft agreement described above, for instance, a grievance procedure has been carefully worked out to insure as completely as possible the settlement of any dispute. First, the employer appoints a Labor Relations Committee and the workers, a Plant Grievance Committee, each of five members. Whenever a complaint is made by a worker, it is referred first to the shop steward in his unit of the plant. If he can settle it directly with the head of the department, the grievance ends there. If not, a member of the Plant Grievance Committee goes with the complaining worker and the shop steward to the plant superintendent. If they settle the question satisfactorily to all concerned, no further action is necessary. Each of these steps must be completed within 24 hours. If not, the Plant Grievance Committee decides whether to carry the question further. It judges the merit of the grievance and may decide for or against the worker. It tries, first of all, to obtain an agreement with the shop foreman and the department head. If it is not successful, the complaint then goes formally to the company's Labor Relations Committee.

The two committees then consider the complaint. Each committee votes as a unit, but three of the five members of each must agree on the decision. Unless they do so, the question then goes to representatives of the local union and the general manager of the whole plant. If they fail to agree on a settlement of the grievance or dispute, a special arbitration committee of five members is appointed, two by the union, two by the management, and one by the four other members. The fifth member serves as chairman. Even if they cannot agree on the choice of the fifth member, a settlement of the dispute is not endangered. The four members must ask a representative of the United States Department of Labor to submit a list of five names of persons suitable to act as chairman. If the four members cannot agree on a name, each side may reject two; the fifth automatically becomes chairman. The decision of the arbitration committee is "final and binding" on both parties.

This somewhat detailed account of how grievances and disputes are to be settled in one company has been given to show that employers and workers can adjust their differences peaceably. It is typical of many of the collective-bargaining agreements in force in this country today. Some of these agreements have been in effect for many years. They have worked well because both the employers and the workers have been ready to follow the rules which they themselves have set up.

Mediation and Arbitration

Such collective-bargaining agreements are the best possible evidence that workers and employers can, when they are willing to sit down together to work out their problems, establish sound and cooperative industrial and labor relations. Although there are a great number of collective-bargaining agreements in force, many workers and employers have not yet voluntarily adopted this way of adjusting their disputes. To meet this situation, we have acted through government to aid these employers and workers who have sought to maintain peaceful relations by establishing public conciliation agencies. The two methods which these agencies employ in seeking to maintain peaceful industrial and labor relations are called mediation and arbitration.

What Mediation and Arbitration Are

Although mediation and arbitration are intended to reach the same goal, the peaceful settlement of industrial disputes, their roads to that goal are different.

Mediation involves helping the people decide for themselves. The mediator asks each party in effect, why don't each of you give up a little bit and try to work out your own problem? Arbi-

MEDIATION

EMPLOYER AND WORKER DISAGREE

MEDIATOR TALKS WITH BOTH

MEDIATOR ADVISES WITH WORKER
AND EMPLOYER

EMPLOYER AND WORKER SATISFIED

MEDIATOR HELPS PEOPLE TO DECIDE FOR THEM-SELVES BUT DOES NOT IMPOSE BINDING DECISION

ARBITRATION

EMPLOYER AND WORKER FAIL TO
AGREE

WORKER AND EMPLOYER SUBMIT TO
ARBITRATION

ARBITRATOR STUDIES CASE AND
PREPARES DECISION

BOTH LISTEN TO DECISION OF
ABITRATOR AND ARE BOUND BY IT

THE ARBITRATOR RENDERS A DECISION BY HELPING TO INTERPRET AGREEMENT OR CONTRACT

tration, on the other hand, involves helping the people by deciding for them. The arbitrator says, I have heard both your claims and I decide as follows.

Each of these methods—mediation and arbitration—is especially suited to a different kind of dispute. For example, when a new labor agreement is being worked out between workers and their employer, disputes may arise as to just what terms should be included in the agreement. The two parties may not agree on the terms under which they will work together in the future. In such a situation it is always better to try to bring the two sides together with a friendly third party. If the two sides are really interested in coming to an agreement, the presence of a third person who is impartial will often help them to do so. Talking the dispute over with a friendly and impartial outsider, with no power to enforce his decision but with a desire to help each side to see the other's point of view, is called mediation. It is often the best way to achieve a fair settlement.

Sometimes, however, the dispute may not be about what terms should be included in an agreement which is being drafted. It may relate to an action which one side has taken under an agreement already in force. For instance, an agreement may include some special provisions about how workers are to be hired or fired. The workers may claim that a fellow-worker had been fired or hired contrary to the agreement. The dispute really involves only a difference of opinion over the interpretation of the agreement. Both parties feel that they are right. The situation calls for an impartial judge who can hear both sides and decide which one presents the correct interpretation of the agreement. Arbitration, as this method of determining the meaning of a contract is called, offers a sound way of settling the dispute.

Most of the democratic countries of the world have established mediation and arbitration machinery for the settlement of labor disputes. Although there is a general similarity in the organization and procedures of these public agencies, there is a wide difference in their powers in different countries. In Great Britain, for instance, the emphasis in the law is placed on voluntary joint action between industry and labor. Elaborate machinery is established within the industries themselves and every effort is made to settle the disputes directly. The government steps in only as a last resort. Republican France, on the other hand, required all labor disputes to be settled finally by one procedure or the other. Where private efforts failed, the law imposed the duty on the parties to accept compulsory arbitration by a state-appointed board.

In the United States, arbitration of labor disputes cannot be made compulsory by law. Our courts have held that no person can be compelled to enter into an arbitration agreement against his will. If he does submit a labor dispute to arbitration voluntarily, the finding of the arbitration agency can, as we have seen, be enforced in the courts. This might occur under an arbitration agreement already in force, for instance, if the parties do not agree as to its meaning. Because both parties have adopted the agreement voluntarily, they must arbitrate their dispute over its meaning.

Mediation is also generally voluntary in the United States. As we shall see, there have been only a few experiments in this country with compulsory mediation. For the most part, however, public mediation agencies have not been given final authority to settle a dispute. Members of these agencies feel, moreover, that they will accomplish more in the long run if employers and workers appeal to them of their own accord. If mediation is imposed by law upon the parties to a dispute, it is all too likely that they will be unwilling to cooperate wholeheartedly. Unless, therefore, the law establishing a public mediation agency includes a compulsory procedure, the parties to a dispute need not accept the good offices of a mediator.

177

We Act Through Government to Promote Mediation and Arbitration

Government action in creating mediation and arbitration machinery began in the states. The first arbitration law was passed by Maryland in 1870; it did not, however, provide a permanent agency for mediation and arbitration. The first permanent boards of arbitration were set up by New York and Massachusetts in 1886. Today, 36 out of the 48 states provide by statute in one form or another for mediation or arbitration— sometimes both. Most of the states which have not established such machinery are industrially unimportant.

More recently, a number of cities also set up some form of mediation or arbitration machinery. In some cities, city officials are assigned to mediate local labor disputes. In other cities, citizen-panels have been set up from which to draw mediators or arbitrators. Two cities, Newark, New Jersey, and Toledo, Ohio, have established their own municipal labor boards. New York City created an industrial relations board in 1927. When the New York State Board of Mediation was set up, three months later, it absorbed the work of the New York City board. It is interesting to note that during its three months of operation, 187 disputes were brought to the New York City board and every one was settled successfully.

In addition to public mediation and arbitration machinery, many states as well as the national government have set up fact-finding bodies to investigate labor disputes. These agencies examine the claims of the parties and make public their findings as to the merits of the conflicting claims. They are designed to bring public opinion to bear on those disputes where no settlement by the parties themselves seems possible. The principle on which these agencies have been established is that public opinion, thus formed, can influence the parties to come to a fair settlement among themselves.

A number of private, non-profit arbitration agencies have also been created by public-minded citizens to aid the adjustment of industrial disputes. The most important of these is the American Arbitration Association, established in 1926. Since 1937, it has carried on arbitration of industrial disputes in 23 states, through panels of impartial arbitrators selected by it. Many collective-bargaining agreements include a clause making the Association the only agency for settling all grievance disputes occurring under them. Other agreements designate the Association as the final agency for settling a dispute when the arbitration does not result in an adjustment. Fifteen states,* including New York, have enacted laws giving to arbitration decisions made through the Association the force of law. That is, no further trial of the merits of the dispute need be held before these states will act to enforce the decision.

National Government Agencies

The national government plays an especially important role in preserving industrial peace because it regulates all those industries which are interstate in character. It has exercised control over all interstate transportation facilities since 1887. More recently, it has, as we have seen (see Chapter 6, pp. 124 ff.), extended its control of industrial and labor relations in those industries, the activities or products of which cross state lines.

When the Department of Labor was created in 1913, Congress authorized the Secretary of Labor to act as a mediator and to appoint conciliators in labor disputes. The United States Conciliation Service was established as an independent agency of the department in 1918. It has been active ever since in helping

* Arizona, California, Connecticut, Louisiana, Massachusetts, Michigan, New Hampshire, New Jersey, New York, Oregon, Ohio, Pennsylvania, Rhode Island, Washington, Wisconsin, (and Hawaii).

to adjust those labor disputes which occur in interstate industries.

The United States Conciliation Service may enter a dispute on its own initiative but it rarely does so unless the dispute is serious. Generally, it acts upon the request of the parties in a dispute or of some representative of the people, such as the governor of a state. Like other public mediation agencies, the United States Conciliation Service cannot compel obedience to its decisions. Its decision in any case which comes before it amounts to a recommendation which the parties may or may not accept, as they see fit.

The national government has a direct interest in seeing that railroad transportation is not obstructed by labor disputes. A Railroad Conciliation Act was enacted in 1926. This Act,

"DEADLOCKED"   Courtesy of Paul Dou

amended in 1934, provides for a National Railroad Mediation Board of three members, appointed by the President. It also establishes a National Railroad Adjustment Board of 18 representatives of the railroads and 18 union representatives, with an impartial government representative as chairman.

The National Railroad Mediation Board generally enters a dispute only upon the request of the parties involved but it may offer its services in an emergency. Its jurisdiction covers disputes arising out of future railroad labor agreements. It may also determine the proper unit for collective bargaining between the railroad managements and the railway unions—the Railroad Brotherhoods which now cover all the workers in this industry.

The National Railroad Adjustment Board may review disputes involving the interpretation of labor agreements concerning rates of pay, working conditions, and similar matters. It acts upon the submission of a dispute by the parties. Its decisions are enforceable by the Federal District Courts. In this field, both the railroads and their workers must accept the decisions of their arbitration agency—the Board.

Under general powers granted to the President by Congress, several other boards for the settlement of labor disputes in interstate industries have been established. There are, for instance, a National Steel Relations Board and a Labor Policy Board of the Petroleum Administration, which deal with labor disputes in these two industries.

New York State Agencies

As we have seen, New York State was one of the first states to provide for mediation and arbitration of labor disputes. A law was enacted in 1886 permitting employers and workers to choose their own boards of arbitration. It also provided for a State Board of Arbitration of three members, to which either side could take appeals from these voluntary boards. A Board of Mediation and Arbitration was created in 1887. For many years it was the sole agency dealing with labor problems in New York State. When the State Department of Labor was established in 1901, the Board of Mediation and Arbitration was abolished and a Bureau of Mediation and Arbitration was set up within the Department of Labor.

The present New York State Board of Mediation was created in 1937. The policy of the state was stated by the Legislature in the law creating the Board:

> It is the public policy of the state that the best interests of the people are served by the prompt settlement of labor disputes; that industrial strife, regardless where the merits of the controversy lie, is productive of economic waste; and that the voluntary mediation of such disputes under the guidance of a governmental agency will tend to promote industrial peace and the health, welfare, comfort and safety of the State.*

The Bureau of Mediation and Arbitration in the Department of Labor continued to function until 1940, when it was merged with the new Board.

The Board is now composed of five members.** They are chosen for their impartiality and their sense of justice. They are assisted by a staff of six full-time mediators to aid in the Board's dual functions of mediation and arbitration. The Board's executive secretary also acts as both mediator and arbitrator. In addition, the Board has appointed a panel of 75 public-spirited citizens who help the Board in its arbitration cases.

* Declaration of policy in the Mediation Act of 1937. (Sec. 730, Art. 21, Labor Law).

** The law was amended on April 4, 1941, to permit the Governor to increase membership to not more than 7. He can exercise this power when he deems it to be in the public interest. The appointments are for one year and must be approved by the Senate.

In effect, the Board itself acts as a committee of review for those disputes which are not settled directly by the mediators on its staff or on the panel. The Board's mediation activities are voluntary. It is, in fact, opposed to any compulsory mediation authority. As the present chairman has expressed it:

> An increase in (the Board's) legal power would undermine the real power that we possess; it would hurt our simple and cordial relations with both management and labor, who now come to us willingly precisely because they need not come to us at all. If they are swayed by any consideration save their own interests, let them continue to be swayed, as they have in the past, by public opinion and a growing sense of the importance of public relations.*

Under a recent law, if the parties to a dispute do consent to arbitration, they must accept the decision of the arbitrator.**

This insures the effectiveness of arbitration, because it gives the force of law to the decision in a dispute in which both parties have voluntarily accepted the principle of peaceful settlement. The party which does not carry out the decision may be taken into court by the other party and required to do so, under penalty of breach of the law.

The side which refuses to accept a decision in a mediation case will often be unwilling to lay its case before the court of public opinion. If, however, the public knows about the dispute and the decision of the Board, they will often bring their influence to bear on the parties to the dispute. In order to make this possible, a law was enacted in 1941, providing for the establishment of Boards of Inquiry in those cases in which all other available means of settlement fail. A Board of Inquiry is set

---

* Address by Chairman Arthur S. Meyer of the New York State Board of Mediation, before the 4th Annual Conference on Adult Education, April 24, 1941.

** Art. 84 of the Civil Practice Act, enacted in 1937.

up by the Industrial Commissioner whenever the Board of Mediation states to him that it has been unable to settle a case. This action makes it possible for the public to know what the dispute is about, what the Board of Mediation has tried to do about it, and what the Board of Inquiry thinks about the whole dispute. Thus, the people are able more intelligently to reach their own decision about the merits of the claims on both sides. By knowing about the dispute, they are also better able to make their influence felt—and so to help in developing more cooperative industrial and labor relations.

How Mediation and Arbitration Work

Let us look at some typical cases of labor disputes in which mediation or arbitration has been used in New York State. Because mediation is a more informal procedure—inducing the parties to a dispute to sit down around a table together and adjust their own differences—the State Board of Mediation does not keep any written record of its proceedings in a mediation case. We may, however, note the kind of situation in which mediation procedure may be effective.

Take, for instance, the case of a small bus company which operates between two upstate cities. A dispute arises over the terms to be included in a written labor agreement between the company and its workers. The workers demand certain terms which the bus company is not willing to meet. If the workers go out on strike, many people will be inconvenienced in traveling between the two cities.

To avoid a strike, the State Board of Mediation of its own accord appoints a member of its staff to look into the dispute and see what can be done to bring the parties together. He gets in touch with both sides in order to find out exactly what their differences are. He talks with representatives of each side separately and tries to get them to compromise their respective claims or demands. In this way, he attempts to narrow down the points on which the two parties are unwilling to agree between themselves. Then he brings them together informally around the table with him and urges them to accept a compromise agreement. Neither side may gain all that it wants; both may win some of their points.

The State Board of Mediation thus provides an opportunity for the two parties to the dispute to come to an agreement between themselves. In an atmosphere of friendly discussion, they are able to work out their differences in the presence of an impartial third party. The very fact that the representative of the Board is present helps the employer and the workers to stick to the issues and talk them over with one another without bitterness. We can see, therefore, that Mr. Meyer's description of mediation as "helping people decide for themselves" is really the basis of this procedure.

Now let us take an example of arbitration. An owner of a tannery agrees with his workers in a written contract on the conditions of work, holidays and vacations. The workers and their employer disagree in their interpretation of the contract. The employer insists on working in his own shop. He also insists on giving every new worker a trial period of two weeks. Third, he tells his workers that they have no right to strike before attempting to negotiate with him to settle these disputes. For a time, the dispute drags along without any clear-cut settlement. Finally, both sides agree that it would be better to ask the State Board of Mediation to arbitrate their dispute over the meaning of the contract. The parties notify the Board of the dispute. The Board then appoints an arbitrator who, after studying the contract and the differing points of view of the employer and the workers, makes a decision.

In this case, an actual one before the State Board of Mediation, the arbitrator decided, first, that the employer might

185

impose a two-week trial period on the new workers. Second, he held that the employer could work in his own shop only if no regular workers could be found to fill an emergency order for his goods. Finally, he ruled that under the contract the workers in this shop might not strike before negotiating with their employer about their demands.

One important point to note about this case is that the dispute was over the meaning of a written agreement. By submitting it to arbitration both parties could find out, from an impartial outsider who had no interest in the result, what the true meaning of the contract was.

Sometimes, a dispute between workers and their employer may lend itself to both mediation and arbitration. Let us take an example. In New York City, one of the companies running a big office building has a dispute with its workers. The dispute involves differences about the meaning of a written agreement which is already in effect and also about the new demands the workers make in seeking to add new terms to this contract.

First, both parties ask the State Board of Mediation to act under its mediation procedure and help them adjust their dispute. When the Board's representative talks things over with the owners and their workers, however, it proves impossible to get them to adjust their differences directly. One side holds out for demands which the other will not accept. If it proves impossible to get these disputed points settled through mediation, the two parties then may agree to submit them to arbitration.

The points on which they could not agree in the case we have just discussed were: the number of paid holidays and vacation days that workers were entitled to receive; the number of hours each week they were required to work; and the wage rates established by the existing contract. The last two points had been expressly included but not clearly defined in the existing agree-

186

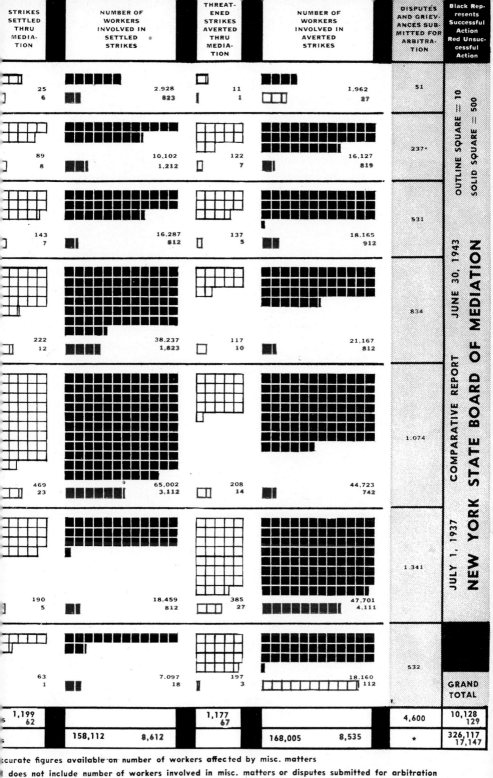

STRIKES SETTLED THRU MEDIATION	NUMBER OF WORKERS INVOLVED IN SETTLED STRIKES	THREATENED STRIKES AVERTED THRU MEDIATION	NUMBER OF WORKERS INVOLVED IN AVERTED STRIKES	DISPUTES AND GRIEVANCES SUBMITTED FOR ARBITRATION	Black Represents Successful Action Red Unsuccessful Action
25 / 6	2,928 / 823	11 / 1	1,962 / 27	51	OUTLINE SQUARE = 10 / SOLID SQUARE = 500
89 / 8	10,102 / 1,212	122 / 7	16,127 / 819	237*	
143 / 7	16,287 / 812	137 / 5	18,165 / 912	531	JUNE 30, 1943
222 / 12	38,237 / 1,823	117 / 10	21,167 / 812	834	
469 / 23	65,002 / 3,112	208 / 14	44,723 / 742	1,074	COMPARATIVE REPORT
190 / 5	18,459 / 812	385 / 27	47,701 / 4,111	1,341	JULY 1, 1937 NEW YORK STATE BOARD OF MEDIATION
63 / 1	7,097 / 18	197 / 3	18,160 / 112	532	GRAND TOTAL
1,199 / 62	158,112 / 8,612	1,177 / 67	168,005 / 8,535	4,600 / *	10,128 / 129
					326,117 / 17,147

:curate figures available on number of workers affected by misc. matters

does not include number of workers involved in misc. matters or disputes submitted for arbitration

misc. requests for advice in drafting collective bargaining agreements; for interpretation of existing agreements; etc.

ment. They were differently interpreted by the employer and his workers. The first was a new claim which the workers were making on the employer.

The arbitrator designated by the State Board of Mediation goes into all the claims made by both sides. On the first point—concerning paid holidays and vacation days—the arbitrator really acts as a mediator and gets the two parties to agree without having to hand down a formal decision. On the second point—the hours per week required by the contract—he defines the working week as 44 hours for men and 40 hours for women. Here, the arbitrator's good judgement on the meaning of the words of the contract as to the working hours required is the basis of his decision. On the third point—wage rates established by the contract—he reviews the questions in dispute and makes a decision on the rates which new workers shall receive. The reason he has to do this is that workers already on the job are receiving different rates of pay for doing the same kind of work. The employer naturally wants to hire new workers at the lowest rates: the workers want them to come in at the highest rates. On this point, the arbitrator's decision may well amount to striking an average of existing wage rates and ordering the employer to take on new workers at this average.

As this case indicates, an arbitrator may also act as a mediator on some points in a labor dispute by getting the parties to agree between themselves on some of the issues. When a dispute is not settled through mediation, it may be arbitrated, if the parties agree to do so. Indeed, the State Board of Mediation tries to induce the parties to include in all collective-bargaining agreements acceptance of both mediation and arbitration. Under such an agreement, both parties accept the principle that, if mediation or any other informal method of settlement fails to adjust a dispute, they will submit it to arbitration.

The creation of mediation and arbitration machinery is one

of the most important services to workers and employers which we have provided through government in the whole field of industrial and labor relations. Because it brings the parties together informally and by their own consent, it stimulates more friendly and cooperative relations between the parties to a dispute.

The Record in New York State

How successful mediation and arbitration have proved is indicated by the record of the New York State Board of Mediation. During its first six years of activity, from July, 1937 to July, 1943, a total of 10,257 questions of all kinds were submitted to the Board. Of these 3,152 involved requests for its advice in drafting collective-bargaining agreements, interpretations of existing agreements, or similar matters. The Board's advice was sought in these cases because one or both of the parties felt that the Board's impartiality would be an aid to the settlement of their difference. The growing number of these informal conferences is an indication of the confidence of workers and employers in its services.

Of the other 7,105 actual disputes submitted to the Board, 4,600 were for arbitration between the parties. All these disputes were settled finally by the Board. The remaining 2,505 were for mediation of an existing or threatened strike. In handling all these mediation and arbitration cases, the Board settled 1,261 existing strikes involving 158,112 employees and succeeded in averting 1,244 others involving 168,005 employees. It was unsuccessful in settling the dispute in only 129 mediation cases involving 17,147 employees. It is gratifying to observe that of the total number of disputes the Board failed to adjust only 1.3%.

☆ · ☆ ☆ ☆ ☆ ☆ ☆ ☆ ☆ ☆ ☆ ☆ ☆

Thus, through mediation and arbitration—or both—we have

acted through government to promote peaceful industrial relations. Not only have we given the force of law to voluntary
collective-bargaining agreements but we have also established
public agencies to aid employers and workers to adjust their
disputes. We have not adopted the principle of compulsory
arbitration found in some other countries. We have, however,
placed the authority of the government, acting for the people,
behind the practice of the peaceful settlement of labor disputes.
By bringing the parties to a dispute together around the table
with an impartial public mediator, differences are often recon-
ciled. By providing for a similarly impartial arbitration of
a dispute about the meaning of existing labor agreements, a
settlement of the dispute is generally achieved. By making
public the facts, through boards of inquiry, about any unsettled dispute, the people can still exert their influence toward a
peaceful settlement. Thus, through both channels—private
collective-bargaining agreements and public agencies of mediation, arbitration, and inquiry—we have acted through government to promote peaceful industrial and labor relations.

There are further questions about how our free-enterprise
system operates, however, which affect not only workers and
employers but the whole community. These relate to the risks—
physical, economic, and social—which the workers face in our
economy. In these fields, how have we acted to protect and
promote the general welfare? In the following chapters, we
shall review some of these aspects of industrial and labor relations and note what policies we have adopted to meet these risks.

AMERICA IN THE 1940's   © Underwood-Stratton

9

Industrial Accidents and Diseases – and Workmen's Compensation

THE FIRST ASPECT OF SECURITY ABOUT WHICH THE WHOLE community became concerned relates to the physical risks which workers face in industry. The hazards of their jobs increased rapidly as the new machines brought many workers together in a single plant and often exposed them to the carelessness of other workers.

The Hazards of Industry

These risks arise from two main causes. First, power machinery, unless protected by various safety guards, and sometimes even then, may cause serious injuries or death to the workers who use it. Second, many diseases occur as a result of the working conditions in some industries. Coal mining and quarrying, for instance, produce dust which gets into the workers' lungs and may cause tuberculosis or other diseases. Painting with aluminum or lead paints may result in lead poisoning. Working in tunnels may result in serious injuries from the "bends", a disease caused by high air pressures. We have succeeded in eliminating many causes of accidents and disease as our knowledge of these causes has increased. Many workers are, however, still necessarily exposed to some of them because of the very nature of the jobs at which they work.

In the first factories in England, employers tried to avoid paying for the injuries and deaths of their workers which occurred as a result of accidents on the job. When they were sued in the courts by an injured worker or by the family of one who had been killed, they claimed they were not responsible for the injury or death. They used as defenses against these suits three old doctrines of the common law—"fellow-servant doctrine", the "rule of contributory negligence", and the "doctrine of assumption of risk".

The first of these doctrines was based on the principle that, if two workers were engaged on the same job, the employer was not liable for the injury of one, unless it could be proved that his fellow-servant had nothing to do with the cause of the accident. The second—contributory negligence—required that the worker prove that he was in no way responsible for the accident. The third—assumption of risk—covered practically every other case of injury or death arising out of the work. This rule provided that, when a worker took a job, he assumed all the ordinary risks of his employment. In order to recover damages for an injury, he was required to prove that it was not likely to occur in the regular course of his work.

These three doctrines of the common law were followed by the courts in this country. For over a century, they were the only rules governing the liability of employers to their workers for industrial diseases and accidents. During the latter half of the 19th century, however, when millions of new workers entered industry, it became increasingly evident that they could neither afford the cost of a court trial nor await a decision on their claims. This meant that many of them or their families were never paid for loss of time or life, even though the accident resulted through no fault of their own but from the inevitable dangers of working on new machines. These accidents often occurred because of faulty machines or the failure to place safety guards on dangerous machinery. Furthermore, as our industrial system developed, the safety of one worker might depend on other workers who were not working on the same machine or even in the same part of the plant.

What Workmen's Compensation Is

More and more people came to feel that it was unfair to continue to apply the old principles of the common law to modern industrial conditions. Contributory negligence, the fellow-servant rule, or the doctrine of assumption of risk did not fit the realities of our modern machine economy. Workers, moreover, realized that those who were injured, often through no fault of their own, had to bear all of the costs of their injuries or diseases. They believed that the ordinary, indeed inescapable, risks of their jobs should be spread over industry as a whole.

This new attitude has resulted in the establishment of new policies by law in order to spread the risks of industrial accident and disease. The principle on which we have acted through government in this field is that the cost of industrial accidents and diseases should not be placed solely on the individual worker. It has become recognized public policy that these costs are really a part of the cost of production. Many people came to believe, therefore, that they should be borne by the whole community. Workers injured in the course of their employment should be compensated, whether or not they were themselves negligent.

The cost of any plan of workmen's compensation, as this policy is called, falls first on the individual employer. Because, however, this cost is really an item in the total cost of production,

194

STATE OF NEW YORK
DEPARTMENT OF LABOR
DIVISION OF WORKMEN'S COMPENSATION

ase No..........................

s. Carrier's No...........................

EMPLOYEE'S CLAIM FOR
COMPENSATION

Injured Person

1. Name of...
   First Name   Middle Name   Family Name
2. Address: Street and No...City or Town...........................
3. Sex......................Age....................Married or single...........................
4. Do you speak English?........................Nationality...........................
5. State regular occupation...
6. What were you doing when injured?...
7. Wages or average earnings per day, including overtime, board, rent and other allowances
   $...
8. Were you paid full wages for the day of accident?..
9. Piece or time worker...

Employer

1. Employer...
2. Office address: Street and No...........................City or Town...........................
3. Nature of business...

Place and Time

1. Location of place where accident occurred...
2. Name of Foreman...
3. Date of accident, the..........day of.......................19........, at................o'clock..........M

The Accident

1. How did accident happen?...
   ....
   ....

Nature and Extent of Injury

1. State fully nature of injury...
   ....
2. On what date did you stop work because of injury?..., 19........
3. Have you returned to work?................If "Yes," on what date............................., 19........
   (Yes or No)
4. Does injury keep you from work?........................(Yes or No)
5. Have you done any work during period of disability?........................
6. Have you received any wages since your accident?........................If so, from and to what
   date?...
7. Has injury resulted in amputation?........................If so, describe same........................
8. Did you secure medical attention?...
9. Attending physician (Name)........................(Address)........................
10. Hospital (Name)........................(Address)........................

Notice

1. Have you given your employer notice of injury?..........When?........................ 19........
   (Yes or No)
2. If such notice was given, to whom?...
3. Was it given orally or in writing?...

I hereby present my claim to the Industrial Commissioner for compensation for disability resulting from an accident arising out of and in the course of my employment and not occasioned by my willful intention or solely through intoxication, and in support of it I make the foregoing statement of facts.

Signed by..
(Claimant)

Dated...................................., 19........   Mail address..

(SEE OTHER SIDE FOR IMPORTANT INFORMATION)

BE SURE TO NOTIFY THIS OFFICE OF ANY CHANGE IN YOUR ADDRESS

Direct all correspondence to office covering your county as listed on back of this form.

it is spread over the whole community in the price people pay for the manufactured goods they buy.

What Types of Compensation Laws Have We Made?

Workmen's compensation as a governmental policy did not originate in this country. As a matter of fact, the first law of this type was enacted in Germany in 1884. England followed in 1897. Today, most large industrial countries of the world have one or another form of workmen's compensation.

The first workmen's compensation law in the United States was enacted by the national government in 1908, covering workers in interstate transportation. Ten states followed in 1911, three in 1912, and eight in 1913. By 1943, all except one state (Mississippi) had enacted some type of workmen's compensation law. Beside two federal acts covering maritime and railroad workers (under the federal admiralty and commerce powers), laws have also been enacted in the District of Columbia and in Alaska, Hawaii, the Philippines, and Puerto Rico.

We may note, first of all, that the principle of workmen's compensation has become the most firmly established and most widely accepted governmental policy in the whole field of industrial and labor relations. When, however, we examine the laws in the various states, the nation, and the territories, we find that there are many types of workmen's compensation.

Perhaps the most important variation is between those laws which compel employers to carry some form of workmen's compensation insurance and those which allow the employer to make his own choice as to carrying any such insurance. If an employer chooses not to protect his workers in this way, he loses the right to use the old common law defenses when he is sued for an accident to or the death of, one of his workers. If the accident or death is not the sole fault of the worker, the employer must pay whatever amount the jury awards.

At the beginning of 1940, of the 54 compensation laws in the United States and its territories, 22 were compulsory and 32 elective. In those states with so-called elective laws, the employer may choose whether to carry insurance or not. Twenty-three of the 32 elective laws require an employer to inform the state that he is not carrying workmen's compensation insurance. In the other nine, he does not have to show that he is not carrying insurance. If he does not carry insurance, however, he is none the less liable for all accidents or diseases covered by the law. In any event, the worker is entitled to the compensation provided in the law.

Another difference in the various workmen's compensation laws relates to the type of insurance which the employer must carry. One type is a state insurance fund, which is, in effect, an insurance company established by the state. Eight states have established this type as the only means of insuring for workmen's compensation. The other type of state fund may be called optional. An employer may insure his workers in the state insurance fund or he may insure them in a private insurance company. Under this system, he may also carry "self-insurance". Self-insurance means that the employer furnishes satisfactory proof to the state that he is financially able to pay any compensation costs for injury or death to his workers. Some states, however, have not set up state insurance funds for workmen's compensation and require all employers to insure their workers in private insurance companies or carry self-insurance.

A third difference in these laws is in the number and kinds of industries which are covered. Many of the earlier laws covered only specific industries which were at that time thought to be especially hazardous. Most states, however, have gradually expanded the list of industries to cover practically every type of employment.

The industries which come within the workmen's compensation principle are always determined by legislation. The states continuously add to the list of occupations for which employers must carry some form of workmen's compensation insurance. As we have gained more knowledge of the hazards to the health and safety of workers, we have acted through government to bring new industries wthin the principle of compensation.

How Compensation Laws Are Applied

Workmen's compensation laws are administered either by a special state board or through the courts. Only a few states still use the courts as a means of enforcing and administering their workmen's compensation laws. Even in these states, however, the courts apply the rules laid down in the law and not the old common law rules. In most states, a board, generally known as the workmen's compensation commission or the industrial board, is established to take the place of the courts in applying these laws.

These commissions or boards are usually appointed by the governor or the head of the state labor department and are generally composed of recognized experts. The boards review claims and make awards to workers for industrial accidents or diseases.

The awards made by these state boards are generally final as to questions of fact. Such questions include, for instance, whether or not the injured worker actually has the injury or disease for which he is making a claim, or whether the injury or disease will result in partial or total disability, or how much the award should be. The awards may, however, be appealed by either party to the courts on questions of law. The question, for instance, whether the accident or disease occurred "within the scope of the employment", that is, whether it resulted while the worker was actually on the job, is a question of law. This

HOW COMPENSATION WORKS

WORKER IS INJURED

WORKER SELECTS DOCTOR; EMPLOYER
PAYS FOR MEDICAL CARE

EMPLOYER REPORTS ACCIDENT TO INDUSTRIAL COMMISSIONER, WHO
FORWARDS TO INDUSTRIAL BOARD

OMPENSATION IS CLAIMED, BOARD'S
REPRESENTATIVE HOLDS HEARING

BOARD'S REPRESENTATIVE DECIDES
THE AMOUNT OF COMPENSATION DUE

IF DECISION IS REJECTED BY WORKER OR EMPLOYER,
BOARD REVIEWS CLAIM AND MAKES FINAL AWARD

EMPLOYER OR WORKER MAY APPEAL TO COURT ONLY ON QUESTIONS OF LAW

question may be stated briefly as follows: was the worker injured while he was actually on the job and while in the course of his employment? His right to recover for an injury or disease will depend on the answer. The principle of workmen's compensation has now become so well established, however, that fewer and fewer questions of law arise.

New York State Acts to Protect Workers Against Industrial Accidents and Disease

New York was one of the first states to establish a workmen's compensation law. In 1909, a legislative committee was appointed to study the whole question of industrial accidents and diseases. The committee recommended a workmen's compensation law which was enacted in 1910. Employers challenged the act in the courts on the ground that it was taking private property without due process of law. The Court of Appeals upheld this point of view and declared the act unconstitutional.*

We, the people, however, were convinced that the principle of workmen's compensation was a fair one. A constitutional amendment (Article XVIII of the Bill of Rights) was adopted by popular vote in 1913, to go into effect on January 1, 1914. By adopting this amendment, the people showed that they desired to establish a new rule in industrial relations as to the right of workers to compensation for accidents or disease "without regard to fault as a cause thereof". The state government followed the people's mandate and enacted new and broader workmen's compensation laws in 1913 and 1914.**

* Ives v. South Buffalo Railroad Co., 201 N. Y. 271 (1911).

** This act was held constitutional by the Court of Appeals in Jensen v. Southern Pacific Co., 215, N. Y. 514 (1915) ; the new constitutional rules which abolished the old common law doctrines quite naturally excepted from compensation workers who were injured through their own "wilful intention" or as a result of "intoxication . . . while on duty".

How the Law Operates

The New York State law, as it has been amended, delegates the administration of workmen's compensation to the State Department of Labor. There is, in the first place, a Workmen's Compensation Division in the Department. It carries on research concerning the causes of industrial accidents and disease and makes suggestions through the Department to the Legislature for extending or improving the law.

There is also an Industrial Board in the Department, composed of five members, appointed by the Governor for six-year over-lapping terms, by and with the advice and consent of the Senate. This Board is responsible for applying the law to individual cases of industrial accident or disease. Its staff includes a number of referees who hear cases and determine the right of the injured worker to compensation. If the employer or the worker disputes the decision of a referee, the Board itself hears appeals and makes an independent decision. If either party does not accept the award made by the Industrial Board, he may appeal to the Appellate Division of the Supreme Court and finally to the Court of Appeals. Any appeals to the courts, however, must be based on acceptance of the findings of facts as to the accident or disease made by the Industrial Board.

When an injury or disease occurs, the injured worker files a claim with the Industrial Commissioner indicating the cause and the nature of the injury. The employee's claim for compensation is a detailed form, concerning all that the Industrial Commissioner should know about the employee, his work, the accident, and the medical treatment he received. In addition to the claim which is filed by the injured workman, the employer and attending physician must also file their reports with the Industrial Commissioner. These forms contain detailed questions, the answers to which give the Industrial Commissioner a clear picture of the type and the seriousness of the injury or disease.

When these forms have been received by the Industrial Commissioner, they are indexed and sent to the Industrial Board.

Hearings on claims are first held before a referee of the Industrial Board. Unless an injury or disease will result in loss of work of at least a week, the worker is not entitled to any compensation. If his injury is serious enough to cause his unemployment for more than a week, he may be entitled to compensation. The period for which no compensation is paid has no relation, however, to the requirement that medical and hospital care shall be paid for by the employer;* the worker is entitled to these benefits immediately. If the worker's disability lasts for five weeks or more, he is given compensation for the one-week waiting period—the first week during which he was out of work because of the accident or illness.

In some cases when the accident is not serious, the injured worker does not file a claim. The Industrial Commissioner, however, always communicates with the injured worker and informs him that, unless he does file a claim, his case will be closed. The worker, therefore, decides whether or not to file a claim. If he does so, he is entitled to a hearing, even though he may not be entitled to compensation for the injury.

This hearing system protects the worker against any possible injustice in a settlement which the employer may wish him to accept. He is always able, therefore, to call on the state to give him an opportunity to present his case before an impartial expert who represents the State and not the employer.

The New York State law allows the employer to choose his own form of workmen's compensation insurance. He may

* The New York State Workmen's Compensation Law always required the employer to provide medical care and treatment for the injured worker. The method of providing such care and treatment was changed in 1935 by an amendment to the Law. It gave to the injured employee the right to select any physician authorized by the Industrial Commissioner to provide medical care. It remained the duty of the employer, however, to pay for medical care and treatment but did not permit the employer to select the physician for the worker.

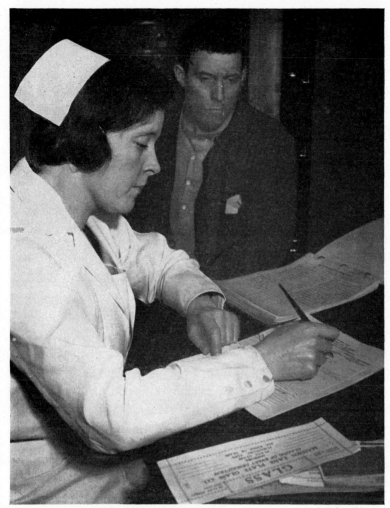

THE WORKER STARTS ON THE ROAD TO COMPENSATION © Ewing Galloway

insure his workers in the State Fund or in private companies. He may also adopt a plan of self-insurance, under which he assumes financial responsibility himself for any accidents to his workers. The law requires the insurance of all workers engaged in a "hazardous employment". The law, however, does not define hazardous employment. Various amendments to the original law have, on the other hand, continually expanded the list of employments which come within the workmen's compensation principle. The list now specifically includes more than 500 occupations.

New York has gone further than some states in including—by specific definition or by a general phrase, "all other employment"—many types of jobs which are not perhaps in themselves directly hazardous. Again, New York, together with 13 other states, has provided that minors employed illegally are entitled to special, and higher, compensation.

What industries will be defined as hazardous will depend upon the judgement of our lawmakers as to the dangers of a particular employment. The State, acting through the people's representatives, the Legislature and the Governor, have final authority to determine what industries shall come under the workmen's compensation principle. Their judgement is based in a large part on the evidence and advice given by the State Department of Labor. Here, the Division of Workmen's Compensation, which is constantly making studies of actual job conditions in different industries, performs a real service.

What the Employer Must Do

The New York State law, as we have seen, allows an employer a choice between insuring his employees in a state insurance fund, in private insurance companies, or by self-insurance. The State Insurance Fund was established in 1914. All of its reserves come from insurance premiums paid by the employers who insure in it. The Fund, therefore, does not cost the State anything. Since 1938, it has been administered by a Board of eight commissioners, all of whom are employers or executive officers of employers insured in the State Fund. The Industrial Commissioner is a member ex-officio. The commissioners are appointed by the Governor for three-year over-lapping terms.

In New York, as in some other states, an employer may make a further choice. He may request the right to insure himself by proving that he is financially able to pay compensation for industrial accidents or disease to his workers. In New York State, in order to guarantee that those employers who choose this plan will really be able to pay their compensation claims, there is a special board to control self-insurance. The Industrial Commissioner appoints a Director of Self-Insurance and an advisory committee of seven self-insured employers to advise on the rules and regulations for operating this plan.

In addition to accidents, New York, with 29 other states, includes within the principle of workmen's compensation various diseases which may result from industry. Some state laws include all "occupational diseases"; others require compensation for specified diseases. New York State now includes in its workmen's compensation law all occupational diseases.

Workers are entitled to compensation, if they are injured while in the course of their employment. New York State, as about two-thirds of the states, has provided that such accidents come within the principle of compensation, even when they occur outside the factory or even the state.

Industries vary in the degree of hazard to the worker. This fact has resulted in setting different insurance rates for different types of industry. This does not, of course, affect the workers' right to receive compensation but it does affect how much the employer will have to pay for his insurance.

In New York State, the rates for different industries are fixed

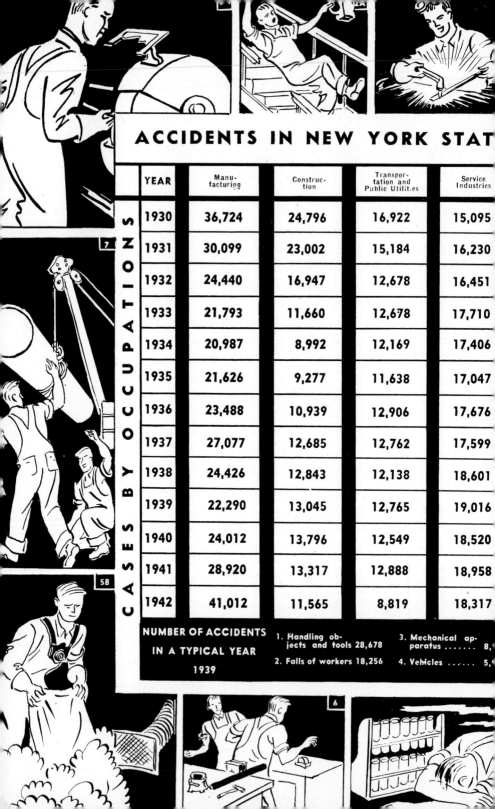

ACCIDENTS IN NEW YORK STAT

CASES BY OCCUPATIONS

YEAR	Manu-facturing	Construc-tion	Transpor-tation and Public Utilit.es	Service Industries
1930	36,724	24,796	16,922	15,095
1931	30,099	23,002	15,184	16,230
1932	24,440	16,947	12,678	16,451
1933	21,793	11,660	12,678	17,710
1934	20,987	8,992	12,169	17,406
1935	21,626	9,277	11,638	17,047
1936	23,488	10,939	12,906	17,676
1937	27,077	12,685	12,762	17,599
1938	24,426	12,843	12,138	18,601
1939	22,290	13,045	12,765	19,016
1940	24,012	13,796	12,549	18,520
1941	28,920	13,317	12,888	18,958
1942	41,012	11,565	8,819	18,317

NUMBER OF ACCIDENTS IN A TYPICAL YEAR 1939

1. Handling objects and tools 28,678
2. Falls of workers 18,256
3. Mechanical apparatus 8,
4. Vehicles 5,

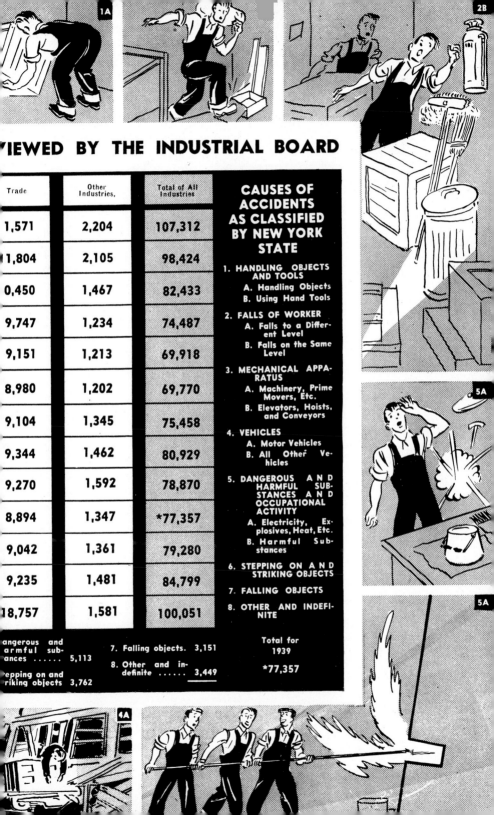

IEWED BY THE INDUSTRIAL BOARD

Trade	Other Industries.	Total of All Industries
1,571	2,204	107,312
1,804	2,105	98,424
0,450	1,467	82,433
9,747	1,234	74,487
9,151	1,213	69,918
8,980	1,202	69,770
9,104	1,345	75,458
9,344	1,462	80,929
9,270	1,592	78,870
8,894	1,347	*77,357
9,042	1,361	79,280
9,235	1,481	84,799
18,757	1,581	100,051

CAUSES OF ACCIDENTS AS CLASSIFIED BY NEW YORK STATE

1. HANDLING OBJECTS AND TOOLS
   A. Handling Objects
   B. Using Hand Tools
2. FALLS OF WORKER
   A. Falls to a Different Level
   B. Falls on the Same Level
3. MECHANICAL APPARATUS
   A. Machinery, Prime Movers, Etc.
   B. Elevators, Hoists, and Conveyors
4. VEHICLES
   A. Motor Vehicles
   B. All Other Vehicles
5. DANGEROUS AND HARMFUL SUBSTANCES AND OCCUPATIONAL ACTIVITY
   A. Electricity, Explosives, Heat, Etc.
   B. Harmful Substances
6. STEPPING ON AND STRIKING OBJECTS
7. FALLING OBJECTS
8. OTHER AND INDEFINITE

angerous and armful substances 5,113

epping on and riking objects 3,762

7. Falling objects. 3,151

8. Other and indefinite 3,449

Total for 1939

*77,357

by a central rating agency called the Compensation Insurance Rating Board. This Board is not an official agency. It has been set up by the private insurance companies. Its rates, however, are subject to the approval and control of the State Insurance Department. The State Insurance Fund is also a member of this rating board, although it is not bound by the rates which are established for private insurance companies.

It is obvious that an employer who makes an effort to prevent industrial accidents or disease in his plant by installing safety guards and medical services should receive a lower rate than an employer who does not protect his workers. This principle has been recognized in the setting of compensation rates in New York State. Those employers whose loss ratios are lower receive lower premium rates. This differential-rate plan has proved a real incentive to employers to improve the safety conditions in their plants.

If an Employer Does Not Insure

There are some employers who do not obey the workmen's compensation law; perhaps they feel they can "get away with it." Obviously, an employer who does not pay for insurance to protect his workers will have a lower cost of production. The State has an interest in seeing that all employers who are subject to the law carry workmen's compensation insurance which pays for the accidents or deaths of their workers.

In the Workmen's Compensation Division of the State Department of Labor, there is a special agency, the "No-Insurance Unit." It checks on whether employers are actually carrying the workmen's compensation insurance required by the law. This No-Insurance Unit first informs the employer of his duty to carry insurance; then it tries to get him to do so voluntarily. If he refuses, the Unit then takes him into court. He may be fined and imprisoned for his violation of the law.

We may summarize briefly the rights of the worker under the New York State Workmen's Compensation Act as follows. As we have seen, a worker does not have a right to compensation for an accident or disease which does not result in more than seven days of disability. During this period, however, he is entitled to complete medical and hospital care at no cost to himself. He may apply at once for this aid. If the injury is a serious one, lasting five weeks or more, whether from an accident or from a disease, he is entitled to compensation from the day of the injury.

The amount which a worker receives for an injury is usually stated in terms of a percentage of his weekly wage. Payments are made to the worker over a given period of weeks, the number of which is prescribed in the law. In New York State, special benefits are provided in cases of "total disability or death".

The New York State workmen's compensation law is one of the most advanced and comprehensive in the country. As experience has shown the need for broadening its protection to the workers, the people have acted through government to extend and improve its terms. The principle of compensation for industrial injury or disease has become thoroughly established —by constitutional amendment and by legislation—as the policy of the State. Not only has the principle become established, but it is being continually extended and made more effective.

☆ ☆ ☆ ☆ ☆ ☆ ☆ ☆ ☆ ☆ ☆ ☆ ☆

We may say that, in this field of industrial relations, the workers' interest in shifting the physical risks of the job from the individual worker to the community has been fully recognized and protected. In what other fields have we acted to apply the same principle in order to protect the workers' stake in economic security?

10

"A Ceiling Over Hours and a Floor Under Wages"

THE VARYING LEVELS OF WAGES AND WORKING HOURS WHICH existed in different industries and in different parts of the country are a second aspect of security about which workers have become increasingly concerned. They have wanted to improve their economic security by reducing these variations, in good times as well as in bad. This is another field in which we, the people, have acted through government to protect and promote this interest of the workers.

Why Wages and Hours Laws ?

Because of the shift from agriculture to industry, from the farm to the city, and because of the rising tide of immigration during the 19th and early 20th centuries, there were, as we have seen, often more workers than there were jobs. As a result, many workers thought that they would benefit both individually and as a group, through shorter hours and higher wages. Workers tried, indeed, to shorten their hours and increase their wages long before the factory system developed. After this system became the basis of our modern economy, the drive grew stronger and stronger among all groups of industrial workers.

One reason is the fact that workers found that more and more women and children were going into the factories. Some of them took jobs, perhaps because they wanted to earn a little "pin money" or because they enjoyed the freedom from homework and housekeeping. In most cases, however, women and children went to work because they had to help to make both ends of the family budget meet. The wages which the head of the family brought home were often not enough to give the whole family the standard of living it wanted.

Many people began to question this trend of women and children into industry. Male workers felt that these newcomers were competitors for their jobs. They feared, too, that because women and children were willing—or had—to work at the same jobs for lower pay, their own wage rates would be threatened. This would result, in turn, in more women and children going into industry to eke out the family income.

Others pointed to the effects of the factory on the health and growth of women and child workers. It was argued that the long hours that women often had to work in order to get a job at all made them less able to keep a good home for the family. Long hours also affected their ability to bear children. Younger children, too, who went into industry lost their freedom for outdoor life and were often stunted both physically and mentally.

For these and other reasons, not only the workers but many other people pressed for laws limiting hours and raising wages. Many state legislatures investigated the effects of long working hours and low wages on the family. It became increasingly clear that there was a special need to protect women and children in industry. Many of our states responded to the growing public concern as to the nation's future generations by passing laws about hours and wages.

Reproduced from The Pageant of America

IN THE 1840's—WHEN WAGES AND HOURS WERE UNREGULATED

We may ask at the outset why the states and not the national government acted first. The answer lies in our federal constitution. As we have seen, the contract which a person makes for his work is a "liberty" or a "property" under the Fourteenth Amendment. These rights may not be taken away by the government without "due process of law". The Supreme Court has held that only the states, not the national government, may exercise the police power to regulate the life, liberty and property of private persons. Hence, if any action were to be taken, it had to be taken by the states. Only recently, during the past decade, when the Supreme Court gave a new meaning to the federal commerce power, was it possible for Congress to enact a national law about hours and wages.

In dealing with these two interests of the workers, we may conveniently divide them. Often, however, our state legislatures and Congress have tried to meet the two problems of hours and wages together. Many laws included provisions covering both views of this aspect of the workers' interest in security. When separate laws were enacted, they were often closely related in time and in operation.

The States Act First

Laws Limiting Hours

The first law regulating the hours of work for children was enacted in Massachusetts in 1842. This law set a maximum working day of ten hours in all manufacturing plants for children under twelve. In 1847, New Hampshire enacted a ten-hour-a-day law for women. These were the first laws limiting working hours enacted in the country. From that time to the present, all the states have, in one way or another, limited hours of work. These laws have covered not only women and children but also, in many states, men in hazardous industries as well.

Most of these laws have applied to all manufacturing industries and have progressively shortened the working day for women and children. Furthermore, most states have enacted laws which limit the hours of the day during which women and children may work. It has become generally recognized that bad effects on the health and morals of these two groups might, and often did, result from night work. Their working at night has now been prohibited in a majority of the industrial states. Many states have also enacted laws excluding them altogether from working in some of the more hazardous industries.

By the end of the 19th century, a general ten-hour limit had become the standard maximum in most states. By 1900, some states had limited the working day of women and children, and of men in hazardous industries, to eight hours. The movement for shorter working hours, however, continued to grow. By the 1920's, the eight-hour day had been generally adopted as a standard except in some of the southern states.

Some employers opposed these laws limiting hours for several reasons. First, it seemed likely that profits would be reduced if hours were limited. This attitude, however, has largely disappeared. It is now generally recognized that the workers' efficiency tends to decrease if he works long hours. Certainly, it decreases after the peak of his physical strength and mental alertness has been reached.

Another and more important reason for opposing laws limiting hours of work arose from our federal system of government, under which the states alone may exercise a police power. As long as different states placed different limits on the working day, employers in the states with higher standards found themselves competing unequally in the market for their products.

Suppose one state set an eight-hour standard and another neighboring state set a ten-hour standard. The extra two hours did not necessarily result in a twenty-five per cent increase in production because the workers' efficiency declined toward the end of the day. Yet there would be some increase in production in the ten-hour state. Because the cost per unit would be reduced, these employers could sell their product for less. Thus, they would have a competitive advantage in the market. Many employers, therefore, whose plants were located in those states in which the legislatures had not yet responded to public pressure for a shorter working day, opposed this type of law. When, nevertheless, such laws were enacted, the battle was carried to the courts.

When these laws were first attacked as beyond the proper exercise of the police power, the state courts distinguished between laws applying to women and children, and those applying to men in hazardous industries. The former type was considered more favorably by the courts. Before the end of the 19th century, many state courts had accepted the principle that it was within the police power of the states to limit the hours of work of women and children but not of men.

Not all state courts, however, accepted this liberal view. It was not until 1908 that the question was finally decided by the United States Supreme Court. In that year, an Oregon law prohibiting the employment of women for more than ten hours a day was carried to the Supreme Court by the employers. They claimed that their rights under the Fourteenth Amendment—a matter of both liberty and property—were interfered with by this law. It was asserted to be beyond the power of the states to regulate their right to contract with their workers for more than a ten-hour working day. The Supreme Court, however, took another view of the police power. It held that it was within the power of a state to protect and promote the general welfare of the people under the Fourteenth Amendment by insuring in this way better health for future mothers. The Court said: "As healthy mothers are essential to vigorous offspring, the physical well being of women becomes an object of public interest and care in order to preserve the strength and vigor of the race".* Since the decision in this case, the right of the states to limit the hours of work of women and of children has not been challenged.

Laws limiting the hours of work for men in hazardous industries, as we have seen, have also been passed by many states. Legislatures recognized the special dangers resulting from fatigue during long working days in these industries. Utah, for instance, passed an eight-hour-day law for miners in 1896. It was held to be a proper exercise of the state's police power by the United States Supreme Court in 1898.** Similarly, in 1898, the people of New York State, finding that there were dangers to the health of bakers from long hours in hot bake-

* Muller v. Oregon, 208 U. S. 412 (1908).

** Holden v. Hardy, 169 U. S. 366 (1898).

shops, enacted a ten-hour law covering all bakeries in the state. The Supreme Court, however, held that this was not a proper exercise of the state's police power, because the workers' as well as the employers' right to make contracts of their own choosing was too strictly limited by such a ten-hour law.*

It was not until 1917 that a general state law regulating the working hours of men came before the Supreme Court. Again the law came from Oregon. The Court held that a state might extend the exercise of its police power to regulate the working hours of men, as well as of women and children, in all manufacturing industries.** In this case, it refused to follow its decision in the New York bakery-shop case.

These instances of the use of the police power by states to limit hours of work indicate that, by 1940, the principle was well established. The states may today limit hours of work for women and children, may prohibit their night work, and may regulate the hours of work for men both in hazardous industries and in manufacturing generally. The question which always arises as to such laws is whether they are a reasonable exercise of the state's police power. During the last quarter-century, there have been relatively few instances in which the courts have found that state laws limiting hours were unreasonable.

Individual state laws did not, however, meet the problem of varying standards among the different states. We shall see (see p. 222 ff.) how this problem has since been met through action by the national government. First, however, let us look at another aspect of the workers' interest in greater economic security through more stable wages. How have our states responded to this concern of the workers?

* Lochner v. New York, 198 U. S. 45 (1905).

** Bunting v. Oregon, 243 U. S. 246 (1917).

Laws About Wages

The states developed policies about wages much later than about hours. The first state law establishing a minimum wage law for women and children was enacted in Massachusetts in 1912. This and other similar state laws were held to be a valid exercise of the police power by the state courts which reviewed them. This was true, for instance, in Oregon, in 1914, in Arkansas and in Minnesota, in 1917, and in Washington, in 1918. The people of these states had learned how necessary such laws were from their experience with the earlier laws about hours of work.

In 1923, a minimum-wage law covering women workers in the District of Columbia came before the United States Supreme Court. This law involved the exercise of the same kind of

Courtesy of Everett Warner
"PROGRESS AND POVERTY" IN THE 1890's, WHEN WAGES WERE STILL LOW AND HOURS STILL HIGH

police power by Congress over the District of Columbia under the Fifth Amendment as is exercised by the states under the Fourteenth Amendment. The question for Congress was the same as for the states. Is such an exercise of the police power for the general welfare, by establishing a minimum wage for women workers, an unreasonable limitation of the employers' and workers' freedom of contract? Although several state supreme courts had declared state minimum wage laws constitutional, the Supreme Court of the United States did not follow their opinion. It held that the national government did not have the right under the Fifth Amendment to enact such a law for the District of Columbia.*

As a result of this decision, all except one state minimum-wage law became automatically inoperative. Most of these state laws, like the District of Columbia law, had been compulsory; a minimum wage, once it had been established, became effective for all workers in that industry. Employers who disobeyed the order establishing minimum wages could be punished. Only in Massachusetts had the law been optional; the state board had no power under the law to enforce the minimum wage against employers. Because it was optional, this was the only state law to survive the Supreme Court's decision as to the District of Columbia Act.

During the next decade, the people in all the states felt increasingly that this type of law was one of the most effective ways of protecting the health and morals of women and child workers. Five states, New York among them, adopted new minimum wage laws. The New York law was passed in 1933 and was reviewed by the United States Supreme Court in 1936. The case involved the arrest and conviction of an employer for forging his accounts to conceal his failure to pay the established

* Adkins v. Children's Hospital, 261 U. S. 525 (1923).

minimum wage. He appealed and the New York law was held unconstitutional by the Supreme Court which followed its decision in the District of Columbia case.*

When the next minimum wage law was brought before the Supreme Court in 1937, this time from the state of Washington, it reversed its decision in both the earlier cases and upheld the power of the states to fix minimum wages. This time it gave a clear-cut decision on the question of whether freedom of contract under the Fourteenth Amendment was superior to the right of a state to regulate wages for women and children. The Court said: "Liberty implies the absence of arbitrary restraint, not immunity from reasonable regulations and prohibitions imposed in the interests of the community."**

As a result of this decision, many states revived their earlier minimum wage laws and others enacted new laws. By 1940, 26 states, including New York in 1937, the District of Columbia, Alaska and Puerto Rico, had adopted minimum wage laws. Most of these laws cover women and children, some, women and girls only. One, Connecticut, covers all men as well as all women and children.

A few of the state laws establish minimum wage rates directly in the law. Most, however, create an official board or commission with power to fix minimum wages in particular industries.

Varying Standards are Made by the States

Various standards to guide these boards are stated in the laws. One standard is that of the "living wage". This was, in fact, the standard in the Washington law which was held con-

* Tipaldo v. Morehead, 298 U. S. 587 (1936).

** West Coast Hotel Co. v. Parrish, 300 U. S. 379 (1937).

stitutional by the Supreme Court in 1937. Here, as the Supreme Court said, a standard which will guarantee the "general necessities of existence" is a proper exercise of the police power. Another standard, less favorable to workers, is a "wage that industry can bear". Under such a standard, a board setting out to establish a minimum wage in a given industry would have to determine what wages an industry could pay while continuing to operate profitably.

A third standard, also one which may be unfavorable to the workers, is that of "commensurate returns". Under this standard, the test would be the value to the employer of the services which the worker performs. This standard is based on the relation between the supply of and demand for workers at any given time. Thus, the standard may vary from time to time, depending on the wage at which an employer can hire workers. In a depression, for instance, workers may be willing to accept wages which will not give them a living wage but which will, in theory at least, reflect the value of their services to the employer. Under this standard, the supply of labor in the market determines for the board—as it does when there are no minimum wage standards—the value of the worker's service.

A few states have adopted an additional standard—"wages paid in the state for work of like or comparable character". This standard may operate in very much the same way as the previous one, because the general conditions in the labor market are made a guide for the board's action.

This brief history of minimum-wage laws indicates that, as of 1940, the states may protect and promote the general welfare by setting wage standards. It seems clear that such laws, applying to women and children, fall within the states' police power. Whether setting minimum wages for men in industry is also a proper exercise of the police power has not yet been settled. Connecticut, has, as we have seen, asserted its power to do so.

It will be interesting to watch whether, as in the case of hours laws, the courts will allow minimum wages for men also to be set by state action.

Here too, as in the case of hours-of-work laws, the states have set up varying standards for different groups of industries. Thus, the same difficulties for employers which we noted regarding state hours laws applies to state wage laws. An employer in a state with higher minimum wage standards may find himself competing for a market with the products of employers in states having lower standards.

Difficulties have also sometimes arisen in making these state minimum wage laws effective in action. Because employers in states with higher minimum wage standards face real problems, they quite understandably use whatever arguments they can to postpone or limit these standards from being applied to their industries. Their resistance is not always because they are opposed to the principle of minimum-wage standards. It is rather because they will inevitably be less able to compete in a free economy with those employers who are not so limited as to the wages they must pay.

From this brief review of state hours and wage laws, we can see why not only workers, but many employers as well, have come to favor more uniform standards throughout this country. Varying standards in different states meant that both workers and employers were at a disadvantage in those states which set the higher standards. Workers often found that the factories in which they worked moved to another state where lower standards, or no standards at all, existed. Employers faced a similar problem. Their competitors in other states could thus undersell them in the market. Either they would have to go out of business if they followed the higher standards, or they would have to find other ways to economize. One of the easiest ways was to "chisel" on the standards of hours and wages set by the states.

Another way was to try to have these standards reduced. Either way, both the honest and humane employers and the workers suffered.

The most direct answer to these problems seemed to be to have a national standard in these two fields of hours and wages. Not only the workers, but many employers as well, favored national action as the surest way of protecting and promoting their respective interests. Here is an area of industrial relations in which we find the long-range interests of both progressive employers and workers meeting. It is worth noting, therefore, what we have done in recent years to insure these interests by national as well as state action.

We Act Through the National Government

One of the first bills laid before Congress in 1933 was the National Industrial Recovery Act. This Act, which was the basis of several of the laws enacted later, conferred on the President the power to prescribe "codes of fair competition." These codes were to be developed by representatives of employers in the different industries. The Act included, among other requirements, that maximum hours and minimum wages be set in each industry. Over 800 codes of fair competition were developed by various industrial groups, most of which were approved by the President. They fixed maximum hours and minimum wages for each of these industries. All employers within each industry were required to adopt the hours and pay the wages prescribed in the industry code. These standards varied but, in general, were from 40 to 44 hours and from 25 cents an hour upwards.

In 1935, the United States Supreme Court held the National Industrial Recovery Act unconstitutional.* This decision ended

* U. S. v. Schechter, 295 U. S. 495 (1935).

SAMPLE COMPLAINT FORM

...siness is your employer engaged in? _Manufacturing shirts_
(Such as manufacturing, mining, transportation, wholesaling, etc.)

...s product move out of the State? _yes_
(Yes or no)

...your job? _Sewing machine operator_
(Such as, stitcher of shoes, truck driver, etc.)

...any hours a week were you hired to work? _40_

...wages you received:

Week Ending	Hours Worked	Total Cash Received	How Much Was for Overtime
Nov. 11, 1940	_46_	_$11.50_	_none_
Nov. 18, 1940	_48_	_$12.00_	_none_

...receive—Board ☐ Lodging ☐ Other Compensation ☐ in addition to above? _no_

...ame? _Mary Doe_ Address? _532 Main St., Blanktown, Pa._
...hu Smith Co. _620 Broadway, Blanktown, Pa._
(Name of employer or firm) (Employer's business address)

WHEN A WORKER DOES NOT RECEIVE HIS MINIMUM WAGE

the binding effect of the codes on employers and, of course,
ended national regulation of hours and wages. Congress,
however, continued to seek ways of meeting the problem of
hours and wages on a nationwide basis. The Walsh-Healy
Public Contracts Act of 1936, for instance, established a 40-hour
week and "prevailing minimum wages for similar work" standards for all those employers receiving government contracts
for $10,000 or more. The Act also prohibited boys under 16
and girls under 18 from working on these contracts.

In response to the increasing demand by workers and others
for a general policy as to hours and wages throughout industry,
Congress took a further step under the interstate commerce
power. The Fair Labor Standards Act, generally known as
the "Wage and Hour Act", was enacted in 1938. Under Section
2 of the Act, Congress made a "finding" and a "declaration of
policy" which illustrated how broad its power over interstate

commerce really is. By the Act, the federal commerce power is extended to cover the field of industrial relations in the new area of wages and hours. It provides in Section 2:

> (a) The Congress hereby finds that the existence, in industries engaged in commerce or in the production of goods for commerce, of labor conditions detrimental to the maintenance of the minimum standard of living necessary for health, efficiency, and general well-being of workers (1) causes commerce and the channels and instrumentalities of commerce to be used to spread and perpetuate such labor conditions among the workers of the several States; (2) burdens commerce and the free flow of goods in commerce; (3) constitutes an unfair method of competition in commerce; (4) leads to labor disputes burdening and obstructing commerce and the free flow of goods in commerce; and (5) interferes with the orderly and fair marketing of goods in commerce.
>
> (b) It is hereby declared to be the policy of this Act, through the exercise by Congress of its power to regulate commerce among the several States, to correct and as rapidly as practicable to eliminate the conditions above referred to in such industries without substantially curtailing employment or earning power.

New National Standards

Under the Fair Labor Standards Act, an ultimate goal of a 40-hour maximum work week and a 40-cent an hour minimum wage was established. The Act, however, did not attempt to impose this "ceiling over hours and floor under wages" at once. Instead, it provided a sort of sliding scale by which to reach the goals of the 40-hour week and the 40-cent wage. A maximum of 44 hours was established for one year from October 1938, of 42 hours for the next year, and of 40 hours after October 1940. The minimum wage for the first year, from October 1938, was to be 25 cents; from October 1939 to October 1945, it was to be not less than 30 cents; after October 1945, the minimum of 40 cents was to apply. These standards are substituted by the Act for any existing standards as to hours or wages enacted by the states in so far as they apply to industries engaged in interstate commerce. If the state standards are higher than the national, they are to continue in force.

This national law regulating hours and wages brings some uniformity into a field in which hitherto there had been widely varying standards between the states. The law applies to any individual, partnership, or corporation which is engaged in interstate commerce or in producing goods which flow in interstate commerce. It is administered by a special Wages and Hours Division in the United States Department of Labor.

How Standards Are Set

In establishing minimum wages for the different industries which come under the Act, the Administrator has the power to appoint an industry committee for each industry. These committees include an equal representation of employers, workers, and the public. They investigate the general conditions within a particular industry and then recommend a minimum wage for that industry during the period between 1939 and 1945. The industry committee—and the Wages and Hours Administrator who is authorized to set the wage—must consider various points in setting minimum wages for any industry. Among them are living costs, costs of production and transportation, and wages for similar work established by voluntary collective-bargaining agreements or by employers who maintain voluntary minimum wage standards in the industry.

After an industry committee has made its recommendation to the Administrator, he shall call a hearing at which all interested persons may appear and object to the report. After the hearing, the Administrator makes a final minimum wage order which applies to all the workers in that part of the industry which comes under the order. All the workers engaged in the main operations of an industry are generally classified together. The Administrator may, however, find that some workers in the plant are not actually "engaged in interstate commerce or in the production of goods for interstate commerce". They would, therefore, not come within the order.

The Act also specifically excludes workers in certain industries or occupations from the new wage and hour standards. Among these are executives, professional workers, employees of local retail stores and service establishments doing mainly an intrastate business, agricultural workers, seamen and fishermen. Similarly, workers for weekly or semi-weekly newspapers with a circulation which is mostly local, workers engaged in processing or canning agricultural products, and telephone operators in small exchanges (with fewer than 500 stations) are excluded. Railroad and bus workers are also excluded because they come under federal wage and hour laws covering interstate transportation.

Another important feature of the Act is its provisions regarding child labor. As we have seen, the earlier attempts of Congress to regulate child labor by a general law were held unconstitutional by the Supreme Court. No child-labor amendment to the Constitution has, moreover, been adopted. The Fair Labor Standards Act (as well as the other national acts noted above which apply general regulations to child labor) does, however, meet this problem. It prohibits the shipment in interstate commerce of goods which have been manufactured in whole or in part by "oppressive" child labor. Those under the age of 16, except when employed by a parent or a guardian or granted permission by the Children's Bureau of the Department of Labor, come within the law. It also includes minors between 16 and 18 in occupations found to be hazardous by the Children's Bureau. Children under 16 may be employed (except

OW THE WAGE AND HOUR ACT WORKS

AGE AND HOUR ADMINISTRATOR APPOINTS AN INDUSTRY COMMITTEE—EQUAL NUMBER OF EMPLOYERS, WORKERS AND PUBLIC

INDUSTRY COMMITTEE HOLDS HEARINGS

INDUSTRY COMMITTEE RECOMMENDS A MINIMUM WAGE TO ADMINISTRATOR

MINISTRATOR HOLDS FURTHER HEAR-GS ON OBJECTIONS TO RECOMMENDA-TION

ADMINISTRATOR MAY REFER RECOMMEN-DATION TO ORIGINAL OR NEW INDUSTRY COMMITTEE FOR FURTHER STUDY

ADMINISTRATOR MAKES FINAL DECISION AND ISSUES MINIMUM WAGE ORDER

in mining and manufacturing) if the Children's Bureau finds that their health, schooling, or general well-being will not be injured.

Employers who violate the terms of the law are subject to a fine of not more than $10,000, or imprisonment for not more than six months, or both. Each separate offense—that is, the employment of each worker contrary to the terms of the Act—is a separate violation.

This Act, of course, greatly expands the control of the national government over private industry. What industries are and what are not interstate in character will always remain a matter for the courts to decide, in the light of findings made by the National Wage and Hour Administrator. The Act does, however, bring about much greater uniformity regarding hour and wage standards throughout our whole industrial system than had been achieved through the action of the 48 states individually. From this point of view, it does meet some of the difficulties which employers had faced under state action. We can say, indeed, that so far as interstate industries are concerned, we have now established a single national standard.*

Just what industries may we expect to come within the regulatory power of the national government? The question is an important one from the point of view of both federal and state powers and policies in the whole field of industrial and labor relations. No very clear answer can be given at present. From the way in which the United States Supreme Court has expanded the power of the National Labor Relations Board we may expect a very wide extension of national authority.

An example or two of actual questions now before the Wage and Hour Administrator will illustrate the difficulty of drawing any very clear lines between national and state authority. A

---

* The act was held constitutional by the Supreme Court in 1941. U. S. v. Darby Lumber Co., 312 U. S. 100 (1941).

button manufacturer, for instance, sells all his product to a shirt manufacturer in the same state. The shirt manufacturer puts the buttons on shirts made in his plant and then ships the shirts in interstate commerce. Does the button manufacturer come within the national commerce power? Or again, a clothing manufacturer sends his garments out of his plant to be sewed by an independent contractor. Is this contractor also engaged in interstate commerce, if after he has sent the garments back to the original manufacturer, they are shipped outside the state? Are the freight-elevator operators in a building, all the tenants of which are engaged in interstate commerce, also within the terms of the Act because they work in this building?*

Such actual situations as these indicate how indefinite the line is today between those industries which are interstate and those which are intrastate. They show, too, how far Congress has already gone in establishing national standards.

New York State Acts

Hours

New York State, although not one of the earliest states to regulate hours for women and children, has set continually higher standards regarding hours and wages. The first hours law was enacted by the Legislature in 1886, limiting the work of girls under 21 to 60 hours a week. The same limit was extended in 1896 to all women working in stores. By 1927, the eight-hour-day and the 48-hour-week law had been extended in New York to include all women working in factories as well

---

* In these cases the Wage and Hour Administrator has answered *Yes*. On June 1, 1942, the United States Supreme Court sustained the findings of the administrator and held further that elevator operators, engineers, porters, and other maintenance employees of a loft-building in the City of New York were within the jurisdiction of the Federal Fair Labor and Standards Act. The courts ruling places these employees within the Wage and Hour Law, setting minimum wages and maximum hours.

as in stores. Since 1938, state regulations have included women workers in hotels, restaurants, elevators, railroads, telegraph and messenger services, and beauty parlors. Clerical and other office workers do not, however, come under this law. In New York City, this group includes more than half the women workers.

New York State follows the principle that "women and minors employed in any occupation should receive wages sufficient to provide adequate maintenance to protect their health." Under the law, no child under 16 may work in a factory more than six days or 44 hours a week, or more than eight hours in any one day. Further, children under 16 may not work between 5 P.M. and 8 A.M. Children under 16 may not be employed even outside factories except when the schools are not in session or an employment certificate has been issued to them. Children under 16 may not work at all in hazardous industries such as those which use, for example, circular saws, power punches or shears, steam boilers, grinding or mixing machinery, or explosives.

The principle of an eight-hour day, except in agriculture and domestic service, has also been established by the state as a general policy. A law was, moreover, enacted in 1909 providing "one day rest in seven" for all industrial workers.

Wages

In addition to these hours laws, a law enacted in 1933 provided machinery for setting minimum wages for women and children. After the Supreme Court held minimum-wage laws constitutional in 1937, the New York law was revived.

The procedure for setting minimum wages is on the whole similar to that under the National Fair Labor Standards Act. Fifty workers in an industry may petition the State Department of Labor to set a minimum wage in that industry. The State

Industrial Commissioner is also given power on his own initiative "to investigate and ascertain the wages of women and minors employed in any occupation in the state". If the Commissioner finds that any substantial number of workers are receiving wages which do not provide adequate maintenance or protect their health, he must appoint a Wage Board for that industry. This Board, like that under the national law, must include an equal number of representatives of the employers, the workers, and the public.

The Wage Board may require witnesses to appear and testify. It may obtain any records from private sources which are essential to determine the facts about wages in the industry. It must submit a report to the Industrial Commissioner within 60 days, recommending a minimum wage for the industry. In establishing a minimum wage, the Board (and the Commissioner) may use as a basis for their finding any or all of the three standards stated in the law. These are: first, the amount necessary to provide adequate maintenance and protect health; second, the value to the employer of the services performed by the workers; and third, the wages paid in the state for work of a like or comparable character.

After the Wage Board submits its report and recommendations to the Industrial Commissioner, he must accept or reject it within 10 days. If he accepts the report of the Wage Board, he must then hold a public hearing at which anyone may appear to support or oppose the recommended minimum wage. If the Commissioner rejects the report, he may submit the question to the same or to a new Wage Board. When the Commissioner is satisfied that a fair finding has been made by a Wage Board, he then issues an order for the industry concerned. Thus, we can see that, once the procedure for establishing a minimum wage has been started, the Commissioner must establish a minimum wage and enforce it for the entire industry.

After the Industrial Commissioner has approved a finding of a Wage Board for an industry, he must issue an order announcing the minimum wage. This order is in the first place "directory"; that is, employers are given the opportunity to adopt the new wage rate voluntarily. It was hoped by those supporting the minimum-wage principle that employers would accept the findings of a Wage Board and of the Industrial Commissioner. If, however, the Commissioner later finds that many employers are not observing the new minimum wage standards, he may make the order "mandatory." This means that thereafter it will be enforced directly by the state by court action against those employers who do not pay the established minimum wage.

Several methods for enforcing minimum wage standards are provided in the Act. First, the Industrial Commissioner may publish the names of employers who do not observe the new standards. This method of enforcement was adopted in the hope that the people would bring pressure to bear on employers to make them conform to the new standards. Thus, public opinion would become an important means of making the policy of the state effective. The Commissioner may publish the names of offending employers whether or not the order is mandatory. This is, in fact, the only method of enforcing a directory order.

A second method for enforcing mandatory orders was provided in the law. An employer who fails to pay the minimum wage may be fined or imprisoned—or both. If he fails to keep proper and correct records of wages paid, or if he discriminates in any way against any of his workers who have served on a Wage Board, he may be fined. The third method of enforcing minimum wage is by a law suit by a worker to recover wages due him under a mandatory order applying to his industry.

By July, 1943, minimum wage rates had been established under this procedure in the following industries: beauty service,

Courtesy of the Ford Motor Company

IN THE 1930's—WAGES AND HOURS LIKE PRODUCTION, ARE CONTROLLED

cleaning and dyeing, confectionery, laundry, restaurants, hotels. It may be noted that most of these industries are service trades rather than large-scale factory industries. It is in the service trades that the workers are often the most exposed to being exploited by their employers because they are often unorganized and frequently unskilled.

A few illustrations will indicate how necessary these minimum wage orders are to protect the living standards of the workers. The Wage Board in the laundry industry, for instance, found that half the women workers received less than $14.19 per week, and 24 per cent less than $600 a year. In 1938, the board established a 40-hour week with a wage rate of 35 cents an hour in New York City, 32 cents in cities of over 18,000 and 30 cents elsewhere. A guaranteed wage of $14 a week with time-and-a-half for overtime above 40 hours was ordered. The Industrial Commissioner has since found that only 3 per cent of the employers were not living up to the order.

In beauty shops, the conditions were even worse. Over 14,000 women worked in 6,200 shops throughout the state. One-third received less than $10 a week, half less than $13.75. In 1938, a Wage Board established a guaranteed wage of $16.50 for beauty shop workers and $15 for maids, on a 45-hour-a-week basis. The order was made mandatory in 1939. The result was to increase average weekly earnings by $3.32. Again, only 3 per cent of the employers refused to comply with the order.

In attacking the conditions in these low-wage industries, the State Department of Labor has followed a policy of helping those who are, in many cases, least able to obtain better conditions through their own bargaining efforts.

☆ ☆ ☆ ☆ ☆ ☆ ☆ ☆ ☆ ☆ ☆ ☆ ☆

Through the laws setting a ceiling over hours and a floor under wages, we, the people, have aided the workers to achieve another of their interests in security. We have regulated hours to reduce both social and economic insecurity in terms of health and a chance for a job. We have regulated wages for the same reasons. We have acted through our governments, state and national, in order to protect the general welfare of all the people by increasing the security of the largest single group within the nation.

Beyond security on the job, however, there remain broader problems of insecurity resulting from unemployment, old age, and dependency. In the next chapter we shall note how we have acted through government to regulate these phases of the workers' interest in security.

11

Spreading the Risks of Unemployment and Old Age

IN OUR MODERN ECONOMY, WORKERS HAVE WANTED, AS WE have seen, to spread the risks of industrial accidents and diseases so that their entire burden would not fall on the injured worker individually. Similarly, they have wanted to stabilize hours and wages in our industrial system in good times as well as in bad. As they have found how our economy works, they have come also to feel that unemployment resulting from the recurring business cycles is not so much an individual as a nationwide problem. Further, they have felt that they have a right to a more adequate economic security than mere public relief in their old age.

Broadly speaking, we have acted through government to spread these two risks—unemployment and old age in two ways. First, we have developed state and national agencies to help workers who are unemployed find jobs by creating public employment services. Through these agencies, we have sought to bring the worker to the job and the job to the worker. Second, we have acted through government to spread the risks of unemployment, old age, and dependency over the whole community by insuring workers against these risks. In these two ways, we have attempted to meet the economic and social effects of unemployment.

By treating them as a nationwide or statewide concern rather than as a problem for the individual worker and his family, we have, in our time, expanded the meaning of the general welfare. This aspect of public policy is, indeed, especially interesting. It illustrates how closely the interests of workers and employers and, in fact, of all the people, actually correspond in this field of industrial and labor relations.

As we shall see, moreover, many employers have pioneered in attempting to meet both these aspects of insecurity. Various plans both for job finding and for taking up the slack of unemployment had been worked out by employers, even before we had acted through government. Indeed, one of the chief reasons why we have acted through government in this field is that the problem had become so large that private groups alone could not meet it. It is out of these experiments conducted by private industry, as well as out of the experience of the European industrial countries, that our governmental policies have been developed.

Out of a Job – Finding Employment

Why is the problem of unemployment a matter of such immediate public concern? We have already noted (see Chapter 4, pp. 60 ff.) some of the reasons for the rise and decline of whole industries as well as of individual plants. Changes in technology, the development of new products which displace older ones, the uneven spread of our national purchasing power, and many other causes affect the chances workers have of finding jobs. Within these broad aspects of our economy, other factors, such as seasonal demand for winter clothing or summer clothing, will affect the individual worker's chances of having a continuous job. Thus, there are many reasons why workers may find themselves out of a job and unable to obtain one—through no fault of their employers or themselves.

Even when industry is running full-strength, there may be as many as 2,000,000 workers out of a job at any one time in this country. When times are not so good, there may be many more millions of workers looking for jobs. For some workers all the time, and for many in bad times, the problem of finding a job is the most immediate and direct concern they have.

Employers Cooperate to Reduce Unemployment

Private industry has done much to meet this problem. Some employers' associations, for instance, have set up employment services in their industries, or provided general information which will help unemployed workers to locate a new job in the industry. Many civic groups have also established employment services, free of charge or at little cost to the workers who are looking for jobs.

Some employers have gone even further. Many progressive industrial leaders today realize that a high labor turnover in their factories is an expensive luxury. Not only do they have to train new workers, which is in itself a direct expense to them, but they may not be able to find the workers needed to fill jobs. Although there may be more workers than jobs available in the country as a whole, the employer may find that constant hiring and firing reduces the efficiency of his plant.

Individual employers have adopted various plans to meet this problem. Some have developed welfare and social services in their plants or have set up private insurance plans for sickness and old age, as incentives to their workers to stay on the job. More important than these plans is the movement for improved personnel management in private industry. Many employers have come to see that providing an impartial method

of hiring and firing or of hearing and settling complaints helps
to keep workers satisfied.

Many employers, too, have recognized that workers have a
right to share in the profits which they help to create. Several
hundred profit-sharing plans have been set up by individual
employers. During the past decade, a few employers, seeking
to solve this problem of high labor turnover, have gone even
further and developed a program of guaranteed jobs and wages
to their workers.

The way in which employer-cooperation with workers operates in practice is illustrated by the experience of the Hormel
Company, one of the largest meat-packing concerns in the
country. In 1939, the company established a guaranteed wage
and profit-sharing plan. Workers on different jobs in the Austin,
Minnesota, factory were organized into teams. Each team was
guaranteed a total yearly wage, determined according to the
skill of the individual workers. The rate was based on the
company's past experience of production, sales, and profits.
The workers were told that if they maintained the average rate
of production, they would receive the guaranteed wage—
whether or not the company sold all the year's production.

In addition, the company agreed to share any additional
profits which it made in any year. A substantial part of each
year's profits was put into a special fund, of which the workers
were to receive 80 per cent and the stockholders 20 per cent.
In this way, the workers were given an incentive to save costs
in the factory—for instance, by not wasting any of the materials
they were packing as well as by working more efficiently. The
results, from the stockholders' point of view, have been most
satisfactory. The company's financial record has steadily improved. This, like many other examples of cooperation through
sharing profits, shows that workers respond to fair treatment
from their employers.

TO CLAIMANT

Please print. Use indelible pencil.

Be accurate.

Sign your name the same way each time you sign a claim.

If you used any other Social Security account number in employment since Jan. 1, 1942 or if you obtained your Social Security account number since Jan. 1, 1942 ask for Form UI-LO 333.1 Claimant's Statement of Covered Employment.

1 SOCIAL SECURITY ACCOUNT NUMBER

NEW YORK STATE DEPT. OF LABOR
D. P. U. I.

REGISTRATION FOR WORK AND CLAIM F

LAST DAY I WORKED: MONTH_____ DAY____

I LEFT OR LOST MY JOB BECAUSE:_____

2 FULL NAME

FIRST NAME   MIDDLE NAME   (MAIDEN NAME IF MARRIED)   LAST NAME

I hereby register for work and claim unemploy benefits. I certify that I am now unemployed, th willing and able to work and that the statem herein are true and correct.

3 HOME ADDRESS

NUMBER   STREET

CITY OR VILLAGE   STATE

4 OTHER NAME

OTHER NAME UNDER WHICH I WORKED IN 1942

5 PLANT OR JOB

CLOCK OR PAYROLL NUMBER

CLAIMANT SIGN HERE AFTER READING THE ABOVE

6 LAST EMPLOYER

DO NOT WRITE IN THIS SPACE   L.O. N

7 BUSINESS ADDRESS OF LAST EMPLOYER

REP. DA

YOUR LAST EMPLOYER WILL BE NOTIFIED THAT YOU HAVE FILED THIS STATEMENT. THE LAW PROVIDES SEVERE PENALTIES FOR FALSE STATEMENTS TO OBTAIN BENEFITS
LABOR UI - LO 333 (REV. 3 - 19 - 43)

INITIAL

Under this and similar plans, workers receive an assured yearly total wage and may also share in any profits which result from the increased efficiency of the plant. These plans have often produced higher profits for the employer because they give the workers an increased interest in—and loyalty to—their jobs. None has failed to reduce labor turnover and unemployment in individual plants.

All of these efforts by employers and others have, no doubt, been of some help in stabilizing employment. These attempts, however, cannot meet all the demands for jobs that occur. This is because obtaining accurate and prompt information concerning those who are unemployed and what jobs are open is too large a task for any private group. The problem is, in fact, statewide or nationwide. It is not enough, for instance, to know what jobs may be open in the town or city where the worker lives. If his own plant has closed down, he must be able to find out where else in the state, or perhaps in the nation, his skills are in demand. Accordingly, we have acted through government to make this kind of information available both on a statewide and on a nationwide basis.

National Government Employment Services

A system of public employment services was established in the United States long after they had been created in Europe

240

in the 19th century. One of the first states to establish a public employment service in this country was Ohio in 1890. By 1931, 31 states had enacted laws which authorized the creation of public employment services. Only 23 states had, however, actually set up offices where everyone could register for a job if he were unemployed and where he could find out about jobs which were available.

The national government's first experiment in this field was in 1907; in that year, the Bureau of Immigration opened several offices to help immigrants find farm jobs. In 1915, when the demand for workers in war industries increased, these offices extended their activities into the industrial field.

No really effective nationwide employment service existed, however, until 1918, when the United States Employment Service was established in the Department of Labor. During its first year, it proved its value by placing almost five million workers in jobs, at an average cost of $1.34 per worker. This new Employment Service had been established because of the urgent need to find workers for the rapidly growing war indus-tries. After the war, Congress cut down the appropriation for the United States Employment Service, so that it was unable to carry on direct job-finding activities on the wartime scale. During the 1920's moreover, there was a large demand for labor; most people felt that there was no longer a need for such a national job-finding agency.

When the depression came in 1929, the demand for expanding the services of the national government in this field grew rapidly. Congress enacted the Wagner-Peyser Act in 1933, abolishing the existing United States Employment Service and creating a new and much expanded service in the Department of Labor. In 1939, the Service was transferred from the Department of Labor to the new Federal Security Agency which includes the Social Security Board.

The United States Employment Service cooperates very closely with the Social Security Board in its unemployment-insurance activities. One of the chief purposes of the Wagner-Peyser Act was to bring about a closer cooperation between federal and state employment services. It was felt that job-finding was really a problem common to both the states and the nation. The purpose of the Act was to lend the advice and aid of the national government to the states, as well as to provide direct job-finding aid to workers through the United States Employment Service itself.

Under the Act, the United States Employment Service was to set up national employment offices to help certain groups—for instance, veterans and farm workers—to find jobs. During the first few years of its operation, the Service was also assigned the task of placing as many as possible of the unemployed workers in various government relief and construction services. It was active for several years in finding jobs for many hundreds of thousands in such agencies as the Civil Works Administration, the Federal Emergency Relief Administration, and the Public Works Administration.

The long-range task of the Service was to aid the states in developing more efficient state employment services. That this was a sound policy is indicated by the increase of job-finding activities in the states. In 1933, when the Wagner-Peyser Act became law, there were only 192 state offices in 120 cities, organized by 23 state employment services. By 1940, every state and the District of Columbia, Hawaii, and Alaska had established an employment service through the grants-in-aid provided by the Act. Over 1500 full-time offices, and over 3000 "itinerant points"—part-time offices in smaller industrial cities working in close contact with the permanent offices—were operating. Through these more than 4500 offices, any unemployed worker could register for a job and receive prompt notice of any job-openings in his locality or in his industry in another community.

The Wagner-Peyser Act is one of many passed by Congress to stimulate the states to cooperate in a nationwide program for higher standards of social security. Under the Act, Congress matches the states by grants-in-aid, on a 50–50 basis, to aid them in establishing their own employment services. To obtain a grant, a state must accept the standards prescribed in the Act and defined by the United States Employment Service. If it does, one-half of the cost of its operation is paid by the federal government. If a state does not set up such a service of its own, the United States Employment Service may itself establish offices within the state.

GOVERNMENT REGISTERS UNEMPLOYED WORKERS FOR JOBS   © Wide World Photos

The first law establishing a public employment service in New York State was enacted in 1896. The state made an annual appropriation of $5,000, which was enough to open only one office. This bureau served as an incentive to the people to broaden the state's services to workers in finding jobs. It was closed, however, because of lack of funds. Not until 1914 was a regular Bureau of Employment established in the State Department of Labor. The new Bureau was given authority to open branch offices throughout the state.

After 1921, appropriations for this service, now called the Division of Employment, were so far cut down that some offices had to be closed. In 1929, the New York State Employment Service was created by the Legislature and has been constantly expanded since then. By 1941, there were 26 full-time employment offices in New York City, and 51 full-time and 41 part-time offices outside the city.

This system of intimate and effective state-federal cooperation in job-finding was substantially modified by an executive order of the President on December 19, 1941. Under this order all state employment services came under the direct administration of the United States Employment Service on January 1, 1942. This meant that state employment-service personnel, records, and offices were transferred to it. Administration of job-finding services is, therefore, no longer subject to state control.

In 1935, when the State Unemployment Insurance Law was enacted, the State Employment Service was consolidated in a new Division of Placement and Unemployment Insurance. Until 1942, this Division carried on two functions, job-finding and administering the unemployment insurance law. After the employment function was transferred to the federal government, the Division continued to carry on the latter function. Registering for unemployment insurance, however, may still be done in United States Employment Service offices, except in New York City. There, the state Division of Placement and Unemployment Insurance still maintains independent offices for unemployment registration. In upstate New York, on the other hand, the Division's unemployment-insurance registration is carried on through the federally-operated employment offices.

This brief review of how both employers and the people have tried to spread the risks of unemployment, by bringing the job and the worker together, tells only half of the story. The efforts of private industry to maintain stable employment were successful in many individual plants. This was not enough, however, to meet the problem of mass unemployment when hundreds of thousands, and even millions, of workers were out of a job. The people's interest in seeing this risk of industry spread over the whole community was realized by laws creating state and national employment services. The other half of the story of spreading the risks of unemployment is older—and more dramatic. It relates to our present-day system of social security.

Out of a Job – Beyond Relief

The early settlers brought over with them the ideas about unemployed workers underlying the Elizabethan Poor Laws, that it was a person's own fault if he was out of a job. All public relief in early America and, indeed, until the middle of the 19th century, was carried out by placing unemployed people in local or state poor houses or poor farms. This was called "indoor relief". Later, unemployed people without funds of their own were given "outdoor relief", that is, cash or food for use in their own homes. Both these forms of relief were based on the idea that the unemployed person was an object of charity, to be supported if necessary at public expense. Neither reflected our present-day attitude that the unemployed person has a right to a decent standard of living no less than his more fortunate fellow-citizen who is employed.

Thus, we have moved from a negative to a positive view of economic security for all workers. We no longer consider that it is a person's own fault if he loses or cannot find a job. As this view of the nature of unemployment, with its resulting dependency of the individual worker and his family on charity, advanced, it was increasingly recognized that the problem of security was a matter of public concern.

The Depression of 1929 turned the nation's attention to this problem as never before. As we have seen, various national relief agencies were established—C.W.A., W.P.A., and, in part, P.W.A.—to supplement local and state relief services. As unemployment figures rose from two to five and then from five to ten to twelve million, more and more people realized that the problem of spreading the risks of unemployment and old age could no longer be met only at the local or the state level. It had to be met by national action if it was to be met at all. Here, as in the field of finding employment for workers out of a job, we shall see that private industry and government have cooperated to find a solution for the risks of unemployment.

What we today call Social Security began in Germany under Bismarck in the 1880's. During the next quarter-century, it spread to England and several other countries in Europe. In these countries, the governments took the initiative in setting up insurance of various types to meet the workers' interest in security. These social security plans were of several different kinds.

Among the plans which were developed in this period were unemployment insurance, sickness insurance, and old age insurance. Some of the plans were compulsory; that is, all workers and employers, at least in certain industries, were forced to accept an insurance plan. Some laws covered one type of insurance; other laws included two or all three types.

The European laws varied in another way. Under some, the worker and the employer carried the whole burden of insurance between them. In others, the government also contributed, so that the public as well as the employers and workers bore a share of the cost.

Finally, these laws varied as to the type of insurance fund established. Some created a state insurance fund very much like that under the Workmen's Compensation Law in New York State. Others allowed the employers and workers to insure in private insurance companies or other insurance agencies of their own choosing. In all cases, these private groups were regulated by the government.

It is out of this variety of experience abroad that our own social security program was developed. There was also another source from which we drew our experience—private industrial old-age pension plans in the United States.

Employers Seek to Meet the Problem

The first industrial old-age pension system in this country was established by the American Railway Express Company in 1875. In this plan, the employer paid the costs; the workers themselves made no contribution. In 1880, the Baltimore and Ohio Railroad established the first contributory plan, under which the workers also bore part of the cost of their own old-age pensions. The workers, however, refused to contribute, so that the company changed over to a non-contributory plan in 1884.

In this country, old-age pension plans spread most rapidly in the railroad field. By 1927, about 95 per cent of all workers on our large railroads were covered by some kind of pension plan, maintained by the railroads on a non-contributory basis. Under these plans, workers paid nothing toward the cost of their old-age insurance and the benefits were usually low.

Various other private pension plans were developed after 1890, mainly in banking and public utilities and, after 1900, in various other industries. By 1929, 139 non-contributory plans had been established in the industrial field, covering nearly a million and a quarter workers. All of these private industrial plans were controlled by the companies which had set them up. When the Depression of 1929 resulted in rapidly increasing unemployment, many of the plans collapsed. Although the movement had taken root in private industry, these plans were not strong enough to withstand the impact of a long and a deep depression.

Many workers, moreover, were suspicious of some of these plans. They felt that too many strings were attached to the payments to which they were entitled. Most of the plans provided, for instance, that a worker must have been continually employed by the company for 15 or 20 years to be eligible for an old-age pension. Companies often refused to pay a pension because a worker who reached the age limit had been laid off for a short time during the period of his employment. Few workers were, in fact, likely to continue working for a single company long enough to become entitled to a pension.

We must remember, too, that none of these plans went beyond old-age insurance. They did not cover sickness or unemployment—the two most immediate risks which workers face. They did, however, offer valuable experience about the working of old-age pension plans.

The demand for governmental action grew rapidly, as people came to realize that it was necessary to organize old-age, sickness, or unemployment insurance on a statewide or a nationwide basis. The first state unemployment insurance law was enacted in Wisconsin in 1931. The movement for spreading the risks of industry was already under way in a number of other

BEFORE SOCIAL SECURITY

© Underwood and Underwood

states. During 1931 and 1932, unemployment insurance bills passed at least one house of seven state legislatures. The legislatures were beginning to respond to the people's interest in a broad program of social security.

As the depression spread and deepened, the problem of unemployment was increasingly recognized as national in scope. It became evident that, if we were to develop an effective social security program, it, too, would have to be on a nationwide basis. In 1934, a bill was introduced in Congress for a national unemployment insurance system based on state cooperation. In brief, the plan was to levy a payroll tax on all employers, amounting to 5 per cent of the wages they paid. A refund on the tax was to be allowed to employers in any state which passed a compulsory unemployment insurance law. Thus, from the very beginning, national policy has looked toward cooperation with the states in spreading the risks of unemployment.

Several other bills were introduced at this time. On June 8, 1934, the President addressed a special message to Congress. He stated that "some safeguards against misfortunes which cannot be wholly eliminated in this man-made world" should be provided by the national government. He announced that he was appointing a special Committee on Economic Security to study the whole problem and to propose a program to Congress.

In the meantime, many private groups were pressing for an old-age pension law. The best known of these is, perhaps, the Townsend Plan which received much popular support all over the country under the slogan, "$200 a month for everyone over 60". Another movement, sponsored by Representative Lundeen in 1935, pressed for a national law to provide unemployment payments of $10 a week, plus $5 for each dependent.

We Act Through the National Government—The Social Security Act of 1935

These movements did not divert the President or Congress from seeking to work out a social security program. After a study of all existing social insurance plans in this country and abroad, the Committee on Economic Security made its report on January 15, 1935. A bill, which the Committee recommended, was enacted by Congress in an amended form and it was signed by the President on August 18, 1935. The Act created a Social Security Board of three members, to be appointed by the President for six-year over-lapping terms. This Board was to supervise the operation of the new social security program. Under the law, both the state and the national governments were charged with important functions. What were some of these functions?

Unemployment

We may divide them into three broad fields. First, a plan for insuring workers against unemployment was established; under which the national government was made responsible for collecting unemployment insurance taxes. The plan applies to all plants employing eight or more workers. The Act provides, however, that a state may develop its own unemployment insurance program, if it conforms to the requirements of the national law. If a state establishes its own unemployment insurance plan, employers of eight or more workers in that state pay only 10 per cent of the national tax to the national government. The national tax is at present 3 per cent of payrolls; thus, they would pay .3 of 1 per cent to the national government. In addition, they pay whatever tax is required under the state law. The percentage of the tax collected by the national government is to be used primarily for administrative purposes—to see that the entire program for social security is carried out effectively.

Congress did not, however, allow the states to enact any kind of unemployment insurance laws they might choose. The Social Security Act establishes certain standards to which the states must conform. Under the Act, the states might adopt any scale of unemployment benefits and any period during which these benefits should be paid. They were, however, required to set up a public unemployment insurance fund and to pay insurance benefits through public employment offices. Furthermore, they were required to keep their funds in the Federal Unemployment Trust Fund. Finally, they had to pay unemployment insurance to all persons who were entitled to receive it.

It can be seen at once that Congress intended to give the states a great deal of freedom in setting up their own unemployment insurance programs. Congress, however, did not delegate to the states authority to alter the basic principles of the law. The policy of making insurance available to the unemployed was established by Congress. All employers subject to the law were required to contribute to an unemployment insurance fund, whether or not the state in which they lived enacted an unemployment insurance law. In this way, Congress guaranteed to unemployed workers the protection of insurance. The principle of spreading the risk of unemployment was placed on a national basis. How much insurance the unemployed worker should receive was left, in a large measure, to the states.

Congress established a general national standard. The payroll tax, which employers must pay on all wages and salaries, was fixed at 1 per cent for 1936, 2 per cent for 1937, and 3 per cent for every year after 1937. Payments from the fund were not to begin until two years after the Act went into effect.

The Social Security Act did not cover all kinds of work. Several groups of workers were excluded in 1935 from the benefits of the Act. Among them were (1) agricultural workers; (2) domestic servants in private homes (hotels, laundries, and restaurants employing more than eight workers are included); (3) services of immediate members of the family when they are employed in a family business; (4) civil servants—national, state, and local; (5) workers in religious, scientific, charitable, and educational agencies and organizations. All other workers in a plant or office employing eight or more persons, except those specifically excluded, may qualify for unemployment insurance.

It is too soon to tell whether the payroll taxes which Congress established will provide enough money in the fund to take care of another deep depression like that of 1929. When the Social Security Act became law, contributions were paid into the fund for the first two years, but no benefits were to be paid so that the reserves of the fund would be built up to enable the payment of benefits in the following years. During 1936 and 1937, approximately $98,000,000 were paid into the New York fund. By June 30, 1943, for instance, the New York State Unemployment Insurance Fund had reached a total of $498,408,397. Since 1938, annual payments into the fund have averaged $144,-000,000, while the average annual unemployment benefits paid out from the fund during this time were $75,000,000. It would appear, therefore, that New York State is in a sound position to meet a real unemployment emergency. In general, an unemployed worker is now entitled to a maximum of 20 weeks' unemployment benefits in any one benefit year. The amount of unemployment insurance he will receive varies with his earnings in the previous year; it ranges between $10 and $18 a week. To be entitled to any insurance benefits, he must have earned at least $250 in the previous year and not less than $100 in any one quarter of the year.

Old Age

The second type of insurance provided for by the Social Security Act covers old age. Here too, Congress gave much power to the states to determine their own policies. Briefly, the national government gives outright grants-in-aid to the states, up to one-half of all old-age pensions of not over $30 a month paid by the state to eligible workers 65 years of age or over. The states are required to pay one-half up to the $30-a-month standard. The states pay all of any pension over this $30 standard.

If, for instance, under a state law, a person 65 years of age or over is entitled to $20 a month, the state will pay $10 and the national government $10. If a state law provides a pension of $40 a month, the state will pay $25 and the national government $15, or one half of the $30-a-month standard established by the Act.

WHO BENEFITS BY UNEMPLOYMENT

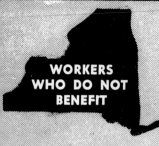

WORKERS WHO DO NOT BENEFIT

a. FARM WORKERS, INCLUDING CROPS, NURSERIES, AND GREENHOUSES.

b. FARMERS WHO PROCESS THEIR OWN PRODUCTS.

c. ANY EMPLOYEE WHOSE EMPLOYER EMPLOYS 3 OR LESS PERSONS.

d. STUDENTS ACTUALLY ATTENDING SCHOOL.

e. WORKERS EMPLOYED BY STATE, MUNICIPAL OR LOCAL GOVERNMENTS.

WORKERS EMPLOYED BY RELIGIOUS, CHARITABLE, SCIENTIFIC, LITERARY OR EDUCATIONAL INSTITUTIONS.

g. SPOUSE OR MINOR CHILDREN OF THE EMPLOYER.

h. GOLF CADDIES.

i. MARITIME WORKERS OTHER THAN THOSE ON INLAND WATERWAYS.

j. RAILROAD EMPLOYEES.

WORKERS WHO DO BENEFIT*

SOME

EXAMPLES

* TO BE COVERED WORKERS MUST WORK IN NEW YORK STATE.

a. CONSTRUCTION WORKERS

b. SHIPYARD WORKERS

c. CLOTHING WORKERS

d. PRINTERS

e. OFFICE WORKERS

f. INLAND MARINE WORKERS

g. LOCAL TRANSPORTATION EMPLOYEES

h. BANK EMPLOYEES

i. RETAIL AND WHOLESALE EMPLOYEES

j. MINERS

k. LUMBERMEN

l. THE WHOLE GAMUT OF FACTORY WORKERS FROM A TO IZZARD

m. UTILITY WORKERS SUCH AS GAS, ELECTRIC LIGHT AND TELEPHONE

Under the Act, the grants-in-aid for old-age pensions will gradually disappear and a compulsory old-age insurance plan will take its place. A pension plan had to be established at first, because no insurance plan could build up the necessary reserves in time to meet the needs of those older workers who would soon reach 65 after 1935. For younger workers, however, these reserves can be built up by a regular old-age insurance plan.

The details of the plan are complex, but the principle is simple. Under the Act, both the employer and the worker contribute equal amounts to the national old-age insurance fund. The payment begins at 1 per cent of the annual wage or salary of each worker for the period 1937–1939, and will reach 3 per cent in 1949 and thereafter. Neither the states nor the national government make any direct contribution to the insurance fund. The national government, however, pays the cost of managing the whole old-age program.

What the worker will receive in the way of old-age insurance is defined in the law. If we take as an example a worker who has been employed for 30 years at an average wage of $1500 a year, we find that he will receive old-age insurance at the rate of $50 a month from the time he is 65. No one may receive more than $85 a month or $1020 a year, no matter how large his average earnings over his whole working life have been.

The national government has set up a special plan, under its complete control, for one group of workers. Under its power to regulate interstate commerce, Congress enacted a law in 1934, the Railroad Retirement Act, setting up a compulsory pension and retirement plan for all railroad workers who reached 65 years of age or who had completed 30 years of service.

Under this plan, both the workers and the railroads contribute to a pension fund at rates which begin at 2 per cent for the workers and 4 per cent for the railroads. All the existing private pension plans of the railroads are merged under the new government plan. A Railway Retirement Board of three members, appointed by the President for five-year over-lapping terms, administers the plan established by the Act.

The railroads attacked the Act in the Courts on the ground that it covered many workers who were not actually engaged in interstate commerce, such as telegraph operators in railway towers. It was argued that Congress, therefore, did not have the power to regulate their employment under the commerce power. The Supreme Court upheld the railroads' point of view in a five-to-four decision in 1935.*

Congress then re-enacted the same law, excluding those workers who were not clearly engaged in interstate commerce. The right of Congress to include some types of work on the railroads was thus limited more narrowly by the Supreme Court under the federal commerce power than it had been the case, for instance, in the fields of labor relations and wages and hours.

Shortly afterwards, the Social Security Act and a number of state unemployment insurance and old-age pension laws were attacked in the Supreme Court as an unconstitutional exercise of the taxing power. The Court, however, upheld the power of Congress and of the states to enact laws "to provide for . . . the general welfare through a program of social insurance".**

Dependency and Public Health

The third group covered by the Social Security Act included dependent mothers and children and the needy blind. Here again Congress saw fit to match the states by direct grants-in-aid. Under the Act, the national government pays a substantial share, up to two-thirds, of the cost of aiding these groups. Any plan established by the states for aid to these groups must be approved

* Railroad Retirement Board v. Alton R. R. Co., 295 U. S. 330 (1934).

** West Coast Hotel Co. v. Parrish, 300 U. S. 379 (1937).

by the Social Security Board before being put into operation.

In the Act, Congress also provided further funds for state child-welfare and public-health services. Some of these funds— $10,000,000 a year—are to be spent by the United States Public Health Service directly. Four-fifths of the amount is, however, to be turned over to the states to aid them in developing their own public-health services.

☆ ☆ ☆ ☆ ☆ ☆ ☆ ☆ ☆ ☆ ☆ ☆ ☆

There are many other aspects of social security which would be interesting to explore. This brief outline indicates, however, the principal ways in which we, the people, have acted through the national government to spread the risks of insecurity. We have sought to shift the burden from individual workers to all the people in the states or in the nation. First, we have placed on the states the responsibility of working out their own policies for spreading these risks—under a national policy established by Congress. This means that the people in the individual states may develop their own policies under general standards developed by the Social Security Board. Only in the field of old-age insurance did we centralize control in the national government. Even in this field, however, we left to the states the right to work out their own pension plans for workers over 65 years of age.

Second, in working out this cooperative program, all the social services of the national government have been placed at the disposal of the states. On the one hand, the Social Security Act provides funds to help the states to work out their own programs, either by 50–50 grants-in-aid or by direct payments from the United States Treasury. On the other hand, it places the services of several national agencies at the disposal of the states in developing their own social security policies and programs. Some are the Social Security Board, the United States Public Health Service, and the United States Children's Bureau.

In providing this aid to the states, Congress set certain standards in the Social Security Act and permitted the states to meet or even exceed them, subject only to review by the Social Security Board. True, the Board is given power to check on the policies and practices of the states to see that they conform to the standards established by the Act. During the last five years, however, the Board has exercised a check on policy or practice in only a very few states. In most cases, the Board has been a service agency for the state boards, giving them advice and help in working out their own policies.

Here is one of the most significant and challenging examples of how the states and the national government can cooperate effectively to promote the general welfare. The workers' interest in spreading the risks of industry, through a broad social-security program, has been achieved. We, the people, acting through government, have established the principle of public responsibility in another field of industrial and labor relations.

© Underwood-Stratton

THE CRISIS OF 1775—RECRUITING AN ARMY OF MINUTEMEN

PART III

INDUSTRIAL AND LABOR RELATIONS IN CRISIS— WAR AND POSTWAR PROBLEMS

THE CRISIS OF 1941—SELECTIVE SERVICE IN ACTION

12

The Challenge of the War – and of the Peace – to Industrial and Labor Relations in America

The Challenge of Total War

IN THE EARLIER CHAPTERS, WE HAVE SEEN HOW THE PEOPLE have acted through government to regulate industrial and labor relations in this country for the general welfare. Throughout most of the century and a half since 1790, we have been able to frame our state and national policies, largely on the basis of domestic, rather than international, conditions. The fact that we have been at peace for most of this period has made it easier for us to build up our American standard of living and to promote the general welfare at home.

Because we have been for the most part free from the fear of foreign attack during the past century, we have not had to face the alternative confronting the peoples of many other countries. During much of this period, these countries have maintained great armies in order to protect what they considered their national interests. Their cost has been a charge against the national income, leaving less available for other public and for private uses.

Almost inevitably, paying for large armaments has meant lower standards of living for the people. The choice between

262

"guns or butter", which Hitler forced on the German people in order to take part in an armaments race, has not, however, until recently been a matter of great concern to us. That we have not had to divert our energies and our resources from normal peacetime activities to meet the danger of foreign aggression has meant that we have been able to develop more stable industrial and labor relations at home. In previous chapters, we have observed our progress in this field from decade to decade throughout our history, a progress which has been both continuous and notable. Only once in nearly a century—from 1816 to 1914—was our domestic security seriously threatened by foreign war.

War—or the threat of war—disturbs these relations more immediately and more profoundly than any other factor in a nation's economy. The First World War had made us realize how directly war affects every group in the nation—consumers, workers, employers, farmers. When the Second World War broke out on September 1, 1939, the experience of 1914–1918 was repeated on a far wider and deeper scale. It became increasingly clear that we could not escape its worldwide effects on our economic and social as well as on our political relations, whether or not we remained neutral. We were suddenly confronted with the necessity of building up our own national defenses at an unprecedented rate. Again, as the war progressed, we shaped our foreign policy toward increasing aid, in munitions and other supplies, to the countries fighting the Axis powers. Even the threat of war began to be felt throughout our economy.

We followed this dual policy, of expanding national defense and of aiding the anti-Axis governments, more intensively month by month after 1939. When Japan attacked Pearl Harbor on December 7, 1941 and we were forced into war against the Axis powers, the effect of war on our economy was quickly and sharply intensified. As our war effort gathered momentum, its effects spread to every home and store and factory in the nation. The American people were faced by sudden and unexpected changes in their normal activities—their peacetime way of life. Total war had come home to the nation.

Industrial and labor relations are not less important to the general welfare in wartime than in peacetime. How total war affects different groups, how it disturbs these relations is, therefore, a matter of direct concern to all of us. We may well, then, review our war record in those fields of industrial and labor relations in which we have noted the growth of public policy and private action during peace. We shall be better able to appraise how—and how far—we, the people, have succeeded in meeting the challenge of total war to our American practice of free government and free enterprise.

We Meet the Challenge
Preserving the Nation's Standard of Living Within A War Economy

In Chapter 4, we noted how recurring cycles of prosperity and depression affect the standard of living of different groups within the nation. In Chapter 10, we reviewed how we have acted through government to insure an adequate level of living for the workers by setting minimum-wage and maximum-hour standards. What have we done during the war to preserve this interest of the workers—and of all the people—in a high and stable standard of living?

Total war requires the gearing of the total effort of all the people to producing the sinews of war. More and more of a nation's productive capacity must be diverted to making the materials essential to modern mechanized warfare—guns, planes, tanks, ships, munitions, and countless other items. Smaller and smaller quantities of consumers goods will be produced because raw materials and factories will necessarily be converted to war needs. At the same time, as more and more people are employed in war industries, they will have more money in their pockets—to spend for a smaller total of consumers goods on the market. Merchants will charge higher prices for their limited stocks and consumers will be willing to pay higher prices in order to obtain a share of the dwindling supplies of the things they want. This widening spread between purchasing power measured by a rising national income—and available supplies of goods inevitably creates economic instability. Unless the spread is reduced by positive checks, the entire economy runs into a rising spiral of higher wages and salaries, higher costs and prices. What did we do to meet these problems?

Gearing Our Economy To Total War

Even before we entered the war, it was apparent that unless measures were taken to meet the likelihood of inflation, our standards of living would inevitably be reduced. If these standards were to be maintained, a broad attack on many economic fronts had to be launched. Without detailing all the measures taken by government during the past three years, we may analyze briefly how we sought to maintain our living standards and a more or less stable economy in the face of total war.

One of the most urgent problems confronting a government in wartime is to obtain the maximum production of materials needed for total war and at the same time to provide the necessary consumers goods to protect the people's health and welfare. Raw materials must be carefully allocated to the uses most essential to the war effort. Whole plants—even individual machines—must be assigned to producing those items which would best serve the needs of the nation, whether for war or for the home front. Manpower must be used wherever it could be most efficiently applied to the job of winning the war. Only so could our available resources be geared to the production of the ships and planes and guns which we required for victory.

From the point of view of industry, the national government developed several policies which have vitally affected our peacetime ideas and practices as to free enterprise. In order to obtain the maximum amount of essential war materials in the shortest possible time, various controls were established. First, a system of priorities* in the use of raw materials was set up. Under this system, whole industries as well as individual plants were required to shift to war production; otherwise they could not continue to operate.

Later, two further controls were established, affecting particularly the wholesale and retail markets—ultimately the consumers directly. First in order came rationing. It was introduced, both to save critical raw materials from being used in producing non-essential goods and to insure a fair distribution of the available supplies of all goods among those requiring them. Under rationing, the sale of certain producers and consumers goods was altogether prohibited. The sale of other items was regulated, as to who might have how much of these goods (e.g. refrigerators, automobiles, tires, gas, foods, shoes, etc.). As the war developed, rationing spread further and further through our economy until practically all consumers goods were controlled or rationed—to guarantee the fairest possible distribution.

After rationing came price-fixing. Price-fixing differs in

---

* Priorities control of raw materials, semi-manufactured goods (e.g. steel bars), or machinery means that those items under priority could be obtained by various industries or plants only in accordance with a rationing plan set up by the government (first, the Office of Production Management, later, the War Production Board). Thus, one industry might have a 1-A, another a 1-B classification, and so on. Only after the industries (or plants) at the top of the list had obtained what they needed for their war production, could those lower down the list obtain critical materials.

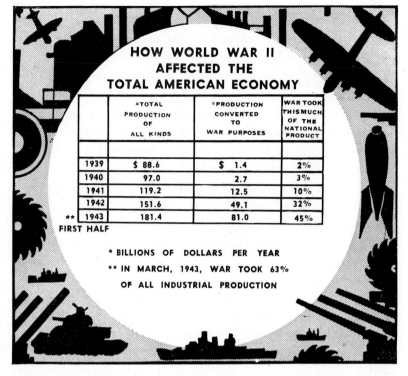

HOW WORLD WAR II AFFECTED THE TOTAL AMERICAN ECONOMY

	*TOTAL PRODUCTION OF ALL KINDS	*PRODUCTION CONVERTED TO WAR PURPOSES	WAR TOOK THIS MUCH OF THE NATIONAL PRODUCT
1939	$ 88.6	$ 1.4	2%
1940	97.0	2.7	3%
1941	119.2	12.5	10%
1942	151.6	49.1	32%
** 1943 FIRST HALF	181.4	81.0	45%

* BILLIONS OF DOLLARS PER YEAR

** IN MARCH, 1943, WAR TOOK 63%
OF ALL INDUSTRIAL PRODUCTION

purpose from rationing. The major objective of price-fixing is not to insure a fair distribution of a limited supply. Rather, it is to prevent inflation by restricting price rises, even though the supply of a given product is not critically short. Price-fixing of raw materials and other producers goods began in 1941 under the Office of Price Administration. At first, it was more or less voluntary. Under the Price Control Act of February 28, 1942, however, compulsory rent and price control over practically our total economy was established by law. Various changes have been made (to May, 1943) in the actual application of price-fixing to particular segments of the economy (e.g. salaries, wages, farm prices). The policy is still, however, in general effect and price-fixing controls are widespread both in the producers and consumers markets and as to wages and salaries of those engaged in war production. The law of supply and demand, which determines prices in a free-enterprise economy, has thus been controlled in order to avoid inflation.

A second broad aspect of gearing our economy to total war related particularly to industrial workers. First, as to hours and wages, the national government sought to maintain the 40-hour-week principle of the Fair Labor Standards Act (Ch. 10) during the shift from a peacetime to a wartime economy. One of the major interests of the workers—a ceiling over hours—was, then, in large part retained. Wherever the basic work-week was changed to 44 or 48 hours, usually in areas of labor shortages, it was done (to May, 1943) by order of the War Manpower Commission (see p. 283) to meet emergency needs in war industries.

As the demand for workers in war industries increased, we were faced by the necessity of drawing upon our reserves of women and young people to fill up the ranks of industry on the home front. Some states, among them New York, enacted laws modifying existing legislative standards as to maximum hours and allowable industrial occupations for women and children.

In general these laws allow women and children to work longer hours, or at night, and to enter industries from which, because of health or other hazards, they had been excluded. In New York, any requests by employers to modify existing standards receive ample review to protect the people's interest in fair labor conditions. First, these requests are reviewed by the State War Council* which sends on the request to the Industrial Com-

* The State War Council was created by an act of the Legislature in 1942 (Laws of 1942, Ch. 544) "for the general purpose of aiding the war effort by formulating and assisting in the execution of plans for the mobilization and efficient utilization of the resources and facilities of the state and for the coordination and direction of state and local activities related to civilian protection and to state and national defense". It includes 20 members, representing the Legislature, the Executive Department, and the public. The Governor serves as chairman.

missioner for determining their necessity. The Industrial Commissioner's decision on the request is subject to further review by the Board of Standards and Appeals.* A request may be denied if the health or safety of women and young people appear to be endangered by granting the request. In this way, again, we have sought to protect new workers against being exploited by requiring adequate safeguards.

If we have sought to maintain a ceiling over hours, what about the floor under wages? In a period of rapidly expanding production, such as that after 1938, the problem of maintaining a wage level adequate to a decent standard of living for the workers hardly existed. The problem, from the point of view of preventing inflation, was, in fact, just the opposite. An increasing proportion of employed workers received large overtime payments under the 40-hour standard as the war industries expanded. The demand for workers in these industries tended, moreover, to push the general wage level rapidly upwards. Competition among employers for new workers made it easy for all workers to demand higher wages. The operation of the law of supply and demand in this field, if uncontrolled, would have resulted in an inflationary spiral of wages—and so prices—no less severe than on the industrial side of our economy.

In an effort to meet this problem, the President suggested to Congress in his message of April 27, 1942, that wages and salaries ("remuneration for work") should be stabilized. "Stabilizing the cost of living will mean that wages in general can and should be kept at existing levels". In a radio address on the next day, he said directly to the workers, "You will have to forego higher wages for your particular work for the duration".

What does this mean in practice? An answer was given by

---

* The Board of Standards and Appeals was created in 1937 by an act of the Legislature, within the Department of Labor. It is composed of three members appointed by the Governor for six-year, staggered terms.

the National War Labor Board in one of its decisions, in which three principles were laid down as to wartime wage fixing.

First, all workmen shall receive wages sufficiently high to enable them to maintain a standard of living compatible with health and decency.

Second, the real wage levels which have been previously arrived at through the channels of collective bargaining and which do not impede maximum production of war materials shall be reasonably protected.

Third, to the extent that it can be done without inflationary effects, labor should be encouraged to negotiate through the processes of collective bargaining for fair and reasonable upward wage adjustments as an offset against increases in the cost of living. Labor should not be put in an economic strait-jacket during the war without redress to some such agency as the War Labor Board, which has authority to grant fair and deserved wage adjustments.*

By these principles, we recognized that, for workers as for employers, the necessity of gearing our economy to total war must be accepted and adhered to. By developing a broad attack upon the causes of inflation, we sought to stabilize the nation's standard of living within a war economy.

The Chance For A Job

In Chapters 5, 6 and 11, we reviewed the workers' efforts to find or to keep their jobs in a free economy with its cycles of boom and depression. This question became more important again after 1939, especially in the new war industries. On the one hand, the shift to war-production created difficulties for many employers. They found it difficult, if not impossible, to keep their factories running at full capacity; much was heard of "priorities unemployment". That question, as we have seen,

* Decision of the War Labor Board in The International Harvester case (April 15, 1942).

soon resolved itself. On the other hand, some employers, and some labor unions, put bars in the way of some workers finding jobs—for reasons of residence or of race or religion. How did we meet this issue?

Residence or Race—On the Firing Line and in the Factory

Even before 1930, many states prohibited migratory workers, or any other persons without financial security of their own, from crossing their state boundaries to seek work. By 1942, 27 states had enacted such laws, limiting the right of residents of other states to cross their borders looking for jobs.

The situation had become so acute by the end of 1941 that a special committee (the Committee on Defense Migration) was appointed by Congress to study this problem. Officials from the 48 states were also invited by the national government to meet in Washington on May 5, 1942. The individual states were requested and, in general, agreed to revise their laws regarding non-resident workers so as to make it possible for them to move wherever war work was available and industrial manpower was needed.

Race and religion were other bars to full employment of all the nation's manpower during the 1930's and 1940's. Some workers, for the most part but not exclusively negroes, could not get jobs in many industries. Some employers would not hire negroes. In other cases, it was the workers themselves who refused to work side by side with negroes or members of other races.

Here was a difficult question for which no clear or easy answer was to be found. Although a number of unions admitted negroes to membership, many still excluded them. Some states, notably New York, had enacted laws prohibiting discrimination in hiring workers because of race, creed or color. These laws, however, were not enough to meet the barriers which some

271

employers and some labor unions had set against these workers. If these barriers were to be allowed to operate, especially in war industries, full production could not be achieved.

New York was one of the first states to seek ways of ending racial or religious discrimination in industry. On March 29, 1941, the Governor announced the appointment of a special committee (under the State Defense Council, later the State War Council) "to consider ways and means of dealing with the problem of discrimination in employment on defense contracts". The Committee included representatives of industry, labor, civic agencies, and state government departments, under the chairmanship of the Industrial Commissioner. Since its organization, it has conducted a number of inquiries into cases in which such discrimination was charged in war industries or by private employment agencies.

Upon recommendation of the Committee a bill was also enacted (May 6, 1942, Laws of 1942, Chapter 677) to help meet this problem. It granted the Industrial Commissioner specific power to enforce those provisions of the Civil Rights Law which prohibit discrimination against workers because of race, color or religion. Hitherto, the enforcement of this law had been left to the person who had been discriminated against. Now, the state itself undertook to make this legal bar to racial or religious discrimination effective directly through an official agency, the State Department of Labor.

On June 25, 1941, a Committee on Fair Employment Practices within the National Office of Production Management was established by executive order. This Committee, consisting of five unpaid members, was "to receive and investigate complaints of discrimination . . . and take appropriate steps to redress grievances which it finds to be valid". The order further provided that all vocational and training programs should be administered without racial or religious discrimination. Per-

WOMEN ENTER INDUSTRY AND REPLACE MEN IN WARTIME

©UNDERWOOD & UNDERWOOD

	TOTAL NUMBER EMPLOYED	NUMBER OF WOMEN EMPLOYED	PERCENTAGE OF WOMEN IN TOTAL EMPLOYED
	12,505,923	1,836,288	14.7
	17,392,099	2,647,157	15.2
	23,318,183	4,005,532	17.2
	29,073,233	5,319,397	18.3
	38,167,336	8,075,772	21.2
	41,614,248	8,549,511	20.5
	48,829,920	10,752,116	22.0
RIL	45,100,000	11,000,000	24.4
ER	47,000,000	10,800,000	23.0
RIL	46,800,000	10,600,000	22.6
ER	50,200,000	12,300,000	24.5
RIL	50,700,000	12,900,000	25.4
R	52,400,000	14,300,000	27.3
RIL	51,200,000	15,200,000	29.7
■ = 5,000,000 TOTAL NUMBER EMPLOYED		■ = 1,000,000 NUMBER OF WOMEN EMPLOYED	● = 30% OF WOMEN IN TOTAL EMPLOYED

haps the most important provision was that all defense contracts must include an agreement "obligating the contractor not to discriminate against any worker because of race, creed, color, or national origin".

A new executive order was issued on May 28, 1943, increasing the Committee on Fair Employment Practice to seven, a chairman and not more than six members. The committee was transferred from the War Manpower Commission to the Executive Office of the President; this shift brought the whole question of discrimination directly under the President's immediate review and possible action. In an important decision shortly afterwards (on June 5, 1943), the National War Labor Board ordered the Southport Petroleum Company of Texas to discontinue using "colored laborers" and "white laborers" in classifying their laborers—with different pay rates for the two groups. In its opinion, the Board stated, "this wage increase (for colored laborers) is made . . . with regard simply for the democratic formula of equal work in quantity and quality in the same classification". Although the Board's order applied to a single company, it marked the first step toward enforcing the principle of no discrimination in our war industries.

In these ways, we, the people, have acted through our governments, state and national, to insure the chance for a job for members of every creed and race, irrespective of where they live. Just as democracy demands equal sacrifice by all in battle, so it should guarantee to all an equal right to work on the home front. By the policies we have established in this field, we have sought to make that principle effective.

Preventing Strikes in War Industries

In Chapters 5–8, we reviewed the ways in which we have acted through government in peacetime to prevent industrial disputes. On the one hand, we have regulated the methods by

274

which workers or employers have sought to enforce their demands against each other. On the other hand, we have established public agencies for mediating or arbitrating disputes between these two groups. What steps did we take to preserve and promote industrial peace during wartime—in order to maintain our production?

Employers and Workers Cooperate for Maximum Production

We have already seen how workers and employers have increasingly adopted collective bargaining agreements for settling every kind of dispute without resort to strikes or lockouts. Many of these agreements had already been made in many basic industries converted to war production after 1939, as for instance, in the aircraft industry. Similar agreements were quickly made in many other war industries, new and old. In some, such as the automobile industry, where collective bargaining was already in force, the agreements had been drafted so as to cover any disputes which might arise even under wartime conditions.

Another development took place in a number of war industries during and after 1939—a cooperative system of management-labor committees. To these committees an equal number of workers' and employers' representatives were appointed by each group to consider ways and means of speeding up production. These committees submitted their proposals—all the way from improvements on a single machine to industry-wide programs for better working conditions—to the employees who were, more often than not, ready to adopt them. Through these committees, the workers were given a further incentive by participating actively in the day-to-day policy-making of their plant or their industry.

Beyond these collective bargaining agreements, the workers acted through their unions to limit voluntarily their right to

275

strike. On January 23, 1942, the A.F of L. and C.I.O. issued a joint declaration of their intent not to engage in any strike during the war. On March 26, 1942, William Green of the A.F. of L. and Philip Murray of the C.I.O. appeared before the House of Representatives' Naval Affairs Committee and repeated the pledge. They indicated that they had already acted to stop several "outlaw strikes" called by local unions without the authority of the national office.

The agreement not to strike was not adhered to, however, in all cases. Some strikes, which have retarded production in war plants for several days or weeks, have actually occurred. Workers desired further guarantees that their interest in adequate security would be protected in a rapidly changing economy. This desire was recognized as reasonable, and we, the people, acted through our government to insure it.

First, the existing national and state agencies for reconciling employer-worker conflicts, which we have already seen in action, continued to operate in wartime. The United States Conciliaton Servce, the State Boards of Mediation, and the National and State Labor Relations Boards were available—and widely used —to settle disputes in war industries as in others. Workers and employers engaged in war production already had available, therefore, various public agencies to aid them in settling their differences peacefully—and quickly.

Congress also granted to the President power to take over and operate any private plant or other private war agency in which either employers or workers were holding up production. The power has been exercised only a few times, chiefly when a labor dispute was not settled promptly and directly between the workers and their employers. The most notable instances were those of an airplane plant in California, a shipyard in New Jersey, a railroad in Illinois, and the coal mines. In each case the government took over the plants in order to expedite production or transportation and returned them to their owners as soon as sound labor relations were established.

Even before we entered the war, we had begun to develop other specialized agencies to deal with labor problems in war industries. As the war-production program continued to expand, the need for a still more effective agency for handling labor disputes was recognized. On March 19, 1941, the National Defense Mediation Board was established by executive order. The membership of this Board, appointed by the President, included 11 members, four representing the employers, four, the workers, and three, the public.

The Board did not succeed in settling one difficult dispute in an important defense industry. The United Mine Workers of America threatened to strike in November, 1941, unless their demand for the closed shop in "captive coal mines" was recognized. These mines, owned by several large industries, such as steel, had not yet been brought within the general closed-shop agreement in effect throughout most of the coal industry.

After the Board's failure to settle this dispute, the C.I.O. representatives resigned. This meant, in effect, that the Board could no longer render useful service in future disputes because one of the two great national labor-union organizations declined to share in its work. It was, therefore, clear to all groups—workers, employers, and government—that some other agency for solving the problem of future strikes must be established.

One recommendation of a labor-management conference called by the President for December 17, 1941, was that the national government should create a new board to try to avoid future labor disputes in war industries. This recommendation was adopted and the War Labor Board was established by executive order on January 12, 1942. By the order, the

AMERICA IN THE 1940's

© Underwood and Underwood

personnel and records of the National Defense Mediation Board were transferred to the new Board.

The Board, appointed by the President, consists of 12 members, four representing, respectively the public, employers, and workers, with an equal number of alternates from each group. The President designates the Chairman and Vice-Chairman. Six members may act in any dispute, provided that at least two representatives of each group serve in the case.

The Board may intervene in a labor dispute only after the voluntary efforts of the parties to settle it and mediation by the United States Conciliation Service have failed. At this stage in a dispute, the Secretary of Labor certifies it to the Board. The Board may also act on its own intiative after consulting the Secretary of Labor. Its powers, as defined by the executive order, are broad. "After it takes jurisdiction, (it) shall finally determine the dispute, and for this purpose may use mediaton, voluntary arbtration (i.e. by the parties themselves), or arbitration under rules established by the Board".

The no-strike pledge of the A.F. of L. and the C.I.O. did not, however, prevent all strikes in war industries. The most important threat to war production came from the United Mine Workers of America in the spring of 1943. The union, through its Policy Committee, made several demands for increased pay during the negotiations with the mine owners for new contracts. After the owners rejected these demands, the union refused to submit the dispute to the National War Labor Board and threatened to call a nationwide strike in the coal mines. When a walkout from the mines was actually ordered, the President intervened to require that both sides submit their cases to the National War Labor Board for a decision as to the merits of the demands made by the miners. After a report by the Board, recommending slight pay increases but denying the miners' major demands, the Policy Committee of the U.M.W.A. again ordered a walkout. This time, the President acted, first, to take over the mines under the power already noted, and, second, to order the miners back to work, under the direction of the Federal Solid Fuels Administrator, the Secretary of the Interior. Each stoppage of work resulted in material loss of production.

This failure to live up to the no-strike pledge by one of the major unions in a critical war industry produced a sharp public reaction. In Congress, the Smith-Connally Bill, one of several which had been introduced to regulate strikes in war industries, was quickly brought up for debate and passed in both houses. Labor groups and others urged the veto of the bill on the ground that it was "coercive", too restrictive of labor's rights, and unnecessary in view of the no-strike pledge. The President vetoed the bill. The President also recommended that Congress consider the extension of the Selective Service System to all men up to 65 years of age. He proposed that all workers be placed under the jurisdiction of the federal government which could thus control their actions to the same degree as those men liable for military service. Without acting on this recommendation, both houses of Congress repassed the bill on the same day the veto message was received—by majorities substantially above the necessary two-thirds. This action reflected a widespread popular feeling that strikes in war industries should not be allowed to occur.

The provisions of the War Labor Disputes Act of 1943 (Smith-Connally Bill) mark a considerable advance in federal control over labor disputes in wartime. It is to remain in effect not longer than six months after the termination of hostilities and may be repealed earlier by joint resolution of Congress. The Act covers labor disputes in any plant, mine, or facility (excep the railroads) contributing directly or indirectly to war production. One of its most important provisions is found in section 7 which gives the National War Labor Board legislative recognition. Its powers are the same as those defined in the executive order creating it, but the Act confers additional power to intervene directly "if (in its opinion) a labor dispute has become so serious that it may lead to substantial interference with the war effort". It is also given power "to decide the disputes, and provide by order the wages and hours and all other terms and conditions (customarily included in collective bargaining agreements) governing the relations between the parties". These powers do not apply to plants, mines, or facilities already taken over by the government. In a government-operated industry, the terms of existing agreements, at the time the industry is taken over shall continue to apply. A majority of the employees may, however, apply to the National War Labor Board for a change in the terms, which the Board may grant after hearings. If granted, the new conditions must be complied with by the government agency operating the industry.

The President's power to take over a plant, mine, or facility is extended and defined by section 3 of the Act. After investigation, he may proclaim that there will be an interruption of war production by reason of a "strike, lock-out, threatened strike, threatened lock-out, work-stoppage, or other cause". Upon such a proclamation, the industry is to be taken over by the designated government agency for a period not over 60 days after the "restoration of productive efficiency". By section 5 of the Act, any person who "coerces, instigates, induces, conspires with, or encourages" others, or aids anyone in doing so, to produce a lock-out, strike, or slow-down in such a plant is subject to a fine of not over $5,000 or imprisonment for not over one year, or both.

Section 8 of the Act, with which the President disagreed in his veto message, provides that employees in any war plant, mine, or facility may notify their employer, and the Secretary of Labor, the National War Labor Board, and the National Labor

Relations Board of any dispute which may lead to a strike or work-stoppage. For a period of not less than 30 days after the notice, production must continue under existing conditions, except as they may be modified by mutual agreement or by the National Labor Relations Board. On the thirtieth day after the notice, the National Labor Relations Board must take a secret ballot of all the employees as to whether "they will permit any such interruption of war production". The ballots must contain a brief statement of the major issues involved in the dispute. The result of the vote is to be certified by the Board—to whom, is not defined by the Act.

A further restriction on labor unions, similar to those applying to banks and other corporations, was written into section 9. None of these groups may make contributions in connection with any election in which a federal official is a candidate for office.

The Act as a whole marks a considerable advance in federal regulation of labor in wartime. It is a significant example of the wide range of the government's war powers.

A special agency to prevent strikes on the nation's railroads during wartime was also created by executive order on May 22, 1942—the National Railway Labor Panel. The Panel is composed of nine members, appointed by the President for the duration of the war and six months thereafter, none of whom may be interested in the railroad industry. This Panel has broad powers as to railroad labor disputes. Any dispute which is not settled by direct action of the parties or by any of the other public agencies in this field (see Chapter 8, pp. 166 ff.) must be finally settled without a strike or stoppage of work. Even in the absence of a strike vote, "a threatened interruption of commerce" is reviewable by the Panel, after the dispute has been referred to it by the National Mediation Board or any other agency. It then has "exclusive and final jurisdiction of the dispute and shall make every reasonable effort to settle" it.

A second broad field in which the problem of expanding our war production called for action by government was that of manpower. The Selective Service System called millions of workers into the armed forces. Their places had to be filled—and millions of new workers recruited—if war production was to keep pace with our own and our Allies' demands. On April 18, 1942, the War Manpower Commission was created by executive, order. Composed of the heads (or their representatives) of eight federal agencies, with the Federal Security Administrator as chairman, it was given general control over the nation's industrial manpower program. The United States Employment Service was placed under it and used increasingly to recruit new workers for war industries and for agriculture. The Commission determined essential occupations, workers in which must be deferred from induction in the armed forces in order to keep production at full speed ahead. It also used its authority to "freeze" workers in those occupations considered most vital in order to prevent competitive "bidding" by employers for workers and thus, perhaps, dislocate the production program as a whole. As the war progressed, the Commission's powers were used to conserve and direct manpower on the entire home front in order to achieve the highest possible efficiency in its use for essential war work.

This brief account of how we have attempted to meet the challenge of total war in this country is only part of the story of the present and the future. Ahead lie new problems in industrial and labor relations. Just as we have had to meet the challenge of war, we shall have also have to meet the challenge of peace. Although the challenge may not be so sudden, it will be hardly less far-reaching—and no less important for us to meet. What are some of the principles which may guide us toward even more stable industrial and labor relations in the America of the future?

The Challenge of the Peace

The American Tradition Has Given Us A Chart for the Future

The preceding chapters have reviewed how we, the people, have acted through government to protect and promote the general welfare in many fields of industrial and labor relations. We have seen how the need for our government to act has developed out of the changes in our economy over the past 150 years. We have seen, too, that the reasons why and the ways in which we have acted have come out of, and indeed become a part of, the American tradition (see Chapters 1–6).

One element in that tradition is our belief in democratic government based on the will of the people expressed through representatives of our own choosing. Through our representatives, we make laws defining the rights and duties of everyone within the nation. What rights and duties we shall regulate by law is (as we have seen in this record of our action to control industrial relations in the past) determined by their bearing on the general welfare. They become a matter of public concern when the actions of private individuals and groups, including workers and employers, affect the whole community. We believe that what shall be defined as questions of public concern can be best determined by the consent of the governed. When we give power to our representatives to act for us, the people, we retain the right to direct them in their use of the powers which we have granted to them. In the last analysis, we, the people, determine the line between private action and public policy.

A second element in the American tradition is our belief that the best way to achieve the general welfare in economic terms is to maintain our system of free enterprise. There have been many changes since 1789 in the way our economy works. As it has developed toward its present urban-industrial pattern, the

WE THE PEOPLE

THE TRADITION LIVES IN GRANITE

TO FORM A MORE PERFECT UNION

relations of employers and workers have become increasingly important tests of the justice and efficiency of our free-enterprise system.

Within that system, we continue to believe, however, that both justice and efficiency can be best achieved by allowing the greatest possible freedom to men and women. We believe, further, that by far the best way to adjust conflicting interests is to induce those who think their interests conflict to try to settle their own differences. The general welfare in economic terms will, we think, be most certainly secured by recalling to private individuals and groups their community responsibility. We believe this because we are convinced that duties as well as rights, obligations as well as interests, are deeply rooted in the American tradition of free government and free enterprise.

This tradition is being challenged today by competing ideas about government and alternative economic systems. Those who deny the principles of democracy in government and in the economy believe that rights belong only to the leaders of government or of industry or of labor. The people have only a duty to obey. The interests of the leaders are the obligations of the followers. Freedom exists only for those on top in government, industry, or labor. Those who do not possess power, or do not seize it for themselves, have no voice or choice in government or in the choice and conduct of their daily work.

These ideas are being promoted by the leaders of more than one nation—by war itself—as challenges to the American tradition, to our way of living and working together. They must be met in the peace which lies ahead if our system of free government and of free enterprise is to endure. They must be met especially in the field of industrial and labor relations for these relations are a major test of free enterprise and ultimately of free government itself. What are the rights and responsibilities of employers and workers in this process and what role does

ESTABLISH JUSTICE

THE TRADITION LIVES IN GRANITE

INSURE DOMESTIC TRANQUILLITY

government have in meeting this challenge of the future?

Rights and Responsibilities in a Free Enterprise System

We have reviewed the actions we have taken, the policies we have pursued in our country to promote the general welfare (see Chapters 5–11). We have observed in the different fields of industrial and labor relations how the rights and responsibilities of employers and workers have, in part at least, been defined through our democratic government. We have seen also how we have left some areas in our economy free from governmental control—in order to allow workers and employers to determine their own actions. It is in these areas that the challenge of the peace will be most direct—that rights and responsibilities will be considered further by the people. It is in these areas, too, that the role which government should play in the economic life of the nation will be tested.

The record we have reviewed in the earlier chapters suggests certain ways in which these questions may be answered in the future. One way is becoming increasingly recognized as fundamental to preserving free government and free enterprise. It is that rights and responsibilities—for groups no less than for individuals—must be balanced. Only as the exercise of a particular right claimed by any individual or group is matched by the recognition of an equal responsibility in its use can a just society be established. Otherwise, dictatorship, economic or political, will result. Rights, in short, must be defined in terms of a balance of responsibilities if freedom is to have meaning.

The idea of balancing the rights asserted by different groups within the nation has been a basic principle of our national life at least since the framing of the constitution. Writing in Number X of The Federalist, Madison explained the principle of balance as essential in a stable society, for a stable government.

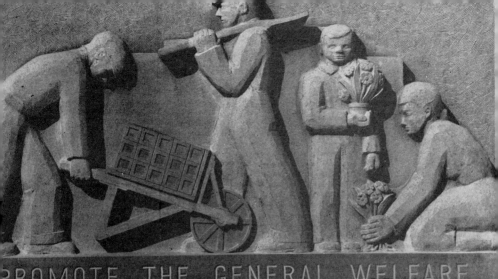

LS, UNITED STATES DEPARTMENT OF JUSTICE BUILDING, WASHINGTON, D. C.   Courtesy of Farm Security Administration

Among the numerous advantages promised by a well-constructed Union, none deserves to be more accurately developed than its tendency to break and control the violence of faction. . . .

Complaints are everywhere heard from our most considerate and virtuous citizens, equally the friends of public and private faith, and of public and personal liberty, that our governments are too unstable, that the public good is disregarded in the conflicts of rival parties, and that measures are too often decided, not according to the rules of justice and the rights of the minor party, but by the superior force of an interested and overbearing majority . . .

By a faction, I understand a number of citizens, whether amounting to a majority or minority of the whole, who are united and actuated by some common impulse of passion, or of interest, adverse to the rights of other citizens, or to the permanent and aggregate interests of the community.

There are two methods of curing the mischiefs of faction: the one, by removing its causes; the other, by controlling its effects . . .

289

The most common and durable source of factions has been the various and unequal distribution of property. Those who hold and those who are without property have ever formed distinct interests in society. Those who are creditors, and those who are debtors, fall under a like discriminaton. A landed interest, a manufacturing interest, a mercantile interest, a moneyed interest, with many lesser interests, grow up of necessity in civilized nations, and divide them into different classes, actuated by different sentiments and views. The regulation of these various and interfering interests forms the principal task of modern legislation, and involves the spirit of party and faction in the necessary and ordinary operations of the government. . . .

The inference to which we are brought is, that the *causes* of faction cannot be removed, and that relief is only to be sought in the means of controlling its *effects*. . . .

By what means is this object obtainable? Evidently by one of two only. Either the existence of the same passion or interest in a majority at the same time must be prevented, or the majority, having such co-existent passion or interest, must be rendered, by their number and local situation, unable to concert and carry into effect schemes of oppression.*

Madison goes on to point out how, in a federation of sovereign states bound together under the constitution, but independent as to their internal affairs, the balance of the "effects of faction" is achieved. It is unlikely that a majority on any question of public policy will exist in all the states at one time. No majority will, therefore, be able even temporarily to override the interests of the minority. A balance of interests will be maintained on which the rights of the minority can rest securely.

We have recognized this principle of balancing rights and duties in many aspects of our life as a nation, not least in

* *The Federalist* (Everyman ed.), pp. 41–44.

industrial and labor relations. Certain basic rights have been guaranteed to employers and to workers in our constitutions and laws. Special responsibilities in the exercise of these rights have been no less clearly defined through government. What are some of these rights and responsibilities which each group now possesses within the framework of our political democracy?

We have already seen, for instance, (see Chapter 5, pp. 100 ff.) that our federal constitution guarantees that no person shall be deprived "of life, liberty, or property without due process of law". This principle guarantees, among other things, the right of everyone to use his property as he chooses, subject to the police power of the states and of the nation. Were this all, the balance of actual power would lie on the side of the strongest individual or group, of those who possessed most property—in whatever form it is measured.

This is, however, not all. We have balanced this right by defining other rights, by stating the responsibilities which must go with the exercise of this right. We have abolished slavery by national action in the Thirteenth Amendment. In New York State, we have gone even further. By an amendment to the State Constitution (Article I, Section 17) adopted by the people in 1938, we have defined the right of private property by limiting its exercise as to persons. That amendment states:

> Labor of human beings is not a commodity nor an article of commerce and shall never be so considered or construed.

By this amendment, we, the people, have acted to balance one right by another, to match one right by a special responsibility in its use.

Other examples will illustrate the same point. In Chapters 5 and 6, we noted how the rights of private property were limited through government in the field of collective bargaining.

The employers' right to "hire and fire" whom they choose was balanced by the workers' right to join unions of their own choosing. In New York State we did not rely on the force of a law alone to guarantee this right; we placed it directly in the Constitution itself by the same amendment noted above:

> Employees shall have the right to organize and bargain collectively through representatives of their own choosing.

Whether we acted through legislative or constitutional channels is not important. We took whatever action was necessary to guarantee this right of the workers against any exercise of the rights of private property which might limit it.

Again in Chapter 7, we reviewed some of the rights which the workers asserted against their employers, such as the right to use pickets to enforce their demands in a strike. Here was an important weapon in the workers' hands, a right which they wished to exercise as they chose in order to gain their ends. It was limited by law in order to prevent the employers' rights in their property or liberty from being unduly limited or even destroyed. Conflicting interests were adjusted by balancing the right of one group to organize and act to win collective bargaining, by requiring certain responsibilities in its exercise.

In Chapters 9–11, we reviewed other ways in which the employers' right of private property has been balanced by the workers' right to just compensation. Industrial accidents and diseases are no longer left to be the individual responsibility of the injured worker or his family. Instead, we have—by our workmen's compensation laws—placed this responsibility on the employers. Under these laws, they must restore the workers' ability to work and to pay for any accident or disease resulting from their employment. Again, by our minimum wage and fair-labor-standards laws, we have acted to guarantee the workers' right to a living wage. Through our unemployment laws, we have recognized the principle of protecting the workers who have lost their jobs through no fault of their own. Finally, through our old-age insurance system we have sought to prevent hardship to our workers no longer able to work. The rights of workers in each of these fields which have been recognized by the people acting through government have been balanced by responsibilities imposed on employers to accept them.

These examples suggest how far we have already gone in applying the principle of a balance of rights and responsibilities in industrial and labor relations—to both employers and workers. The private actions of workers and employers have often recognized the principle in practice. Voluntary collective bargaining is, as we have seen (see Chapter 8, pp. 166 ff.), already generally accepted in American industry today. When workers and employers are unable to adjust their disputes themselves, we have established public agencies of mediation and arbitration—thus calling the attention of both groups to their responsibility to all the people. That responsibility rests on the principle that gains won, interests secured, through private action must not disturb the peace and welfare of the community. We have seen, too, how even in wartime, the same principle is being applied by both private and public action.

The principle has been defined clearly and cogently by our own Legislature in New York State, through one of its committees:

> The rights and obligations of employers in all worker-employer relationships should be commensurate with the rights and obligations of the workers.*

Thus, the American tradition as to a balance of rights and responsibilities in industrial and labor relations is framed for us today—and tomorrow.

* Report of the New York State Joint Legislative Committee on Industrial and Labor Relations (1939) p. 17.

As we review the record of the past and consider the challenge of the future peace, what can we say of the role of government in the days ahead? What does the American tradition suggest as to the part it will play in postwar reconstruction? What principles should guide us here?

In addition to our free-enterprise system, another element lives in the American tradition—representative government on a democratic basis. Throughout our history, we have sought to make it more effective. Today, we are defending it with our lives. Tomorrow, we shall again be using it, as we have in the past, to promote the general welfare in peacetime. How can we, the people, most surely act through government to achieve it?

As we recall how we, the people, have acted in the past in the various fields of industrial and labor relations, we can see one principle of democratic government at work—majority rule limited by minority rights. The policies we make through our legislative representatives and the actions of our executive and administrative officers in applying them are governed by this principle. Whether or not we have always followed the principle in practice, it is a central—perhaps, indeed, the central— foundation of our democratic society.

Government from this point of view is, then as James Madison pointed out in No. X of *The Federalist Papers,* the referee of private interests and conflicting claims. We act through government to protect the rights of minorities as well as to define those of the majority, to register the responsibilities of the majority not less than those of the minority. Through government, we make the rules within which all individuals and groups in the nation carry on their own activities and relations. In order to give as much free play as possible to all persons, we act through government only when the general welfare is threatened by some positive action of one against another.

If the balance of power in a field of conflict between rival individuals or groups swings too far one way, we use governmental powers to establish the balance. If rules already made are broken, we apply penalities to those who are responsible. If new rules are needed to keep the balance even, we make them through our representatives.

In and through our democratic government, then, we have created the machinery by which we can make—and maintain— the rules of private action. As economic and political conditions have changed since 1790, the rules which the majority of the people have believed useful have been altered to meet the needs of all. The process will go on no less in the future than in the past. Minority as well as majority rights have been and will be preserved by defining the responsibilities which parallel the rights. The referee of private claims—our democratic government in response to the people's interest in the general welfare— will continue to operate outside the area of conflicting interests to establish and to enforce the rules.

In these chapters, we have traced the record of government in action as a referee in many fields of industrial and labor relations. After the war is over, how can this principle of balance be best promoted by our government?

Our Legislature has given us a sound and practical rule for the role of government:

> The chief function of government, in dealing with worker-employer relationships, should be to promote good will, to encourage cooperation and, where resort is made to intervention, to be impartial and just, demanding obedience to all law by both parties concerned.*

Any action which our government may take to promote more

* Ibid.

peaceful—and so more stable—industrial and labor relations must rest on the will and the purpose of all the people. The basis of that will and that purpose lies in the spirit in which men and women live together in a free society. It may be found in the time-honored standards of personal and group conduct which underlie the American tradition of free enterprise and free government. In the record we have reviewed in these pages, we have found many examples of these standards in the relations of employers and workers. They are not less significant for the future achievement of the general welfare in these relations than they have been for its historical development. The future of a democratic America after the war requires something more than laws on our state and national statute books. In the final analysis, it is only as men and women live by these standards in their private activities that their statement in our laws can have meaning—and efficiency—in public action. Again, our Legislature has defined this one sure basis for realizing the general welfare of all the people:

> The most satisfactory and happiest human relationships are the product not of legal compulsion, but rather of voluntary determination among human beings to cooperate with one another. Though we may legislate to the end of time, there will never be industrial peace and harmony without good faith, integrity, a high degree of responsibility and a real desire to cooperate on the part of all parties concerned. Without this spirit of good-will, all of the social, economic, and labor laws of man will prove eventually to be in vain.*

AND THE TRADITION LIVES IN ACTION

* See Legislative Document (1940) No. 57, p. 77.

DEMOCRATIC GOVERNMENT | TOTALITARIAN GOVERNMENT

THE PEOPLE ELECT

symbol 100 Representatives   each symbol 20 Senators

**HOUSE OF
REPRESENTATIVES**   **SENATE**

WHO MAKE LAWS

R THE GENERAL WELFARE OF ALL

THE DICTATOR RULES THROUGH

**A FAVORED FEW IN
A SINGLE PARTY**

WHO CONTROL BY FORCE

**FOR THE
ALLEGED
BENEFIT OF THE STATE**

MATERIALS FOR FURTHER STUDY

INDUSTRIAL AND LABOR RELATIONS ARE AMONG THE MOST important and interesting fields—for practical exploration— for the high-school student hardly less than for the adult citizen. The high-school students of today will be the workers and employers of tomorrow, taking their place in the ranks of industry, agriculture, and the trades. Some will become industrial workers or farmers, others, foremen or superintendents, still others, managers or employers on a small or a large scale.

In a very real sense, then, teachers can play a vital role in the future course of industrial and labor relations in New York State. To the degree that they carry out their responsibilities in this respect, their students will become more effective members of a truly democratic society. The materials presented here are offered as examples of activities which may aid in developing their own and their students' awareness—at a time when sound industrial and labor relations are an urgent concern of the state and of the nation.

These materials are suggestive rather than inclusive. They are intended to indicate subjects for further investigation, not to list or develop all the possibilities of individual and group study. Some of these projects are more or less thoroughly worked out, in order to serve as guides in the preparation of other similar projects. Others are presented in outline only, to allow for more individual development by teachers who may wish to emphasize different aspects of the fields covered by the text.

The presentation of the materials in this form is deliberate. It is believed that considerable flexibility in scope and method is inherently valuable in the preparation and use of projects of this type. The more comprehensively developed materials presented here will provide the basis for immediate use in connection with outside work by the students on particular topics. The less fully developed offer an opportunity for experimentation in applying this type of material to differing needs. It is also believed that teachers desire and, indeed, practice, a wide discretion in their classroom procedures and activities. It is the initiative of the teacher which will most surely infuse meaning and vitality for the student into the challenging problems of industrial and labor relations in America today. No manual, however comprehensive or detailed, provides a substitute for the teacher's own contribution to the awareness of his students as to the basic conditions of and issues in a democratic American society.

It is believed, therefore, that what will prove most useful to teachers and others and what is desired by them is a series of signposts, not a set of prescriptions, a broad perspective, not a detailed blueprint. It is with these convictions that the materials are presented both as a guide for study activities on industrial and labor relations and as an experiment in the construction of projects of this type.

The following pages include first, a number of activities centered on library research; second, some suggestions for translating figures into charts and diagrams as visual aids to understanding; third, suggestions for group activities such as debates and conferences; fourth, suggestions for considering controversial issues from different points of view. They can— and should—be expanded as new events in the broad field of industrial and labor relations emerge. They can be developed and refined in use by those on whom falls a primary responsibility for improving our future industrial and labor relations— the teachers of the State of New York.

Although these projects have been designed especially for use in high-school classes, they will, it is hoped, also provide guidance for adult-education leaders and groups in developing their own study programs. Experimentation in the use and further elaboration of materials suggested here for the analysis and appraisal of problems in this field on the part of such groups will do much to broaden the base of sound industrial and labor relations throughout New York State.

1. Library Activities

Where libraries are available in the school or community, secondary school students should learn how to use their resources. Books, documents, newspapers, periodicals, and pamphlet materials should be referred to and used in the classroom as frequently as possible. The school library or the individual teacher on his own initiative can build up at little cost a working file of clippings and pamphlets on industrial and labor relations. News from the daily press gives the most complete and up-to-date treatment of current developments from a nationwide and an international viewpoint. Local papers are useful guides to new events and changing conditions in the community.

Where files of newspapers or periodicals are accessible, the same procedure can be carried back to earlier periods. The possibilities of useful library activity are, of course, limited by the resources available in the community. If only contemporary materials are available, this type of project is still well worth developing.

Government publications are also important sources of general information and statistical data. Every school library should contain the annual *Statistical Abstract of the United States* (Washington, Superintendent of Documents). Current United States Census Bureau publications should also be collected, as far as possible, in the school or community library. Separate pamphlets are often available for particular topics and for New York State. Most of the items listed are free or available at a nominal cost.

The following United States government annuals will be found valuable reference sources:

U. S. Department of Agriculture, *Annual Report of Secretary, Yearbook.*

U. S. Department of Labor, *Annual Report of Secretary* National Labor Relations Board, *Annual Report* Federal Security Agency, *Social Security Yearbook; Annual Report of the Social Security Board.*

(Most annual reports include reports of bureaus and divisions within the departments).

The following United States government serials will also be useful both for classroom materials and for reference:

U. S. Department of Agriculture, Consumers' Counsel Division, *Consumers' Guide.* Also *Consumers' Study Outlines.*

U. S. Department of Labor, Bureau of Labor Statistics, *Monthly Labor Review; Labor Information Bulletin.*

............................, Division of Labor Standards,

Labor Standards; special *Bulletins* and *Press Releases.* Federal Security Agency, Social Security Board, *Social Security Bulletin; Employment Security Review.*

Among the most useful New York State publications are the *Annual Reports* of the Industrial Commissioner, the New York State Labor Relations Board, the New York State Board of Mediation, the New York State Department of Welfare, and the Division of Commerce. The Department of Labor also publishes a useful monthly, *The Industrial Bulletin,* and, through its Division of Placement and Unemployment Insurance, *The Unemployment Review* (quarterly).

The *Annual Reports* of the New York State Joint Legislative Committee on Industrial and Labor Conditions (1939-   ) include valuable reviews of the development of industrial and labor conditions in the state and much information on their legislative and administrative aspects.

The materials distributed by many private organizations, current periodicals, and pamphlets and research studies are easily obtainable, often free or at a nominal cost. The Chamber of Commerce of the United States (Washington, D. C.), the National Association of Manufacturers (14 West 49th Street, New York City), the American Federation of Labor (Massachusetts Ave. and 9th Street, N.W., Washington, D. C.) and the Congress of Industrial Organizations (1106 Connecticut Avenue, N. W., Washington, D. C.) are among the more important national groups issuing valuable free materials on industrial and labor relations. State and local labor unions, employers' associations and trade associations should also be consulted; most of them will gladly supply materials from their files or obtain it on request.

Student assignments to cover specific report, document, magazine, or organization sources can be made a useful exercise in learning how to collect and use such materials. It can also become a cooperative procedure in developing the school's own library resources. Such projects provide valuable additions to the usual texts and reference books found in the school or community library. The following library activities may be considered for individual or group study, and perhaps for classroom report. References (in parenthesis) are to chapters and/or pages of the text.

A. Bibliography

One set of assignments may be to prepare special bibliographies for general use in developing individual studies or classroom activities. Among others, the following can be carried further than the materials presented in the text:

1. Knights of Labor; I.W.W.; Farmer-Labor Party; A.F. of L. and C. I. O.—history and organization (Chs. 3–4).
2. Employer and trade associations—history and organization (Chs. 3–4).
3. Collective bargaining, mediation, and arbitration in the United States (Ch. 8).
4. Social security—unemployment and old-age insurance, employment services (Ch. 11).
5. Labor-relations laws—national and state (Ch. 6).
6. Recent proposals for controlling labor-union activities (Chs. 7, 11).
7. Postwar problems in industrial and labor relations (Ch. 12).

B. Biography

One way to awaken interest in industrial and labor relations is to show how various political, industrial, and labor leaders have viewed them. The standard biographies and histories, as well as newspaper files, should be consulted. In each case, assign several persons or periods to different members of the class. Among topics which may be assigned in this area are:

1. What have the following Americans said about the rights of employers and workers?

Thomas Jefferson	Samuel Gompers	William Filene
Abraham Lincoln	James J. Davis	J. D. Rockefeller, Jr.
Woodrow Wilson	William Green	Henry Ford
Calvin Coolidge	John L. Lewis	Wendell Willkie
Herbert Hoover		
F. D. Roosevelt		

2. Compare the types of labor problem which confronted Presidents about 1840, 1890, and 1940. Why and how have they changed over the past century? What powers under the federal constitution did the Presidents in these three periods possess for settling these problems (Chs. 2, 3, 4, 12)?

3. Write a brief biography of selected contemporary industrial or labor leaders. Trace especially their background (family, education, etc.), the chief events in their lives and their philosophy of industrial and labor relations.

4. Draft a speech or message to Congress which one of the Presidents since 1880 might have written about industrial and labor relations in his time.

C. General Report Topics

Another library activity which can yield useful materials for supplementary classroom discussions can be organized around the more important historical incidents in industrial and labor relations. The following topics are merely suggestive of many others which can be utilized.

1. One of the best ways of understanding how Americans have viewed workers' rights—for instance, the right to strike—is to compare cartoon interpretations in different periods. How have cartoonists treated this and similar questions since, say, 1900?

2. What planks on the following rights of workers and employers have the major parties included in their national platforms since 1880?
    rights of property and of labor
    government regulation of industry and business labor relations
    mediation and arbitration
    workmen's compensation
    social security
    (Many platforms are included in *The World Almanac.*

304

They may also be obtained from newspaper files. The national headquarters of the parties will furnish such materials on request).

3. What provisions relating to the rights of employers and workers are found in the United States and the New York State Constitutions?
   (See U. S. Constitution, Article V, Amendments I, XIV; New York State Constitution, Article I, Sections 6, 11, 17, and 18. The United States and New York State Constitutions are to be found in the current *New York State Legislative Manual*).

4. Compare the "statements of policy" of federal and New York State laws on the following subjects:
   injunction
   labor relations
   mediation and arbitration
   workmen's compensation
   social security

5. What trends in public opinion as to workers' rights, especially the right to strike and to organize unions, do the various public opinion polls since 1936 show? What changes in opinion have occurred since 1939 with respect to strikes in defense industries?

6. Make a survey of current national magazine opinion on industrial and labor relations as to editorial policy on the various questions discussed in the text. Compare and appraise the fairness and adequacy of presentation of facts and issues in each magazine.

7. What positions do representative workers' and employers' groups take on the following questions:
   the right to organize unions
   the right to strike and to picket
   the closed shop

8. Outline the organization of the A.F. of L., and the C.I.O. Show how a national (or international union, a city-central trades council, a local union in each group is organized. (Write to A.F. of L. and C.I.O. for materials. Indicate the materials and data desired).

9. Outline the organization of the National Association of Manufacturers, the Chamber of Commerce of the United States of America, and other employer and trade associations.

Show how a national, regional, state, or local unit is organized.

2. Visual-Aid Activities

Significant factors determining or affecting industrial and labor relations are often much more effectively presented by charts and other visual aids than by the printed page. Maps are, of course, indispensable. A general United States map and, if on hand or obtainable, resources, industrial, population, and transportation maps should be utilized.

In addition, with a small stock of cardboard, a few colored pencils, inks, or paints and brushes, and a dash of ingenuity, a wide variety of illustrated and illustrative materials can be added to other classroom resources. The actual preparation of such materials by the students is, moreover, a valuable type of manual activity in the social studies.

Converting the figures in a table into a bar or trend chart, for instance, helps to fix in the students' minds not only the facts themselves but their relation to each other as well as their significance. The preparation of these materials in the form of graphic illustrations can also be made an exercise in judging the validity of data underlying argument and in accuracy in presenting them. It can also be a fascinating exploration in making ideas come alive. Examples in the text will suggest data for similar visual interpretation by students.

The best nontechnical description of how to construct graphic illustrations is Rudolph Modley's book, *How to Use Pictorial Statistics* (New York, Harpers, 1937). The following books are also useful on this subject; W. C. Brinton, *Graphic Presentation* (New York, Brinton Associates, 1937), which is an elaborate guide to chart making; H. Arkin and R. R. Colton, *Graphs: How to Make and Use Them* (New York, Harpers, 1940); and Hacker, Modley and Taylor, *The United States: A*

Graphic History (New York, Modern Age Books, 1937). The graphic illustrations in the text offer unique examples of the activity suggested here; they will, on comparison with the books noted above, indicate a more highly personalized form of what are usually called "pictorial statistics".

Over the course of two or three years, a file of visual aids can be built up in any class. Their utility for classroom instruction and for general school and community exhibit—and enlightenment—is cumulative.

The following suggestions lend themselves to pictorial presentation:

1. Collect pictures of the early days in your community—the layout of the town, typical houses of the early settlers, mills, etc., public and civic buildings. Set up a "then-and-now" exhibit in the school library or a classroom (Chs. 1–4).
   (Draw or borrow maps showing the street plan in about 1790 (and at later half-century periods). Draw a chart of population changes. Consult local histories and other community records, United States Census, etc.).

2. Trace a map of the frontier in America, 1790–1890. Indicate the spread of population and the growth of cities (number, location, size) 1790–1840 (Chs. 1–4).
   (The *United States Census* for 1890 contains an excellent record of the changing frontier and includes many valuable maps. As to the growth of cities, see National Resources Planning Board, *Our Cities* for maps and other data).

3. Make a chart of changes in occupation since 1880 (by decades) as to proportion of all workers employed in agriculture, industry, service trades (including clerical and professional). What factors have influenced these changes (pp. 36 ff.)?
   (Use United States Census data, well summarized in *Statistical Abstract of the United States*).

4. Make an outline map of the United States, indicating the five principal national resources, agricultural products, and manufactures for each state. How does this distribution affect economic competition among the states (Chs. 3–4)?

5. a. Compare New York State, the next four industrial states,

and the United States as to:
> number of workers engaged in agriculture, industry, service trades
> six principal manufactures
> value added by manufacture
> wealth per capita
>> (See United States Census of Agriculture, Manufactures, Population (Chs. 3–4).

  b. What advantages does New York seem to have in terms of employment for its citizens?
  > (This topic can be expanded and developed into a thorough analysis of New York State economy. The New York State Division of Commerce, (Bureau of Planning) will supply much useful material. See also the 1942 *Report* of the New York State Joint Legislative Committee on Industrial and Labor Conditions).

3. *Debates and Conferences*

One useful device for developing student understanding of the issues involved in industrial and labor relations policies is to hold class debates or conferences on proposed bills, state or national.

Conferences may be set up, for instance, as hearings on proposed bills before the New York State Senate (or Assembly) Committee on Labor and Industry. Four or five members of the class may be assigned as members of the committee (both majority and minority). Others may be assigned to act as witnesses representing particular points of view as experts or as representatives of different interest groups. The witnesses may be allowed three to five minutes each to present their material, and the members of the committee should question them in support or attack of the positions they represent. The committee may draw up a report and present it to the class for discussion at a later meeting.

Such a device offers also an opportunity to develop an understanding of parliamentary procedure. Parliamentary manuals should be consulted; one of the most helpful is Robert D.

Leigh, *Modern Rules of Parliamentary Procedure* (New York, Norton, 1937). See also Roberts' *Rules of Order* (any recent edition). As in legislative committee hearings, committee members and witnesses should be careful to identify themselves in terms of the interest which they represent. An effective hearing can be carried through in two class periods or in a special period outside of the regular class hour. A hearing may follow such a pattern as this.

1. *Committee Hearing: Senate Committee on Labor and Industry.*
   a. *Bill No. 1.* To require a "cooling-off period" before a strike or lockout is called (pp. 157, 158, 282).
      Committee:
      Chairman and three or four additional members.
      Witnesses:
      (1) A representative of the New York State Department of Labor to explain how such a regulation would work and to indicate where it is now found in operation.
      (2, 3) Two representatives of state labor organizations to present the workers' views.
      (4) Two representatives of state industrial organizations to present their point of view.
      (5, 6) Two citizens to oppose and support the bill on different grounds.

   b. *Bill No. 2.* To require compulsory mediation or arbitration of labor disputes not settled through voluntary collective bargaining agreements (Ch. 8).
      Committee:
      Chairman and three or four additional members.
      Witnesses:
      (The same "cast" of witnesses may be used. Others will occur to teachers and students under both *1* and *2*).

2. The following topics are suggestive of many others which may be developed as class debates or as conferences:
   a. The closed vs. the open shop.
   b. Compulsory incorporation of labor unions (pp. 151 ff.).
   c. Making jurisdictional strikes illegal (pp. 55 ff., 160 ff.).
   d. Governmental regulation of labor unions (pp. 163 ff.).
   e. Restricting the prohibition of injunctions against strikes to disputes between an employer and his own workers (pp. 113 ff.).

309

f. The advantages and defects of the War Labor Disputes Act of 1943 (Ch. 12).

g. Retaining control of unemployment insurance administration in the states (pp. 251 ff. See the 1943 *Report* of the New York State Joint Legislative Committee on Industrial and Labor Conditions).

4. Other Activities

Another sort of classroom activity of the same general character as a debate or conference is to raise questions to be considered from different points of view. By casting students in different roles, greater awareness of why there are controversial issues in our society—why people look at the same question differently—can be developed. Similarly, the community investigations suggested here are intended to make the students more aware of the various points of view which are held by those in different economic and social groups. In this way it may be hoped that they will appreciate the difficulties—and the possibilities—of reconciling differing attitudes by mutual understanding and goodwill.

1. Select an industry which has recently recognized collective bargaining. Choose one company and discuss the issues in the light of the following:
   a. a member of the union seeking recognition
   b. a non-union worker in the company
   c. a member of the company management
   d. a citizen of the community in which the major company plant is located
   e. a citizen of an adjacent town or state
      (Other members of the class may be cast in other roles).

2. What are the five major industries in your community? Report on, for each industry:
   a. number and size of factories
   b. total number of workers
   c. number of workers who are members of labor unions
   d. representative wage scales for skilled and unskilled workers.
      (The same type of activity can be carried out with respect to local service trades).

3. How have wages and salaries changed in these industries and businesses since 1935? How do these rates and changes compare with New York State as a whole? What factors help to explain the differences?

4. What major strikes have occurred in your community during the last five years? What were the causes stated in each case? How many workers were affected? How long did each last? How was each settled? How did the local press present the issues?
   (Charts and diagrams can be constructed for questions 2, 3, and 4, if sufficient data can be obtained from local reports or class investigations of New York State documents and reports, especially those of the New York State Department of Labor).

5. Appoint a class committee to visit the local headquarters of an employers' association and of a labor union. The committee should talk with the representatives about their problems in industrial and labor relations; for instance, what issues are important locally; what solutions they suggest; what contracts they have established with representatives of the other group to work out these solutions. The committee should report to the class as a whole on the interviews and present its own findings. The class as a whole may then organize itself as a "clinic" to analyze the problems and solutions submitted in the report.

6. Invite a representative employer (for instance, through the Chamber of Commerce) and worker (for instance, through a city central labor-union headquarters or an individual union) to your class. Discuss with them any of the major questions noted in the unit or in these "activities".
   (Prepare the questions you wish to ask them precisely; inform each of them of the questions beforehand; ask them to come together—and leave time for questions to them from the class).
   (Numbers 5 and 6 are not mutually exclusive. After the procedure suggested in No. 5 has been carried through, it would be especially profitable to invite representatives of both groups to participate in the clinic).

7. What major collective-bargaining agreements are there in your community? What machinery for settling disputes is included in each? Has this machinery ever been used? What were the

bases of the disputes and how was each settled?
(This question can also be applied to other communities. Such agreements can often be obtained from press reports. Some typical agreements can be obtained on request or for a small cost from employers' associations and international labor unions).

8. Appoint a class committee to visit the local war price and rationing board to find out what are the major problems in wartime rationing in your community and what changes in rationing programs people desire.
(Apply the clinic procedure suggested under 5).

9. Appoint a class committee to visit the local office or write to the headquarters of the agencies noted below, requesting copies of all the official forms used in their operations. Have the committee, with, if necessary, additional members of the class, carry out complete presentation of the steps in clearing a case before each agency, from initiation to completion.
New York State Labor Relations Board (an unfair labor-practice complaint or a representation petition).
New York State Division of Workmen's Compensation (an accident report and action upon it).
New York State Division of Placement and Unemployment Insurance (a claim for unemployment benefits).
U. S. Fair Labor Standards Administration (investigation of wages and hours in an industry).
U. S. Employment Service (registration of an unemployed worker for a job and notification of any available job).

INDEX

AGRICULTURE, (1790), 2ff.; (1840), 20; (1890), 36; (1940), 60; shift to industry, 21

American Federation of Labor, history and organization, 51–56; convention (1935), 88; craft unions v. industrial unions, 88–89; no-strike pledge, 276; membership 55, 87–88, 89; split with C.I.O., and 88–89, 160; unskilled workers and, 51–52

Arbitration, American Arbitration Association, 179; Civil Practice Act, 183; definition, 174, 176; enforcement, 183; N.Y.S. Board of Mediation, 181ff.; Railroad Conciliation Act, 181; U. S. Conciliation Service, 179–180, 279; Vultee Aircraft, Inc., 171–174; see also mediation

BEAUTY SERVICE INDUSTRY, 232–234

Blacklist, 57, 101–102, 107, 142

Boycotts, injunction, 110ff.; secondary, 112

Byrnes Anti-Strikebreaking Act (U. S.), 109

CHAMBER OF COMMERCE OF THE U. S., 92

Child Labor, 223, 226–228, 229ff.

Children's Bureau, (U. S.), 226

Civil Works Administration (U. S.), 242, 246

Clayton Act (U. S.), 82, 117, 121

Closed shop, 136, 277

Collective bargaining, 93, 104, 125–126, 134–135, 141–142, 171

Committee on Defense Migration, (U. S.), 271

Committee on Fair Employment Practices, (U. S.), 272–274

Committee for Industrial Organization see Congress of Industrial Organization

Compensation Insurance Rating Board, (N. Y. S.), 208

Congress of Industrial Organizations, history and organization, 88–92; membership, 89; no-strike declaration, 276; split with A. F. of L., 88–89, 160

Constitution (U. S.), 10ff., 288ff.

Contempt proceeding, 113–114, 122

Contributory negligence, 193

Corporations, development, 44ff.; government control of, 45; growth of factories, 65

Craft unions, 15, 30–31, 51–52, 87–88, 89–90

DEBS CASE, 116

Depression, (1837), 32; (1929), 69–72, 76–77, 79–82, 87, 246, 248

Discrimination in employment, 271ff.; New York State Committee on, 272

Division of Placement and Unemployment Insurance (N. Y. S.), 244–245

Dual union, 54

EIGHT-HOUR DAY, 51, 215–216, 229

Elections, 46

Employer organizations, Chamber of Commerce of the U. S., 56–57, 92–93; Employers General Association of Michigan, 56; Master Mechanics of Boston, 57; National Association of Manufacturers, 57, 92; New York Master Builders Association, 57; Trade Associations, 92–93

Employment, labor turnover, 239; migratory workers, 271; service trades, 64; U. S. (1890), 38, (1940), 61

Employment Bureau, (N. Y. S.), 244

Employment Division, (N. Y. S.), 244

Employment Service (U. S.), 240–243

Executive Office of the President, War Manpower Commission, 274

FAIR LABOR STANDARDS ACT (U. S.), 222ff.

Federal Emergency Relief Administration, 242

Federal Security Agency, 241

Federal Society of Journeyman Cordwainers, 14, 30

Fellow-servant doctrine, 193

Franchise, 27–29

Free enterprise, 13, 29, 288ff.

GRANTS-IN-AID, dependent mothers and children and needy blind, 257–258; employment services, 242–243; old-age pension plan, 253; Wagner-Peyser Act, 242–243

Guilds, 13–14

HEALTH, employer organizations, 93; Social Security Act, 257–258

Horizontal unions, 15

Hours of labor, demands for shorter, 15–16, 30, 32, 39; eight-hour day, 51; employer organizations and, 92–93; Fair Labor Standards Act, 222ff.; hours legislation, 213–216; National Industrial Recovery Act, 222; state laws on, 213ff.; ten-hour day, 16; Walsh-Healy Public Contracts Act, 223

313

315

A
NOTE
ON THE
PRINTING
OF THIS BOOK

*This book is set on the
Linotype in 12 point Bodoni Book
2 point leaded.   Headings set in 10, 12
and 14 point Bodoni Black Italic. Chapter numerals
in 60 point Bodoni Campanile. The graphic illustrations
were designed especially for this book.   The photographs
(133 line screen) and illustrations were engraved
by Austin-Empire Engravers, Inc. Composed,
printed and bound by the Williams Press,
Albany, New York.   Paper made by
Consolidated Water Power and
Paper Company*

s